# Sweet 18

Emmanuel D. Fouquet

AF597541

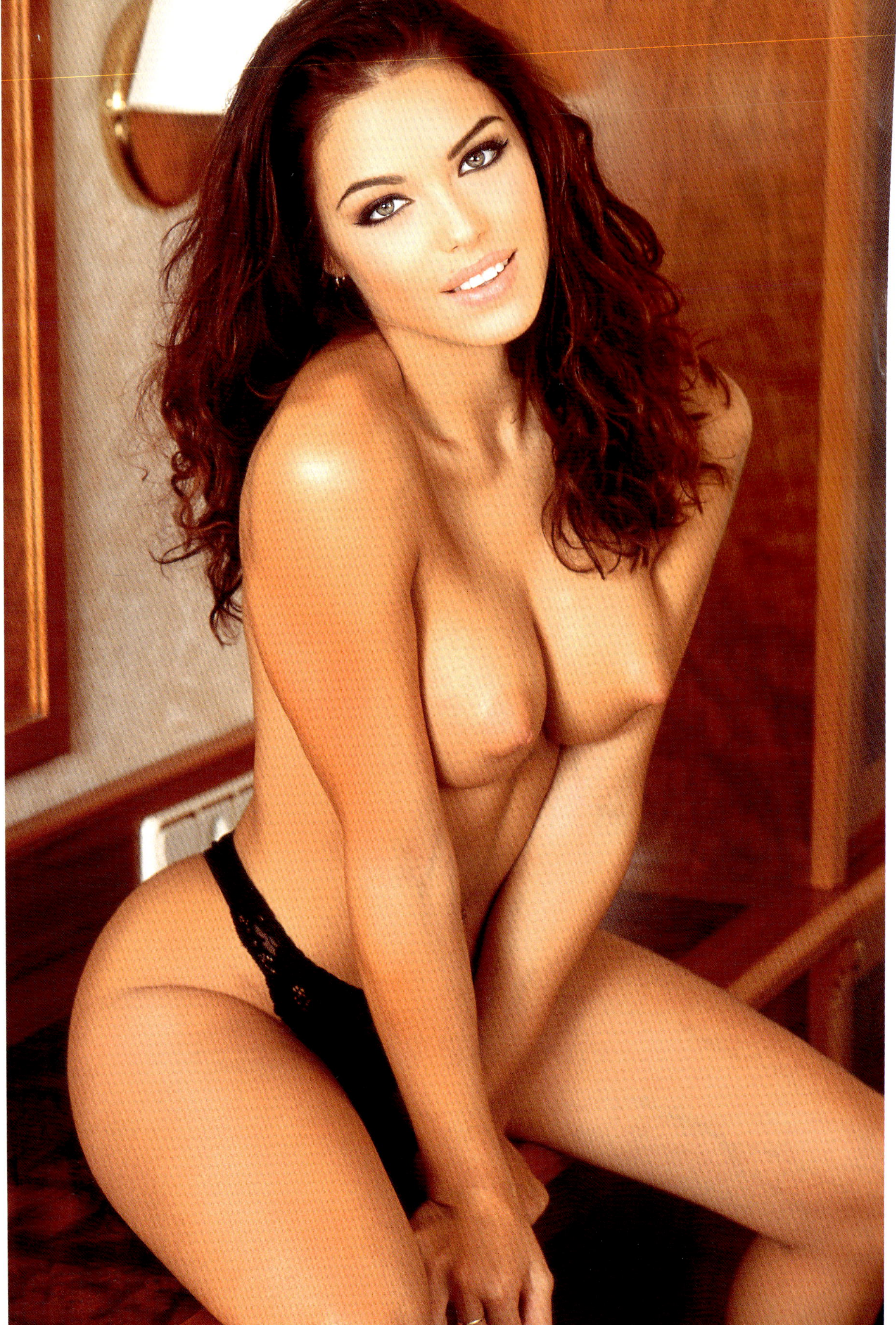

# Sweet 18

Emmanuel D. Fouquet

EDITION Skylight

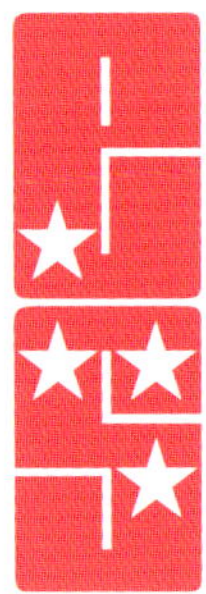

2nd Edition 2024 in Paperback,
revised and enlarged
Copyright © 2012 by Edition Skylight

**EDITION SKYLIGHT**
Rosengartenstr. 13B
CH-8608 Bubikon/Zürich
Switzerland
Mail: info@edition-skylight.com
Web: www.edition-skylight.com

ISBN 978-3-03766-694-4

All rights reserved. No part of this book may be reproduced in any form or by any electronic or mechanical means including information storage and retrieval system without the permission in writing form from the copyright owner.

Bibliographic information published by Die Deutsche Bibliothek
Die Deutsche Bibliothek lists this publication in the Deutsche Nationalbibliografie; detailed bibliographic data are available in the Internet at http://dnb.ddb.de.

Printed in Bosnia and Herzegovina

# preface • vorwort • avant propos

The photographs in this volume were all taken without commercial interest or intent of any kind; without paying attention to taboos or respecting what is forbidden. They are real photos, entire stories that have no need for long words. And even though it could hardly be called a "pillow book", you do risk having sleepless nights after having enjoyed it. I have tried to capture the frank and sweaty atmosphere surrounding teenagers, their charged awareness, as this is what I repeatedly found on my many travels. It was a personal quest that led me far away from my real work. We see young adults (all at least 18 years of age), who become professional models for a day. French and Czech women, Ukrainians, Hungarians and even American women initiate us into the intimacies of their youth, with not too much posing, but occasionally enhanced with accessories of their choice. In this volume, you should see nothing but pictures that are erotic art!

Alle diese Bilder sind ohne jegliche kommerzielle Absicht entstanden … ohne Beachtung von Tabus oder Verboten, echte Fotos, kleine Geschichten ohne große Worte … – auch wenn dieses Buch kein Kopfkissenbuch ist, so riskiert man dennoch nach seinem Genuss schlaflose Nächte: Die ungetrickste und schwitzige Atmosphäre, wie sie Teenager umgibt, in alltäglicher Aufgeladenheit – so wie ich sie immer wieder vorfand auf meinen vielen Reisen. Und für mich eine persönliche Suche, die mich sehr weit weg von meiner eigentlichen Arbeit geführt hat. Wir sehen junge Erwachsene (alle mindestens 18 Jahre alt), Models für einen Tag wie professionelle Models, Französinnen, Tschechoslowakinnen, Ukrainerinnen, Ungarinnen, sogar Amerikanerinnen, wie sie uns in die Intimität ihrer Jugend einweihen, nicht zuviel Posing, nur hier und da mit Accessoires ihrer Wahl. Man sollte hierin nichts anderes sehen als Bilder erotischer Kunst!

J'ai pris toutes ces images sans références ni idées d'un résultat commercial. … Sans tabous ni interdits, des photographies réelles, des histoires sans paroles qui en racontent long … Ce book n'est pas un livre de chevet et au contraire au risque de ne pas pouvoir dormir après l'avoir regardé. Une ambiance teen-ager sans artifice et exécuté dans des conditions naturelles de tout les jours à travers mes voyages, une recherche personnelle qui m'a amené très loin dans mon travail … Nous voyons des jeunes adultes ( toutes les filles ont au moins 18 ans ), modèles d'un jour ou professionnelles, Françaises, Tchécoslovaques, Ukrainiennes, Hongroises, ou même Américaines nous délivrent leurs intimes jeunesses avec une grande fraîcheur sans poses imposées et avec les accessoires de leurs choix. N'y voyez pas autres choses que des images d'art érotique.

*Emmanuel D. Fouquet*

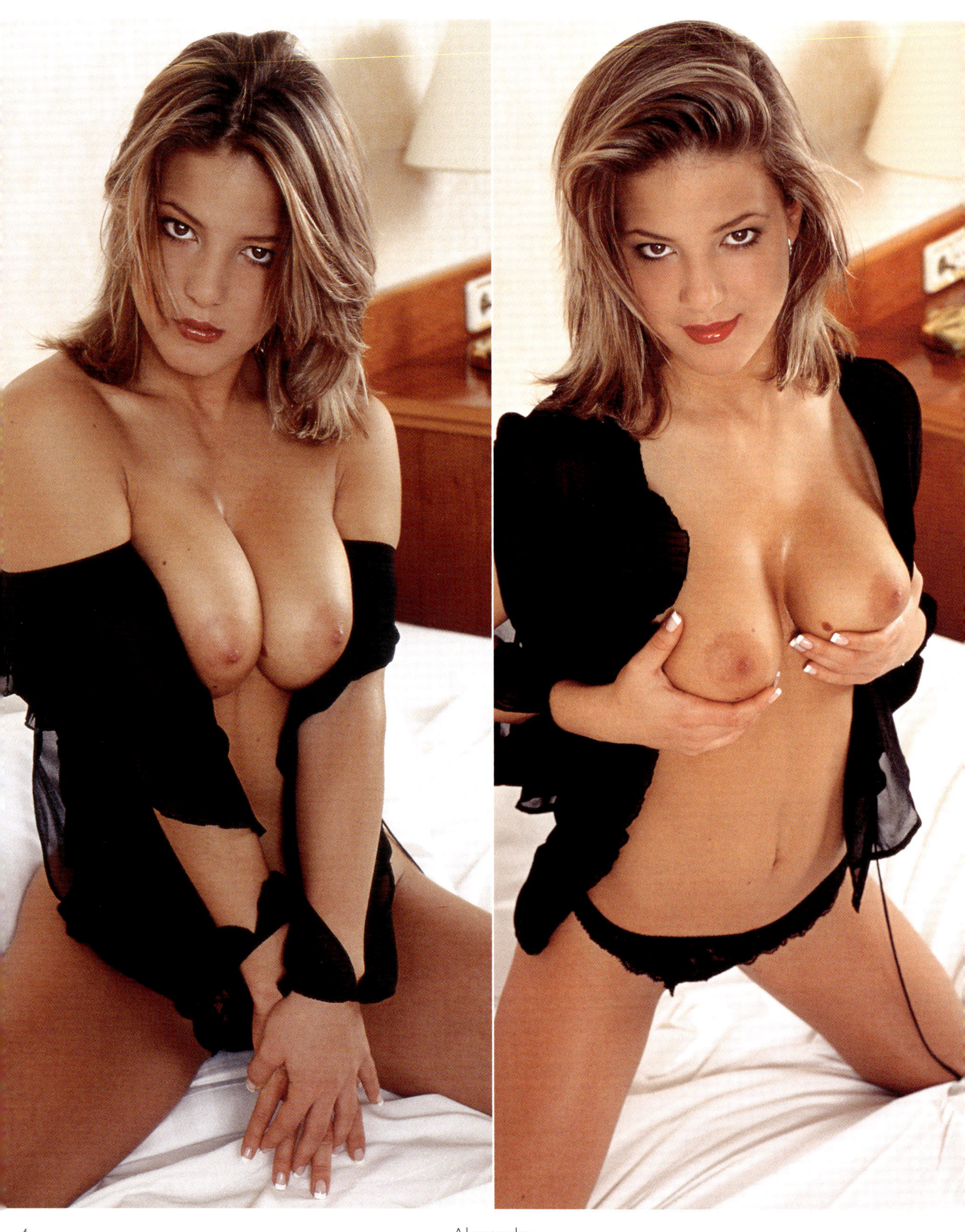

Alexandra

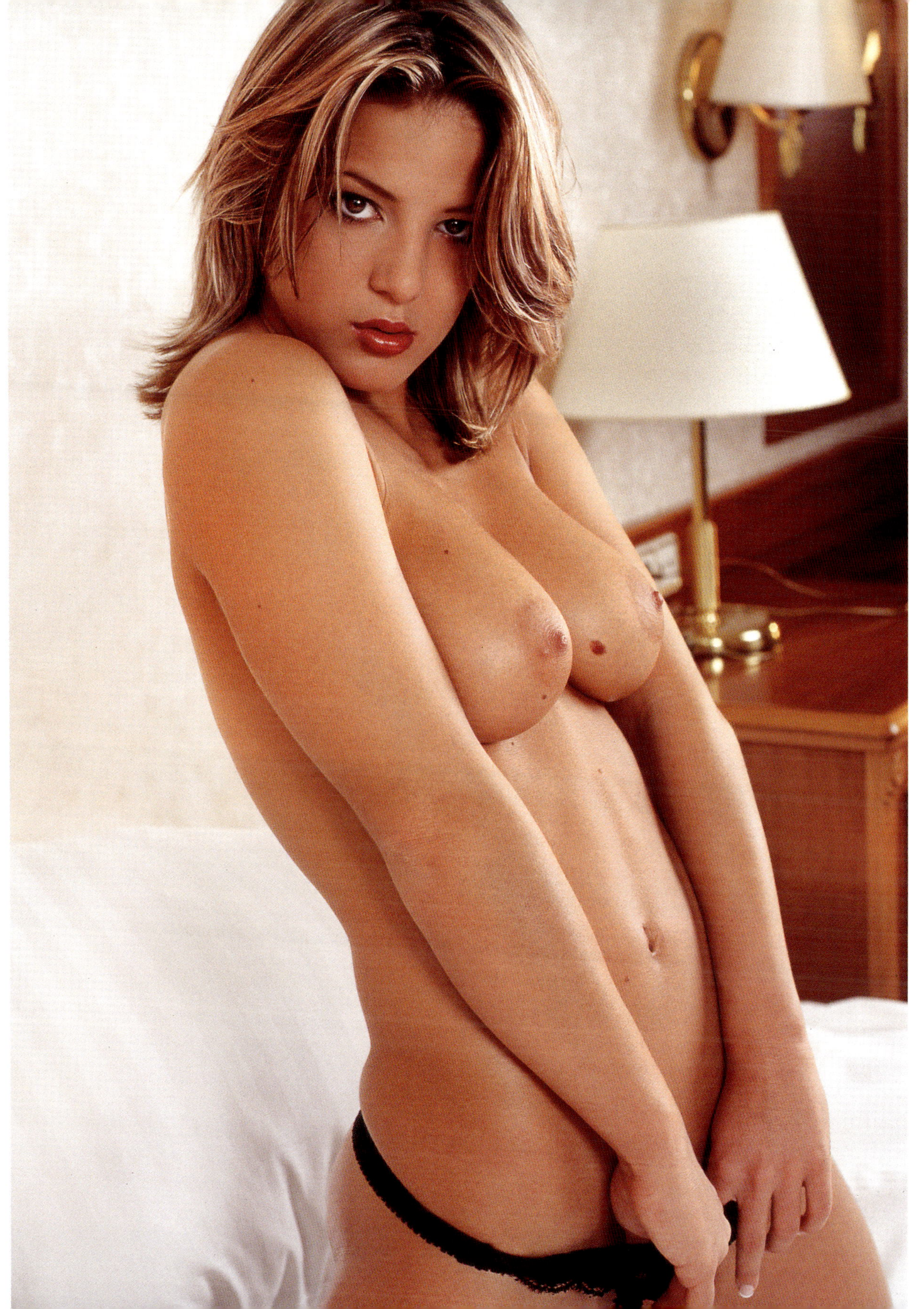

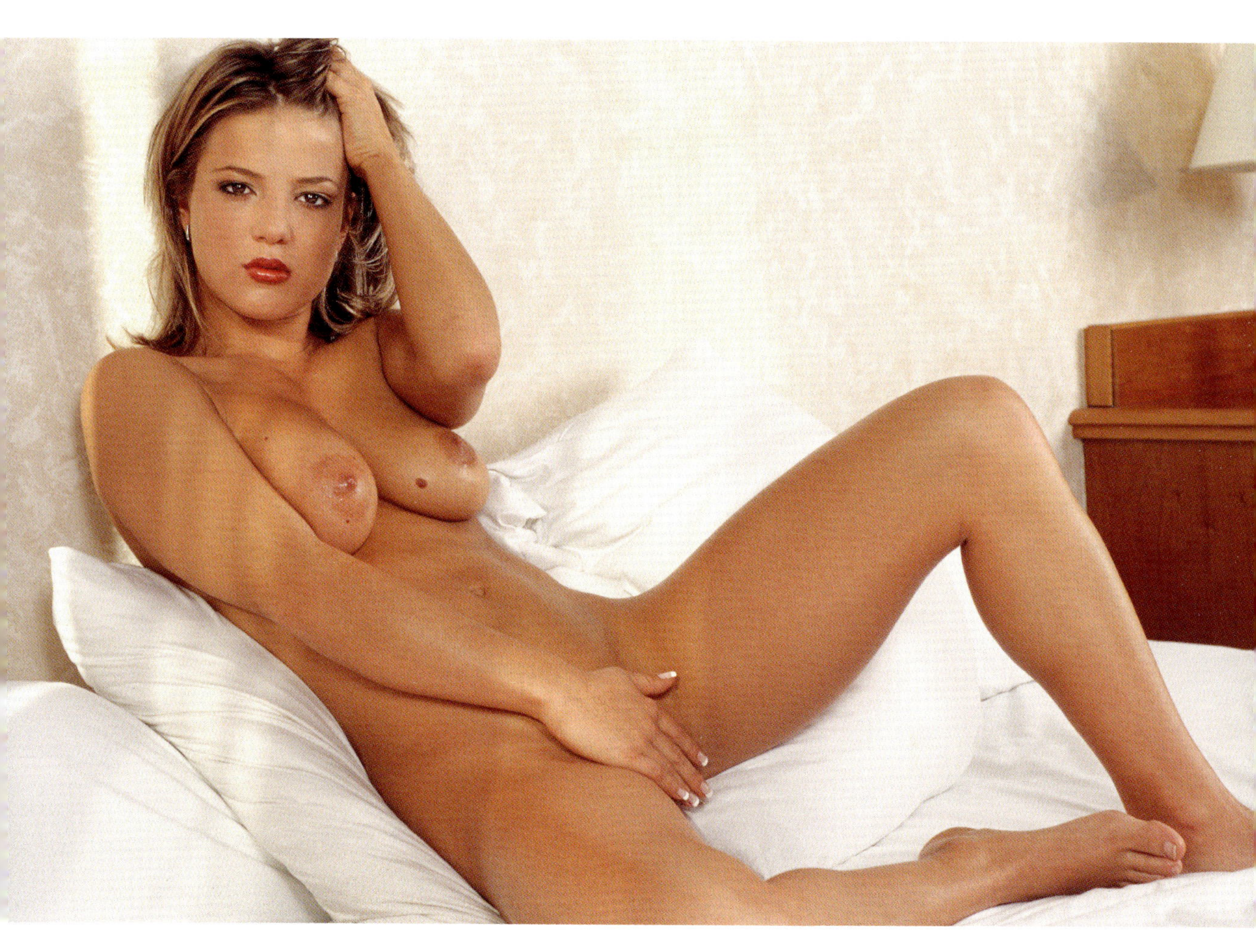

Alexandra

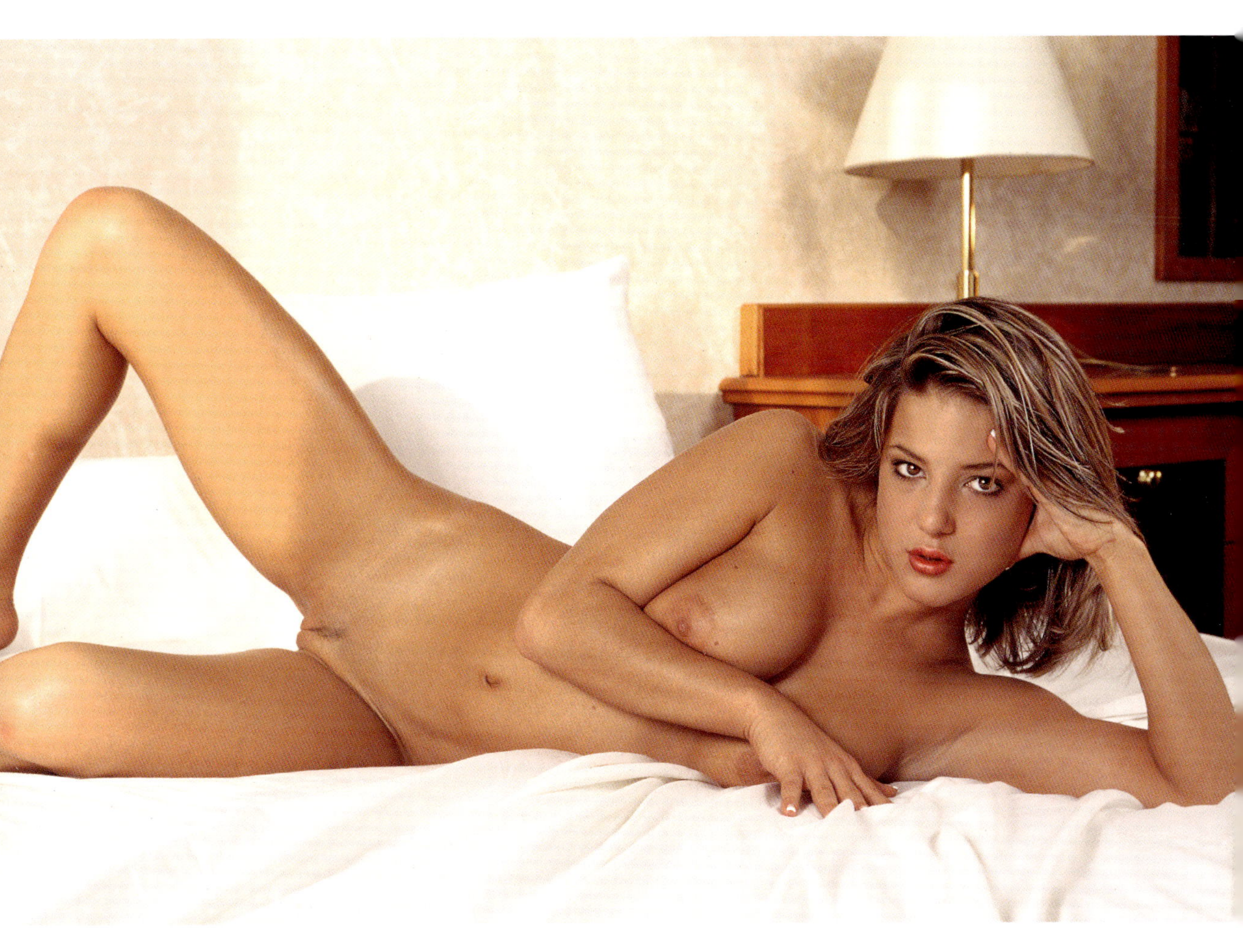

Alexandra

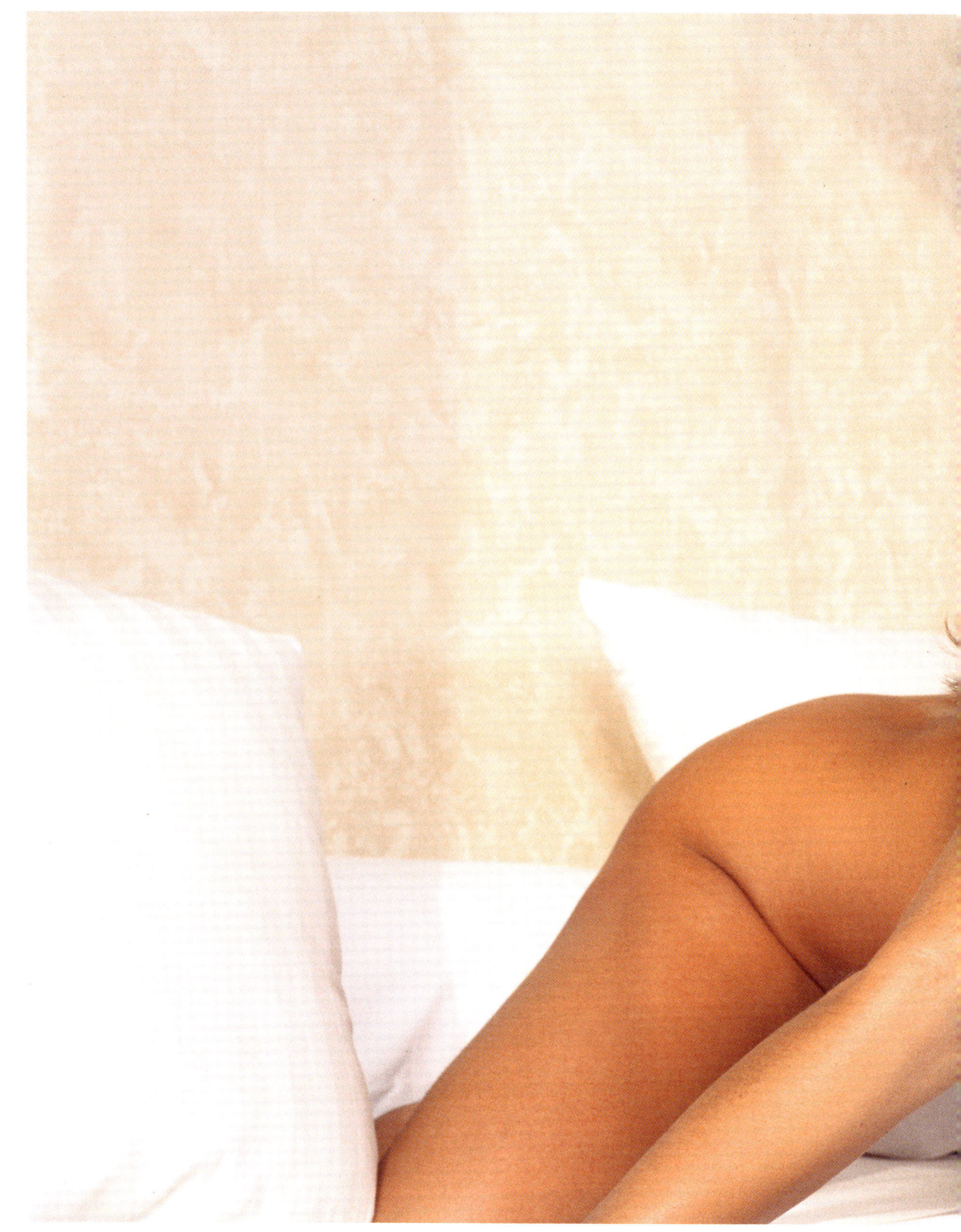

Alexandra

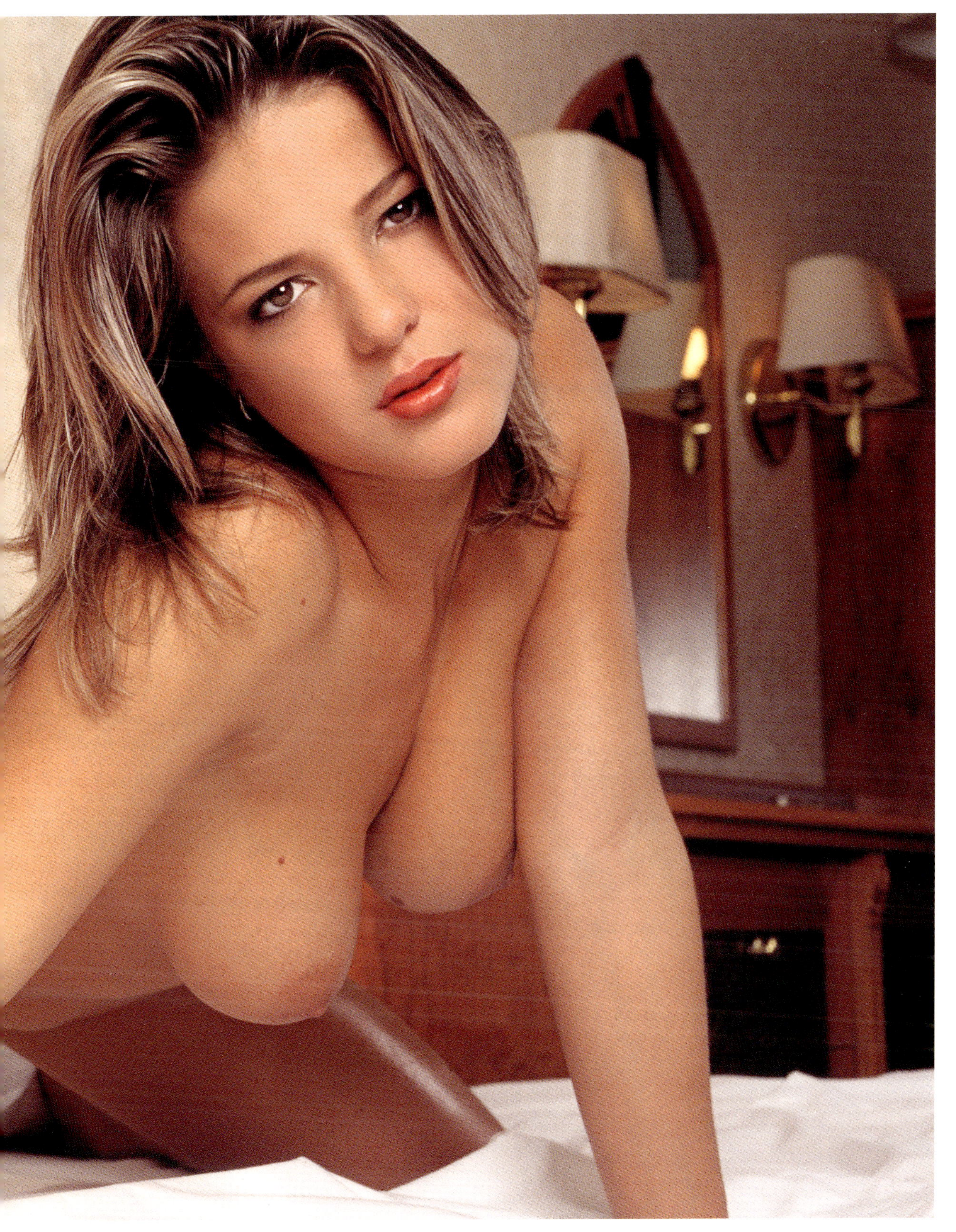

Alexandra

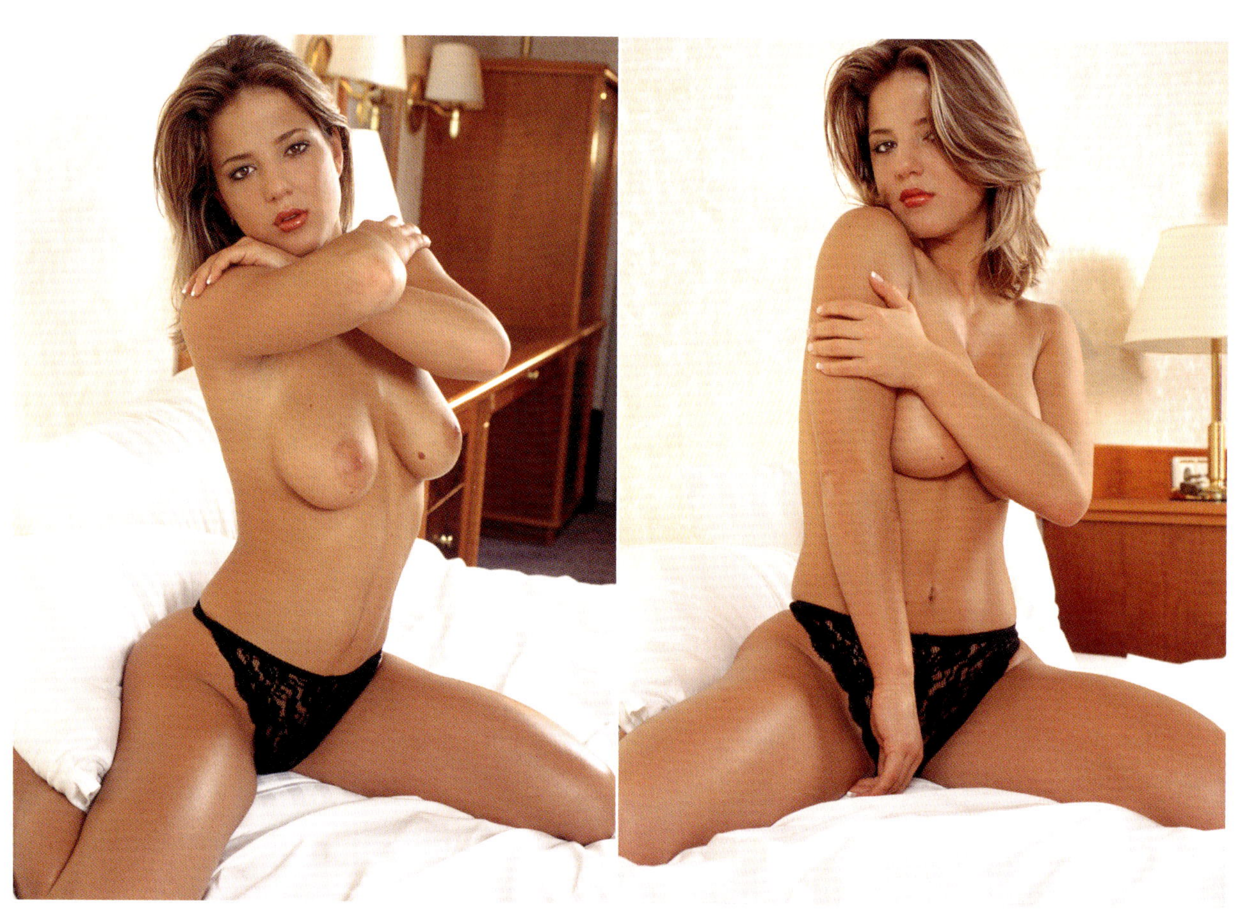



Alexandra

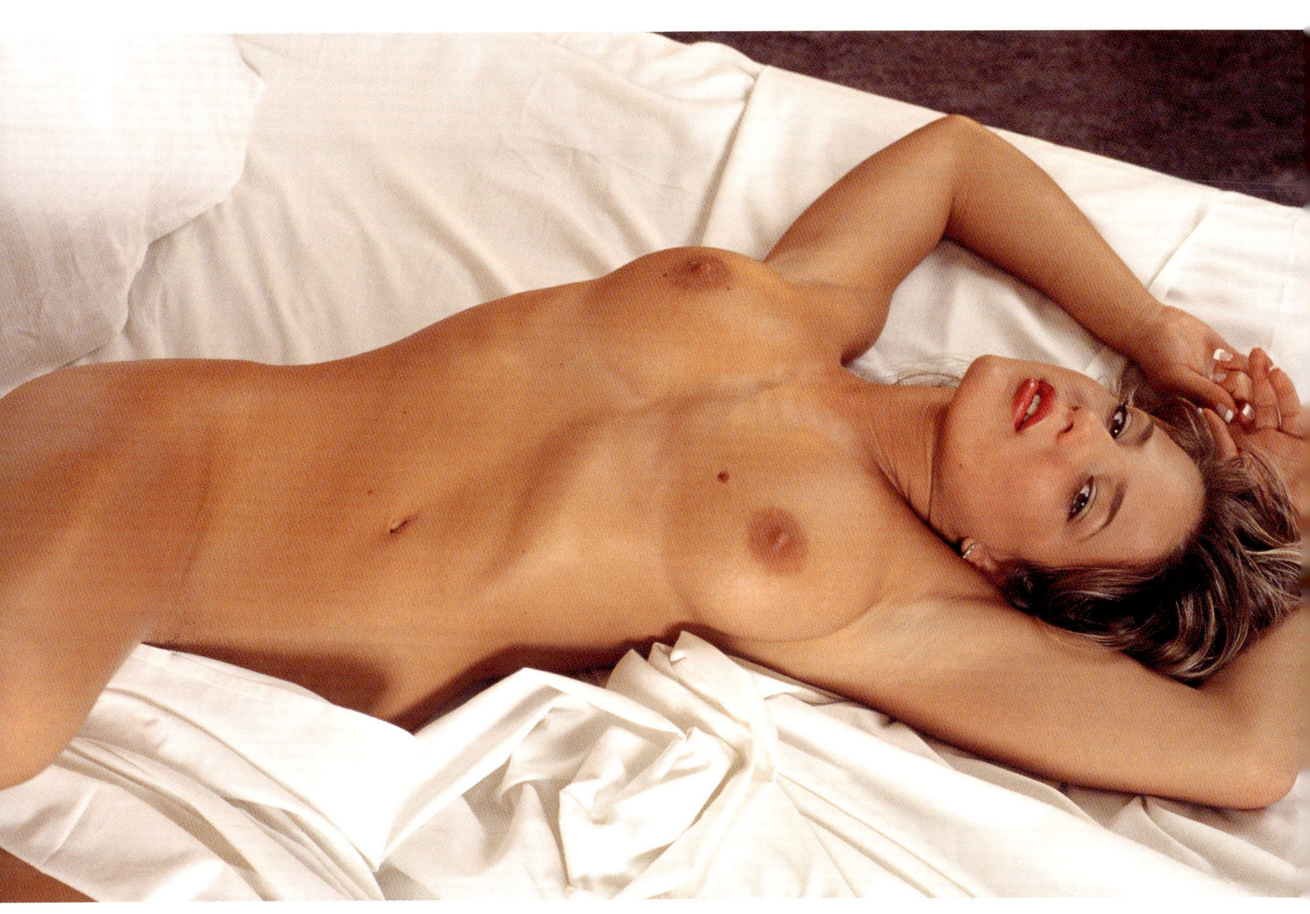

Alexandra

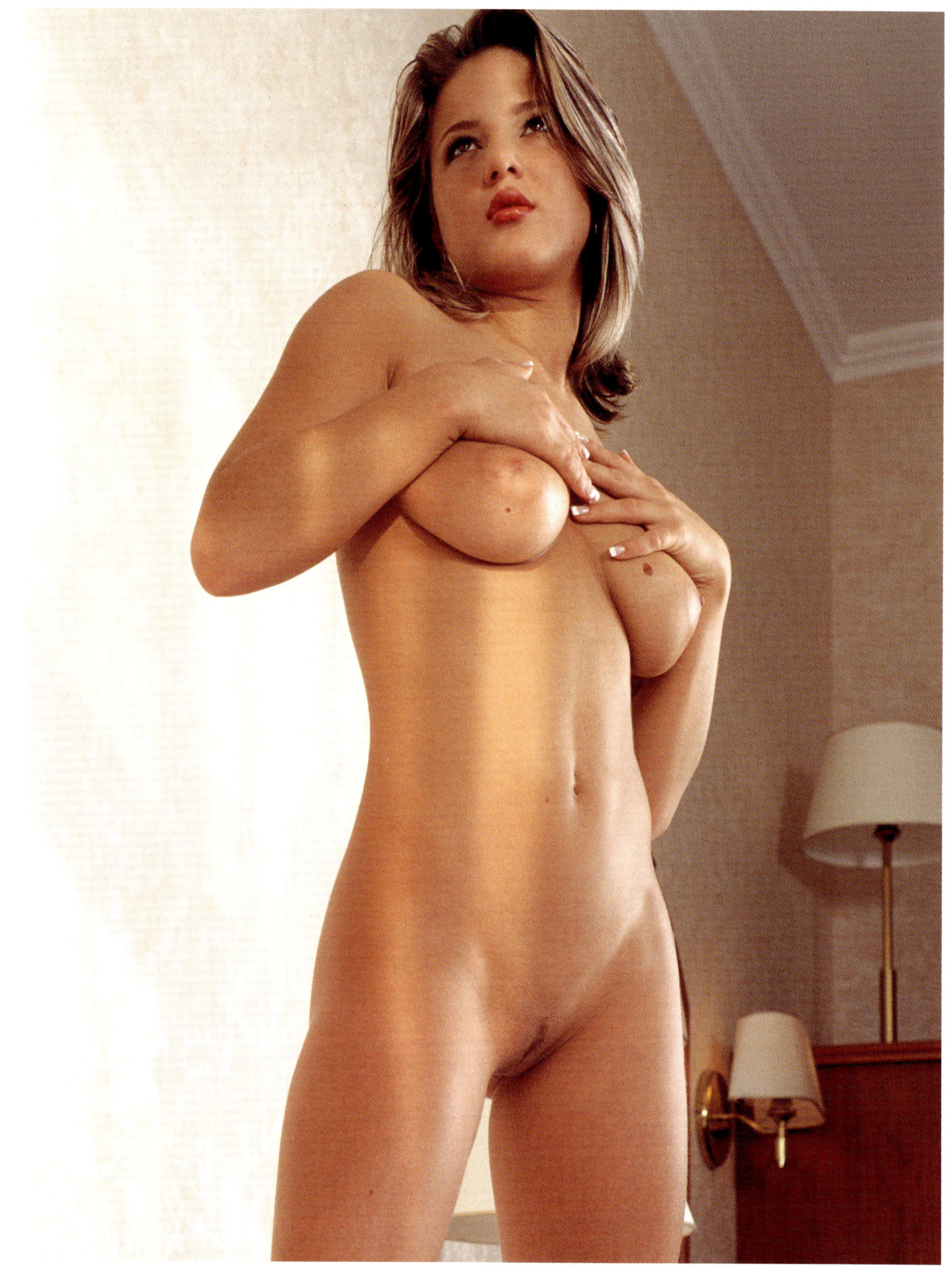

Alexandra

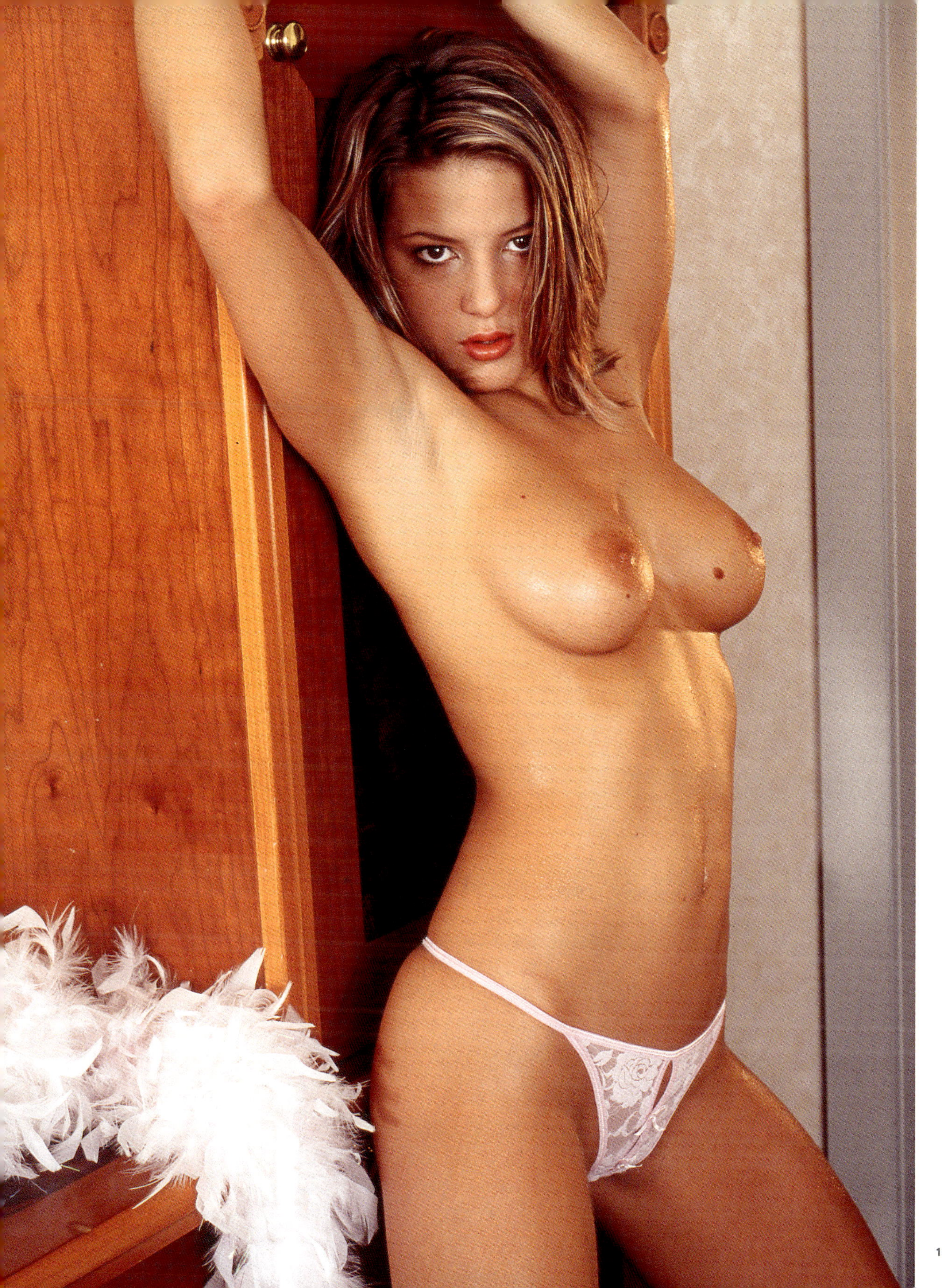

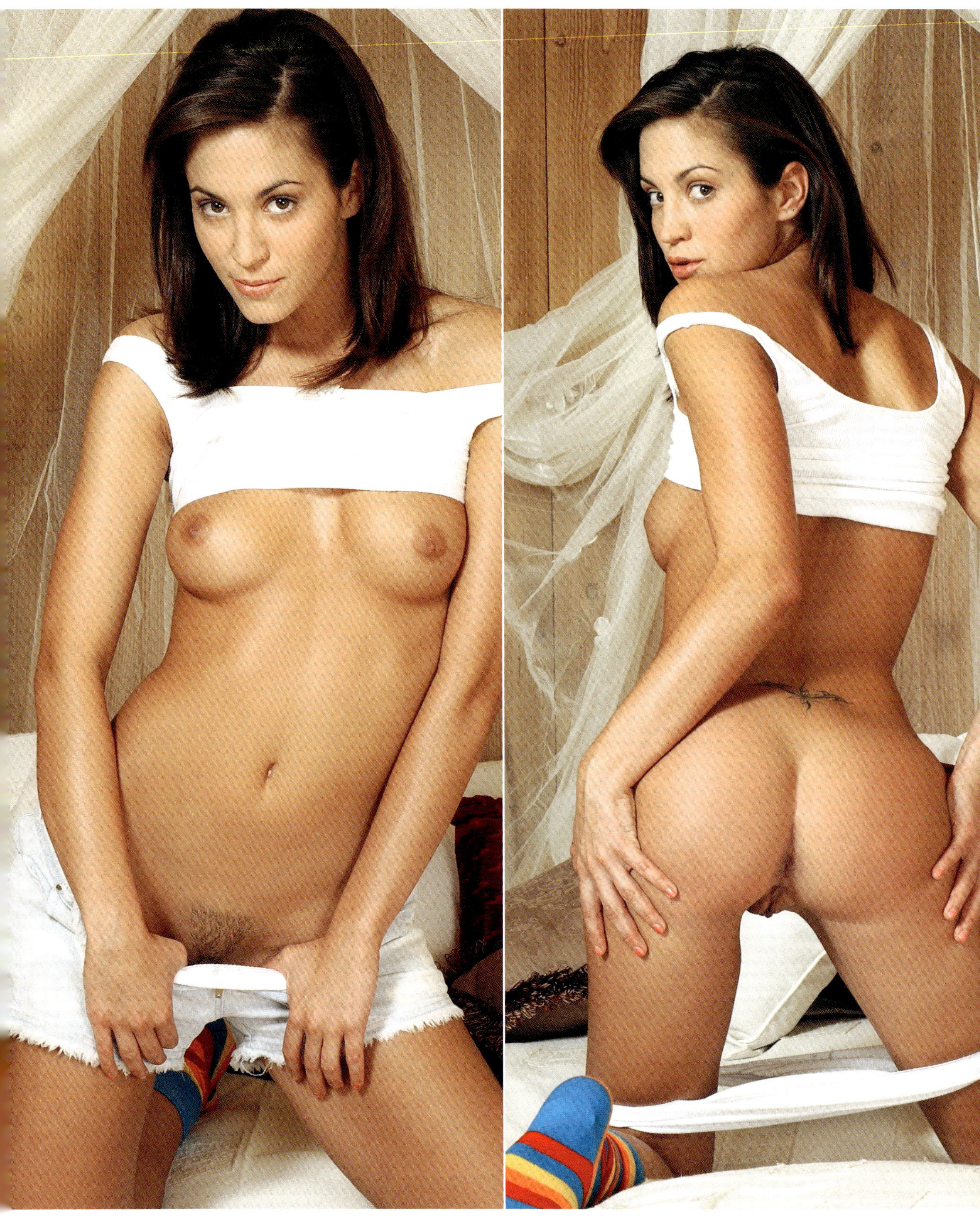



Anita Kiss

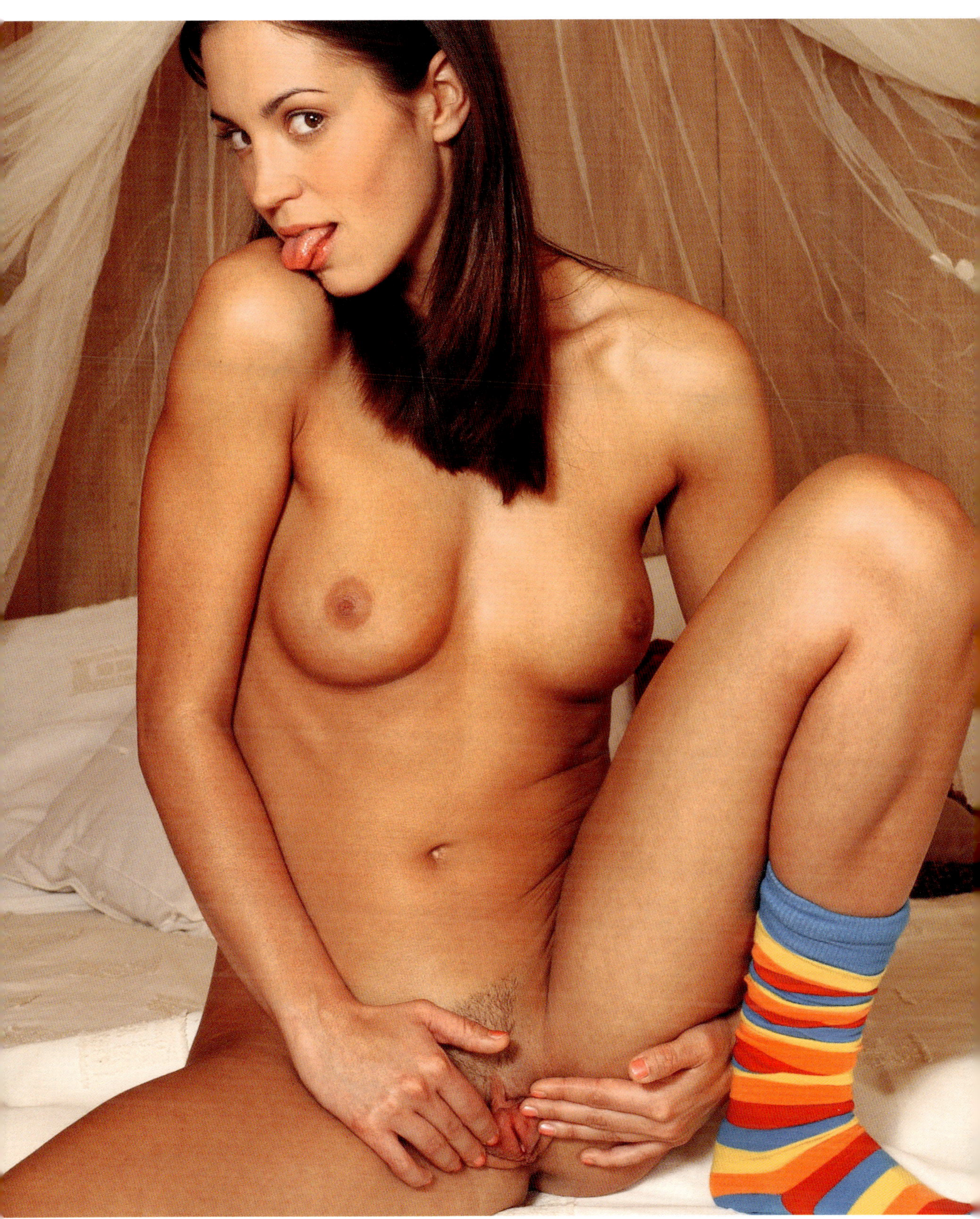

Anita Kiss

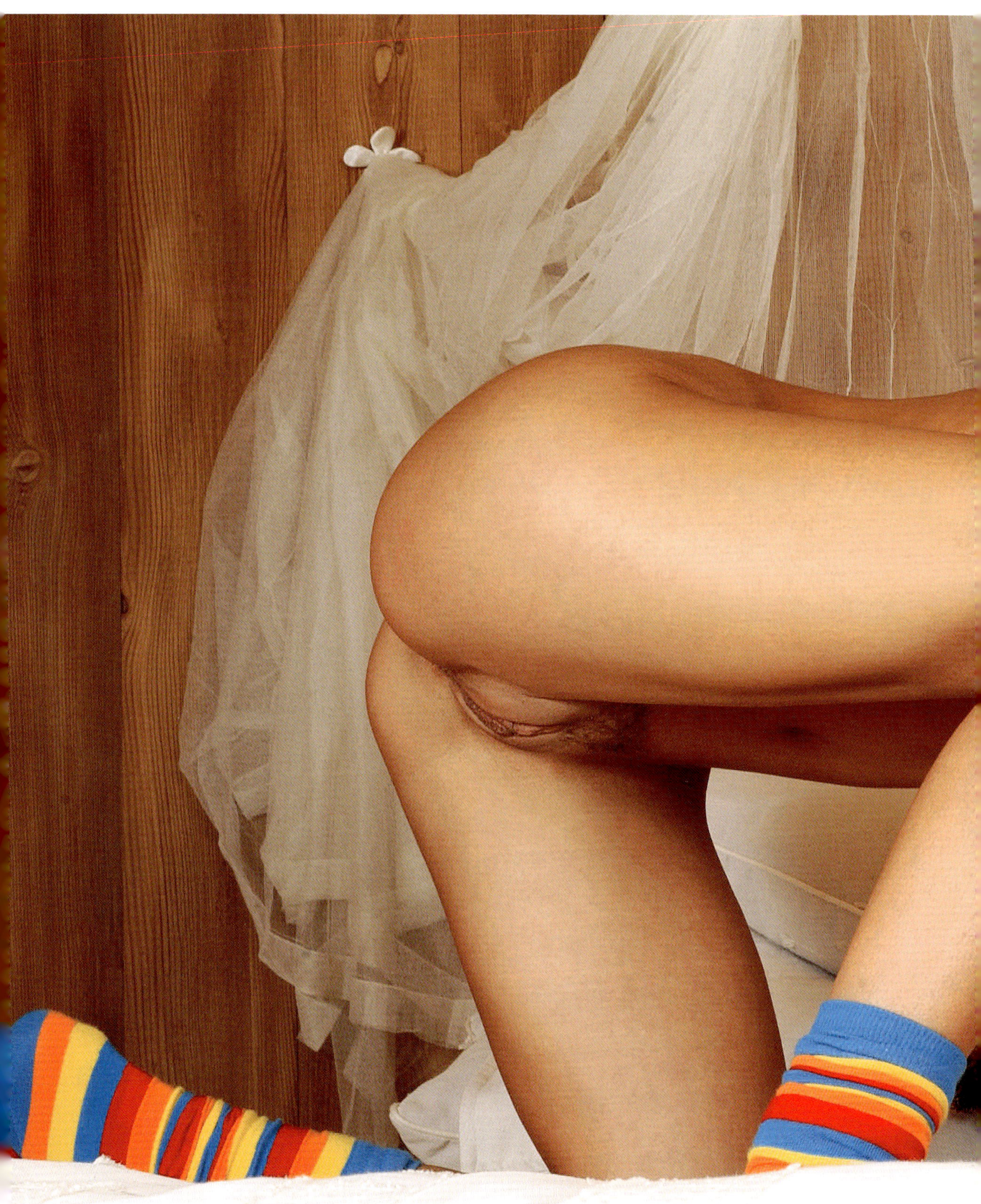



Anita Kiss

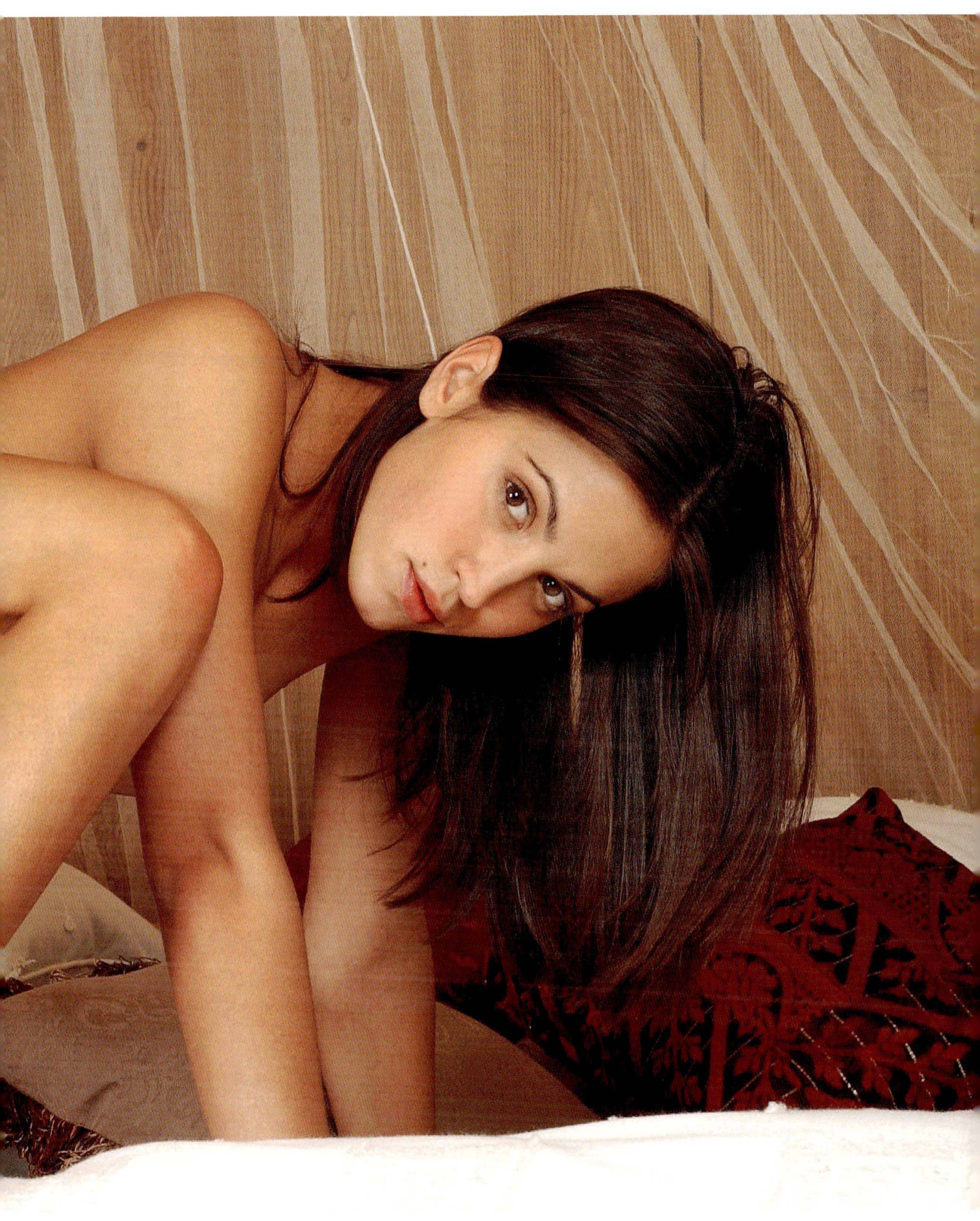

Anita Kiss

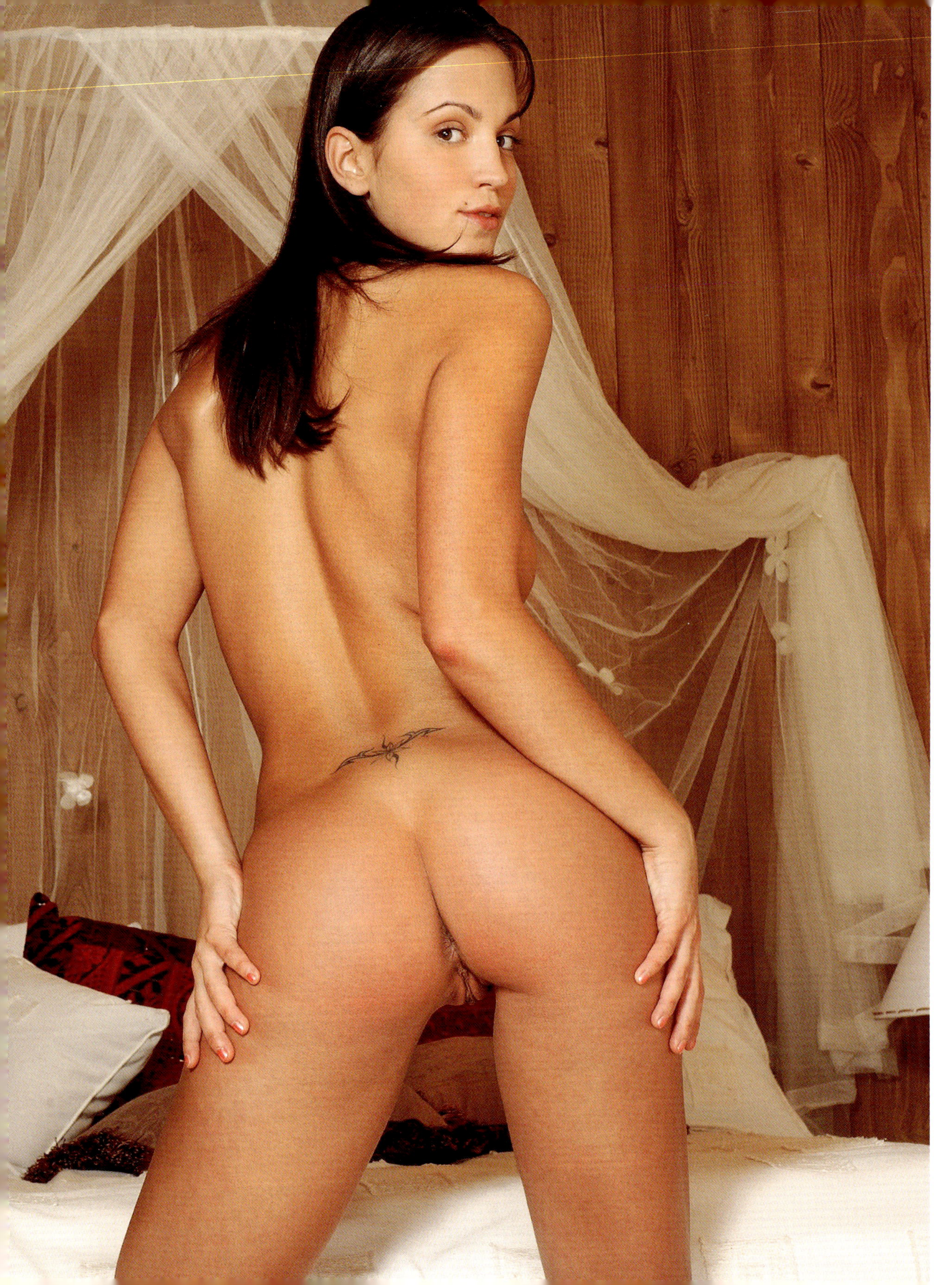

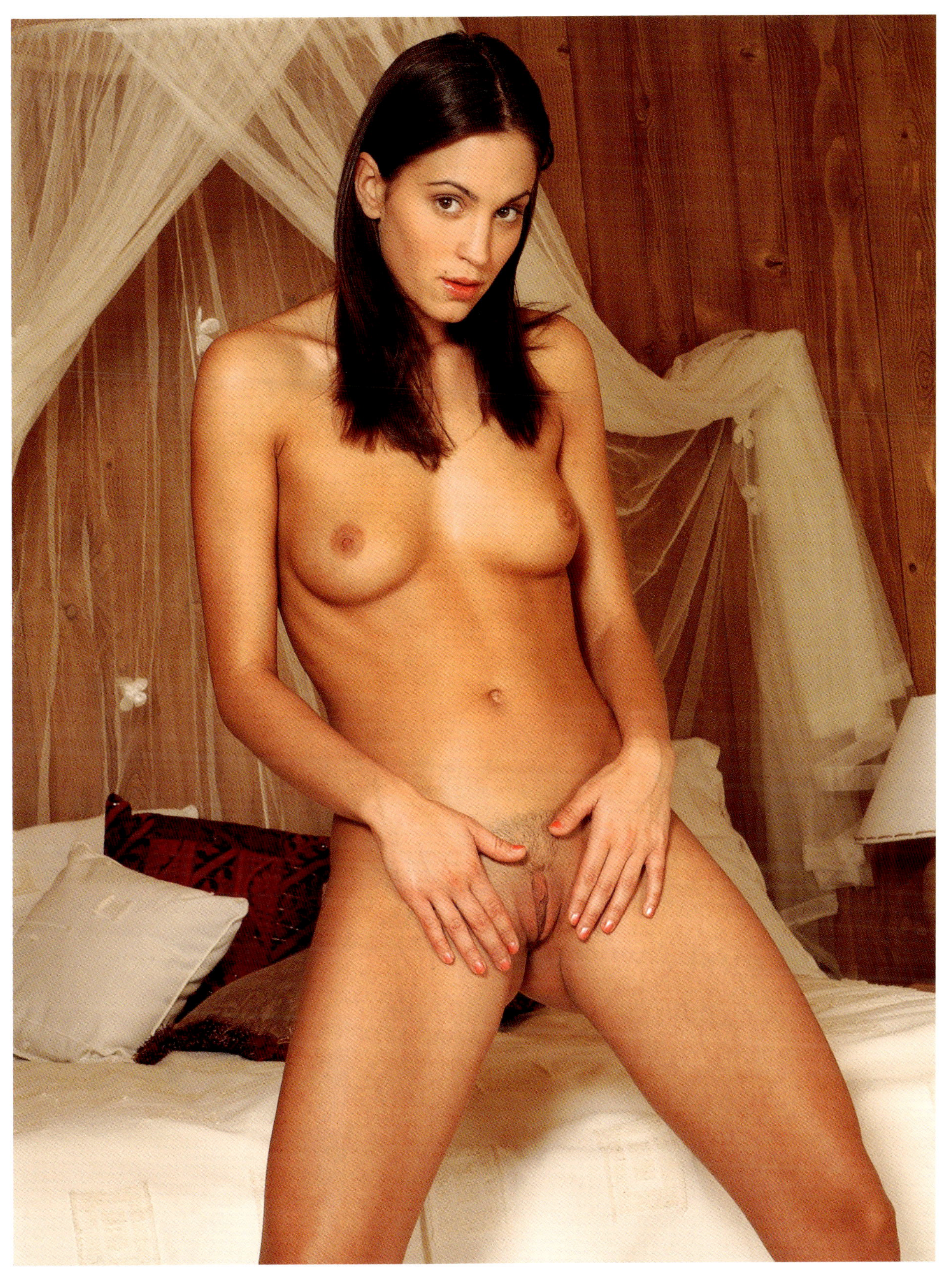

Anita Kiss

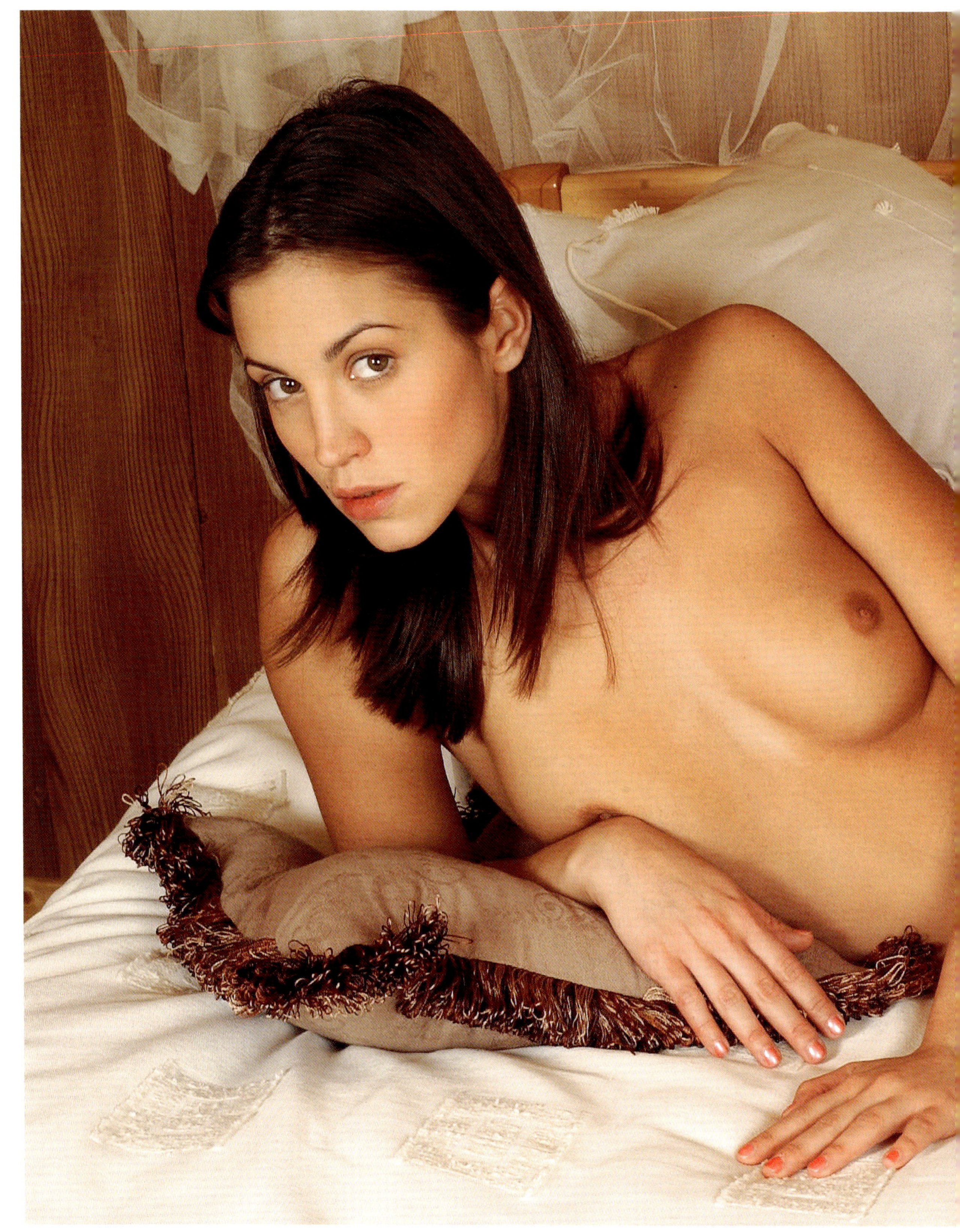



Anita Kiss

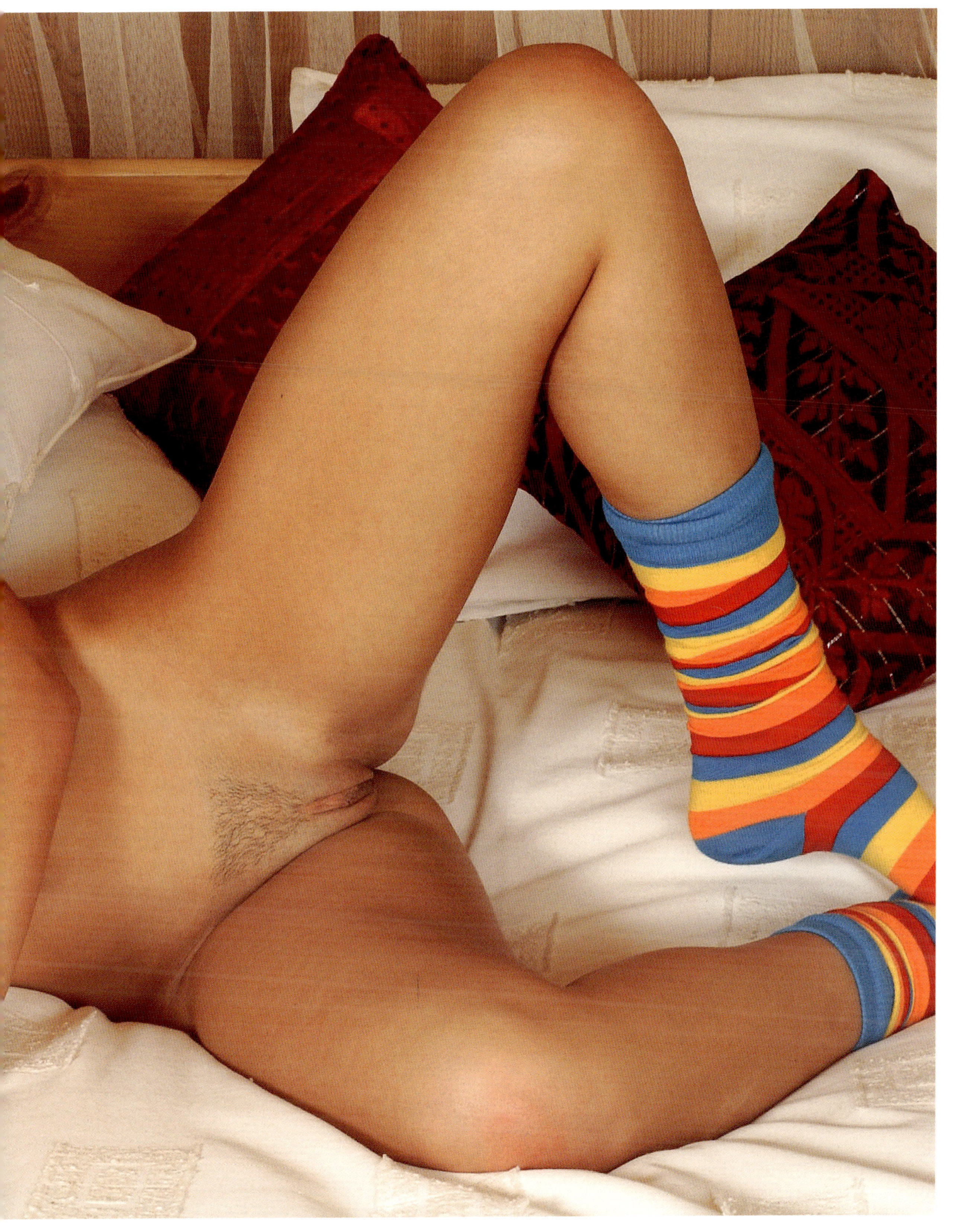

Anita Kiss

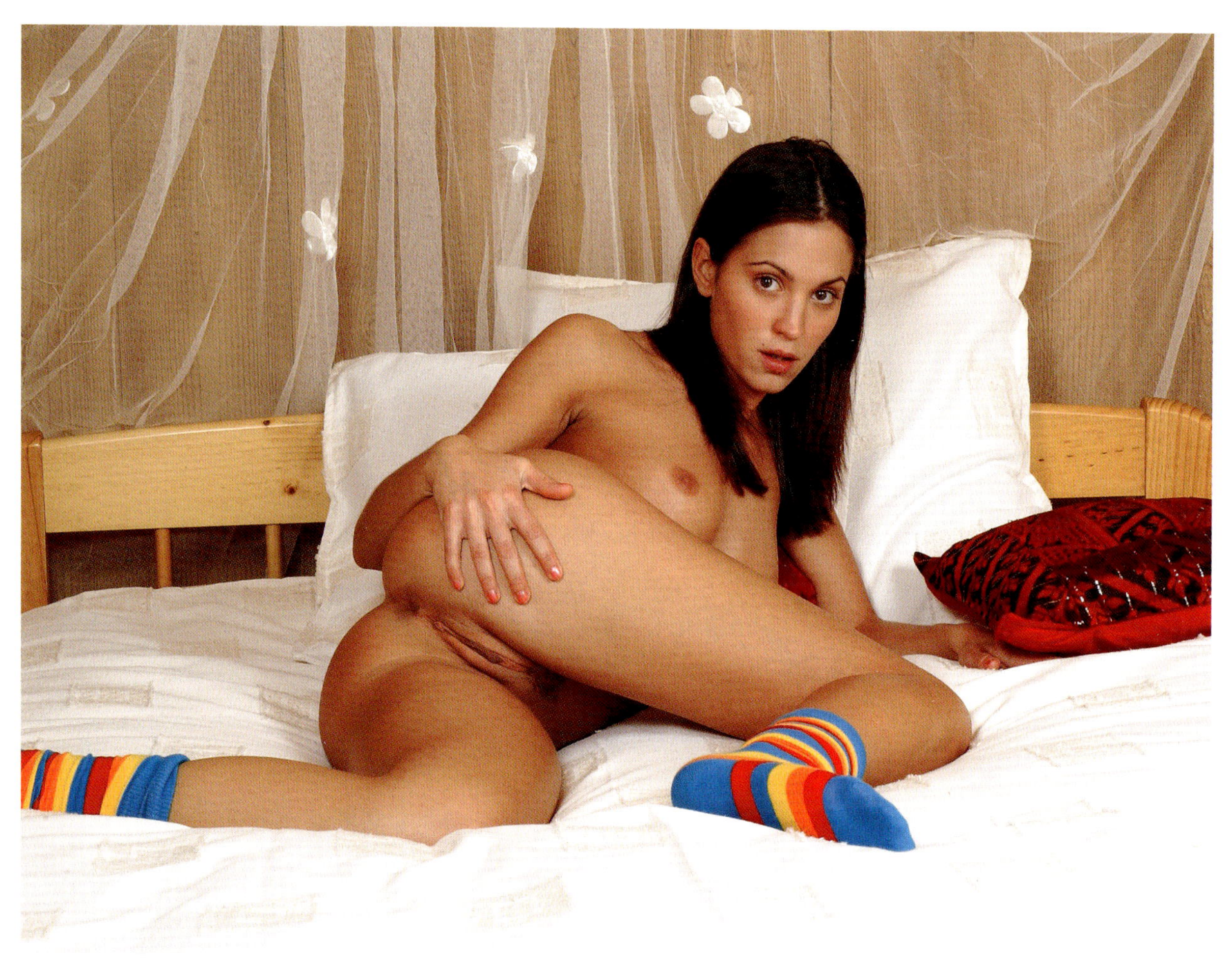

Anita Kiss

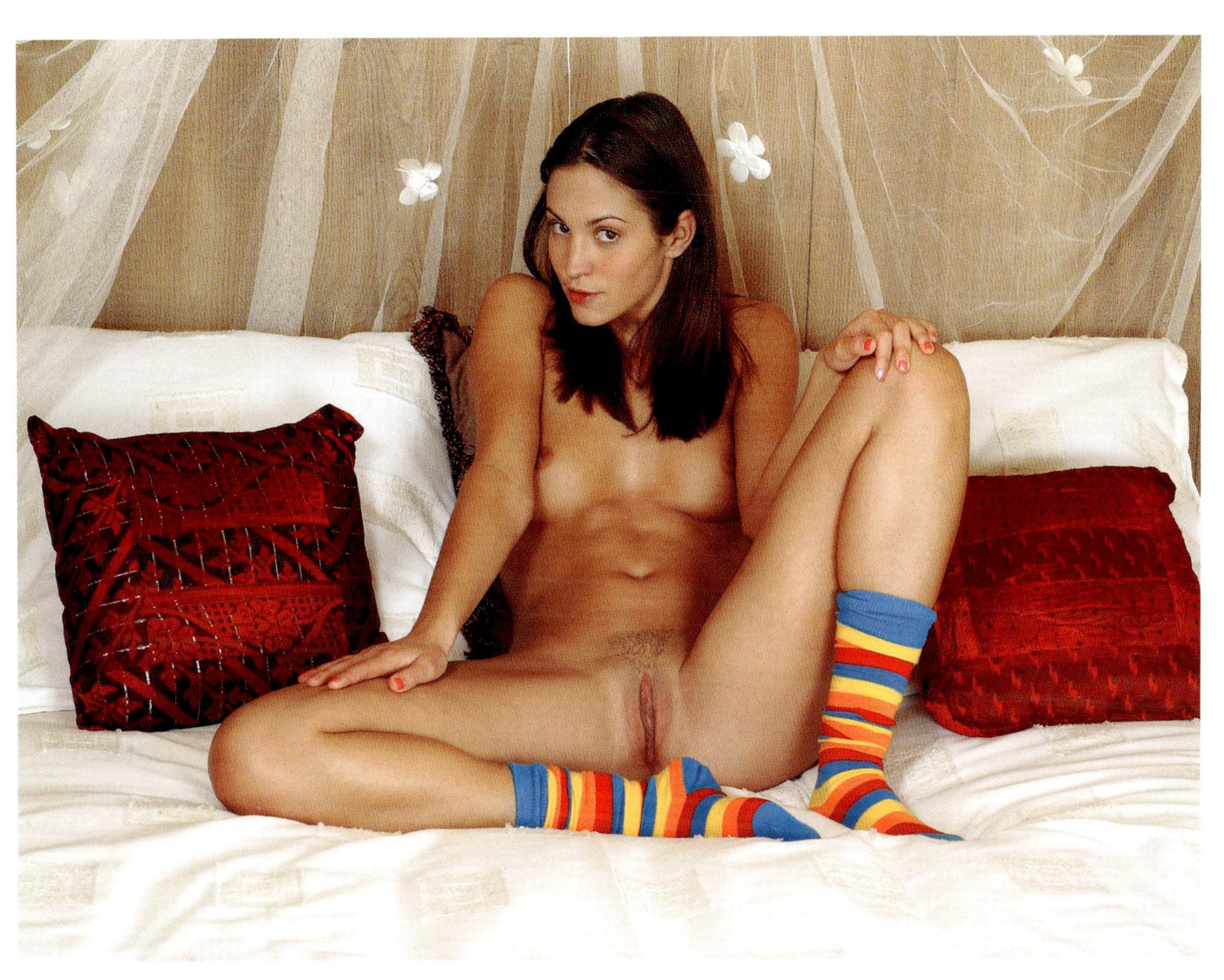

Anita Kiss

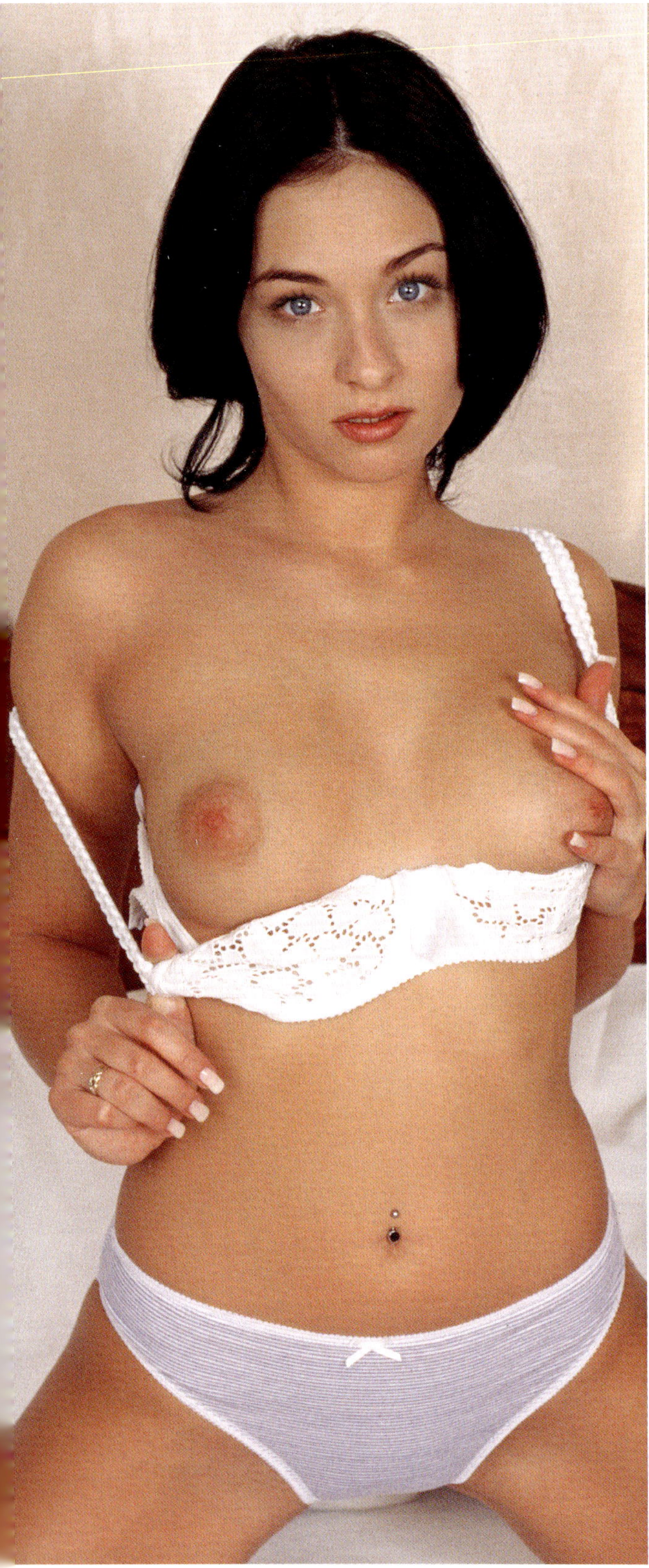

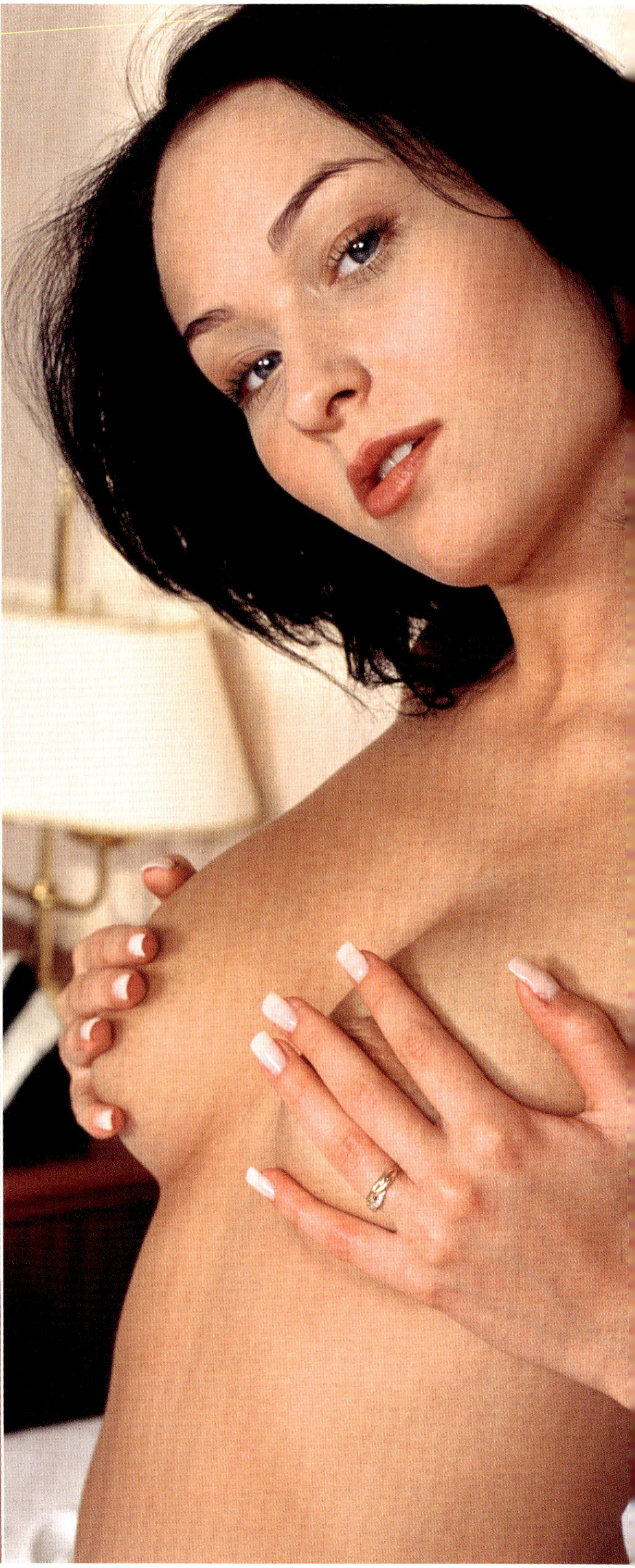

Sofia

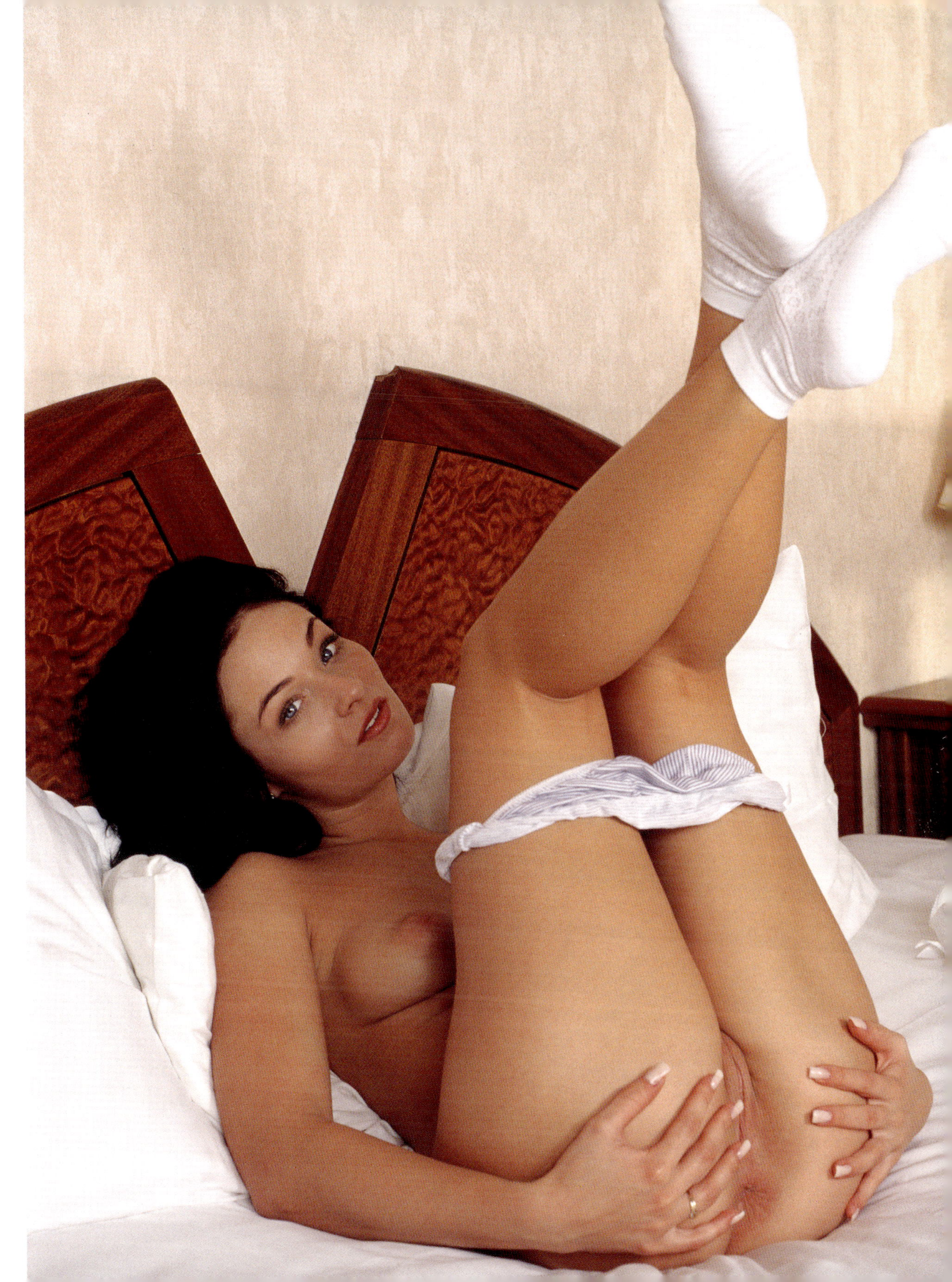

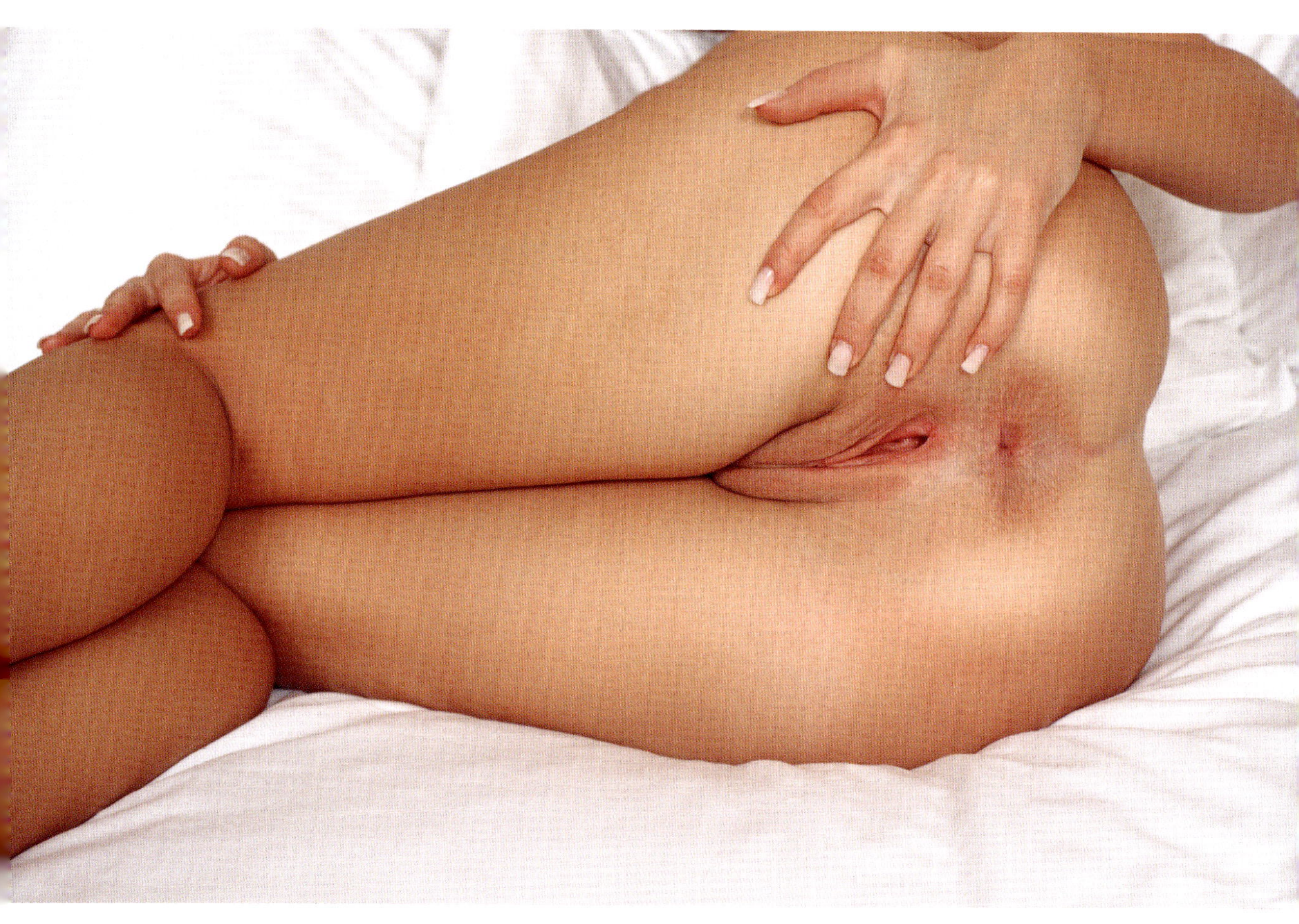

Sofia

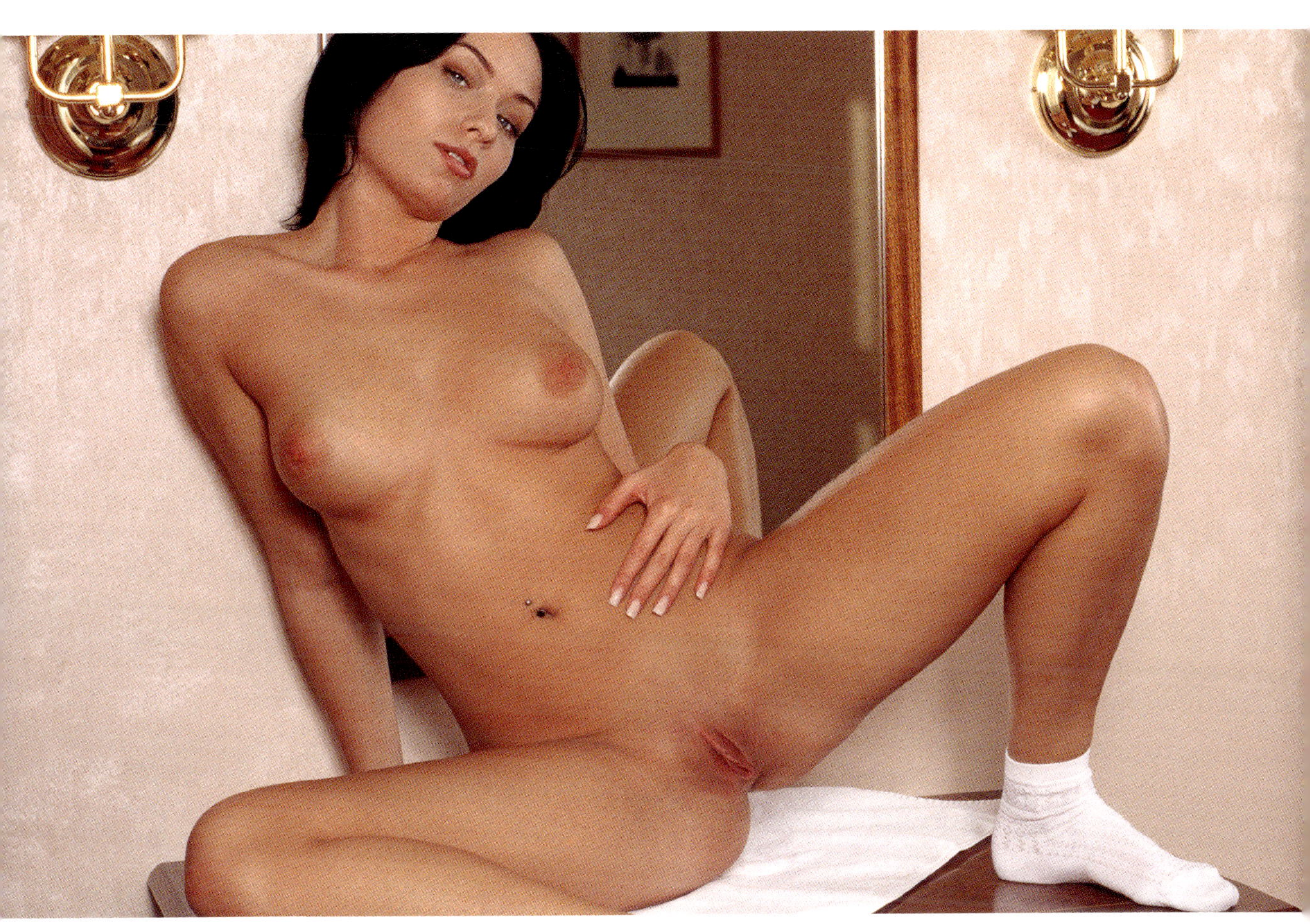

Sofia

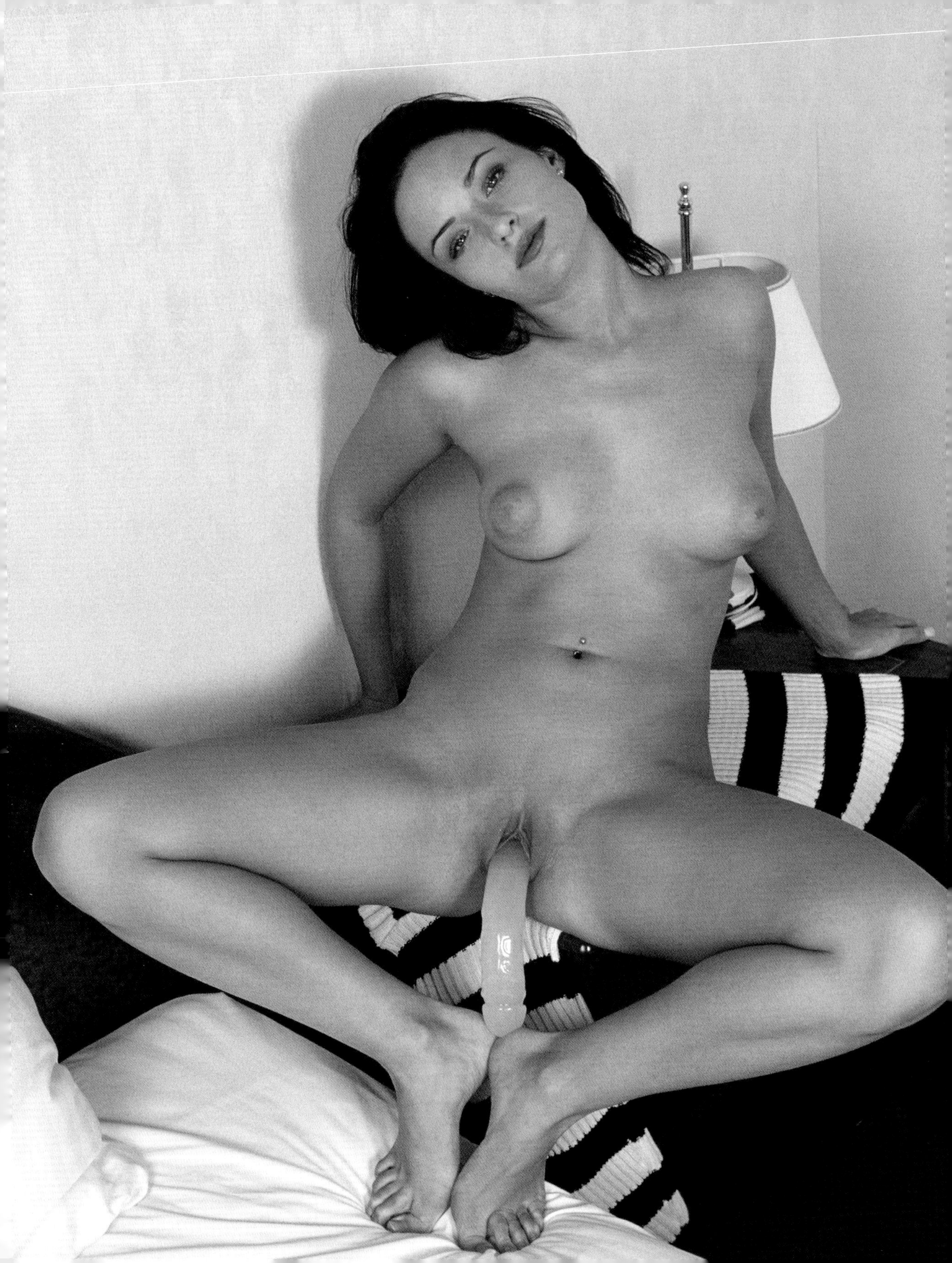

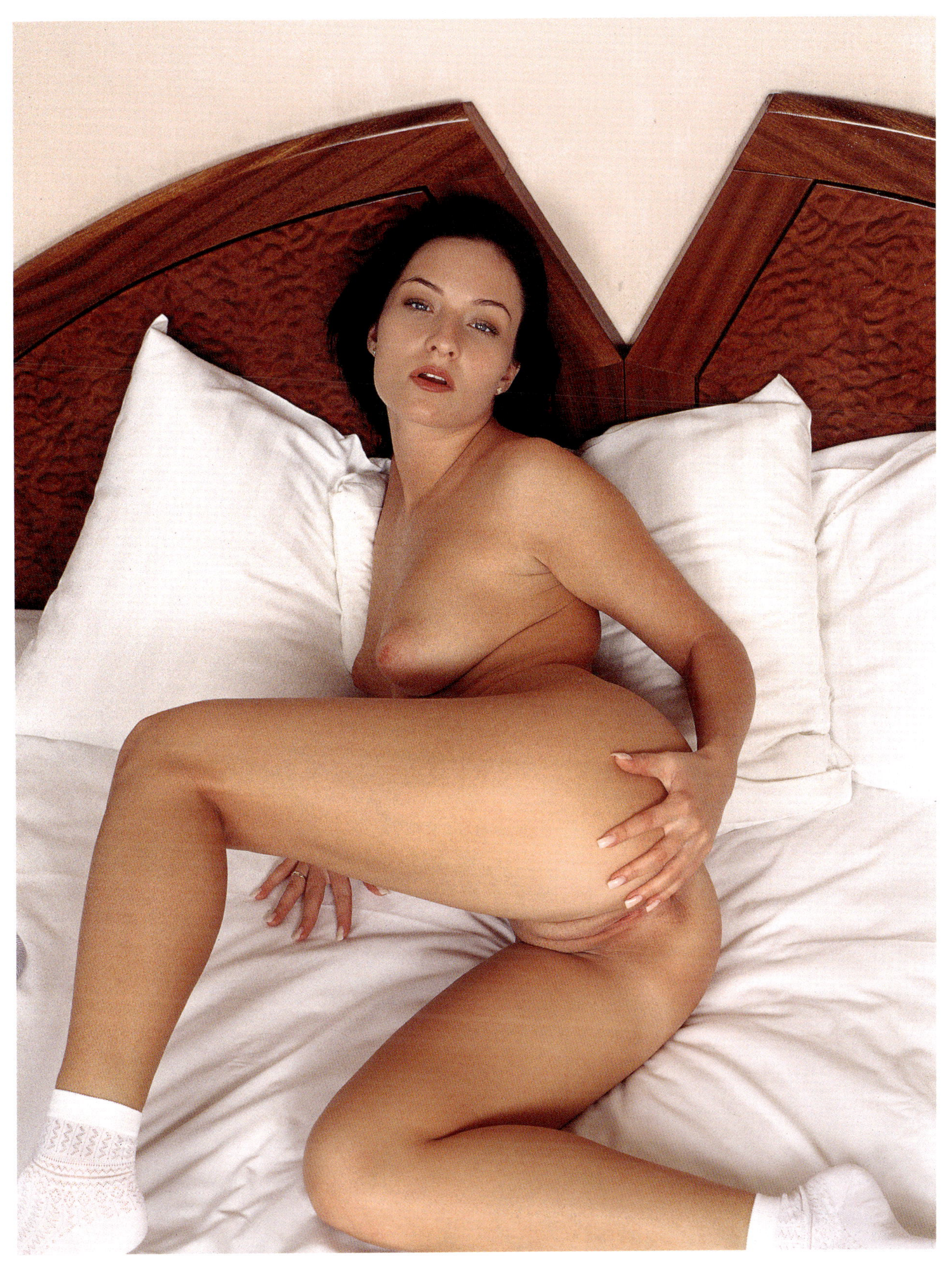

Sofia

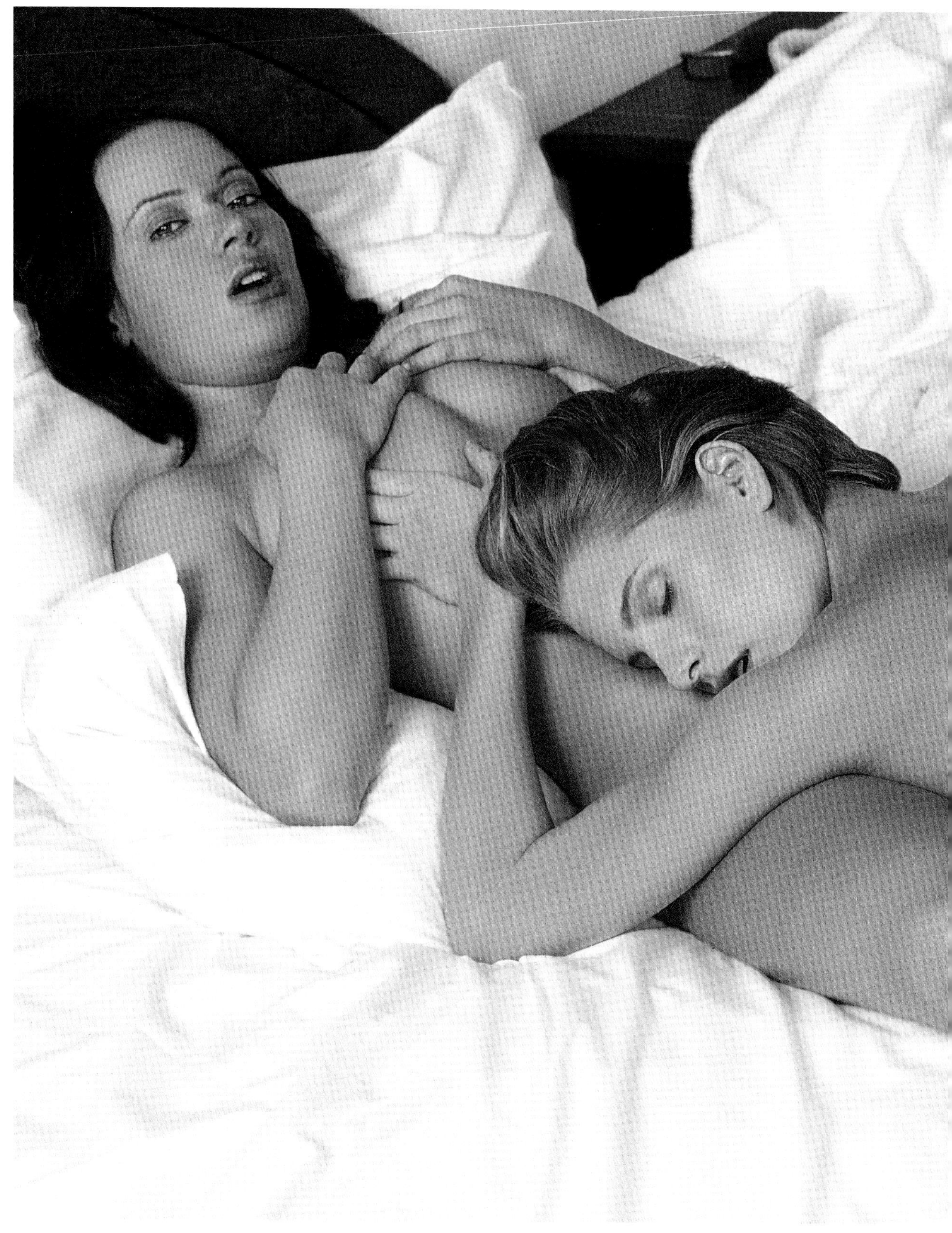

Eva and Anita

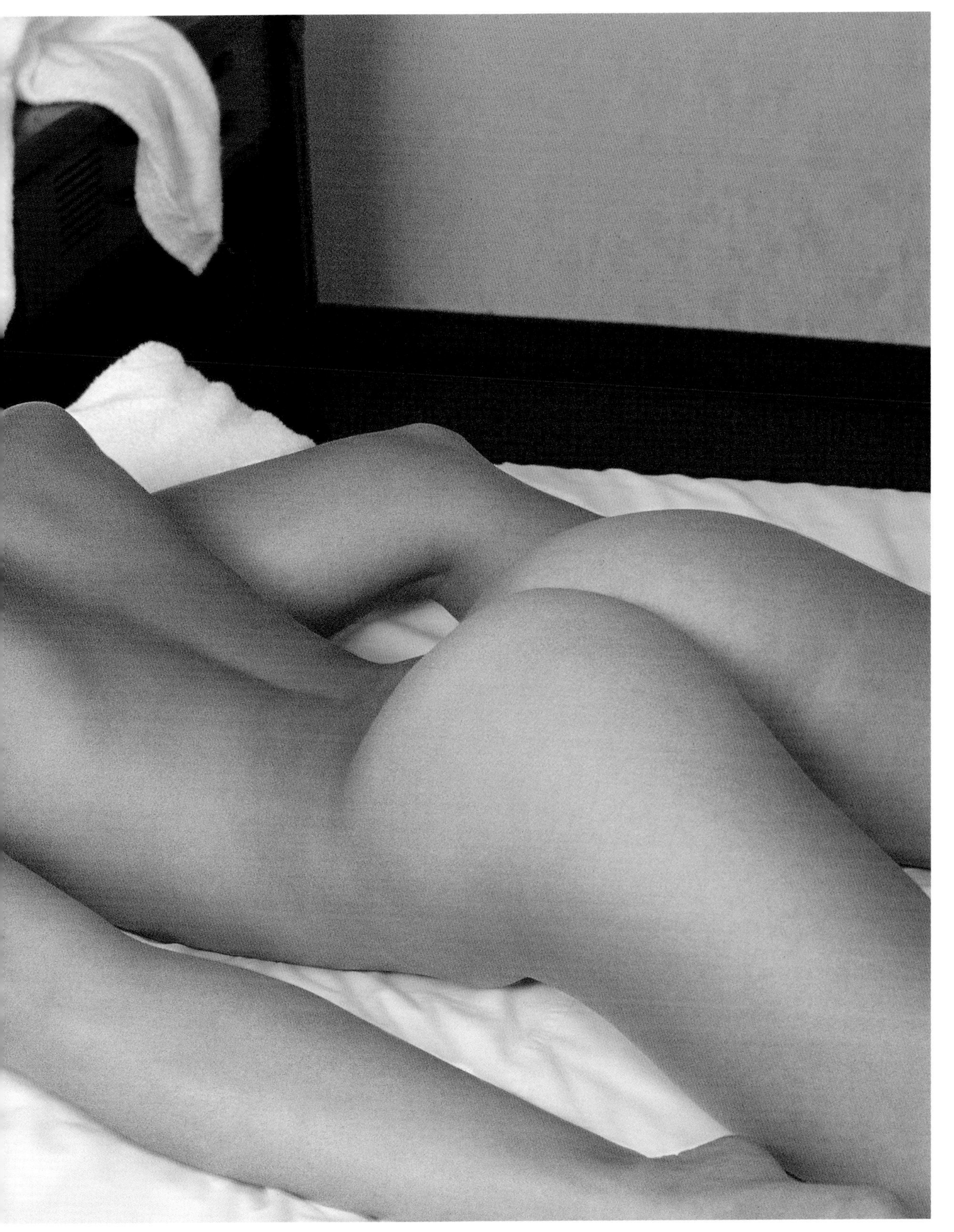

Eva and Anita

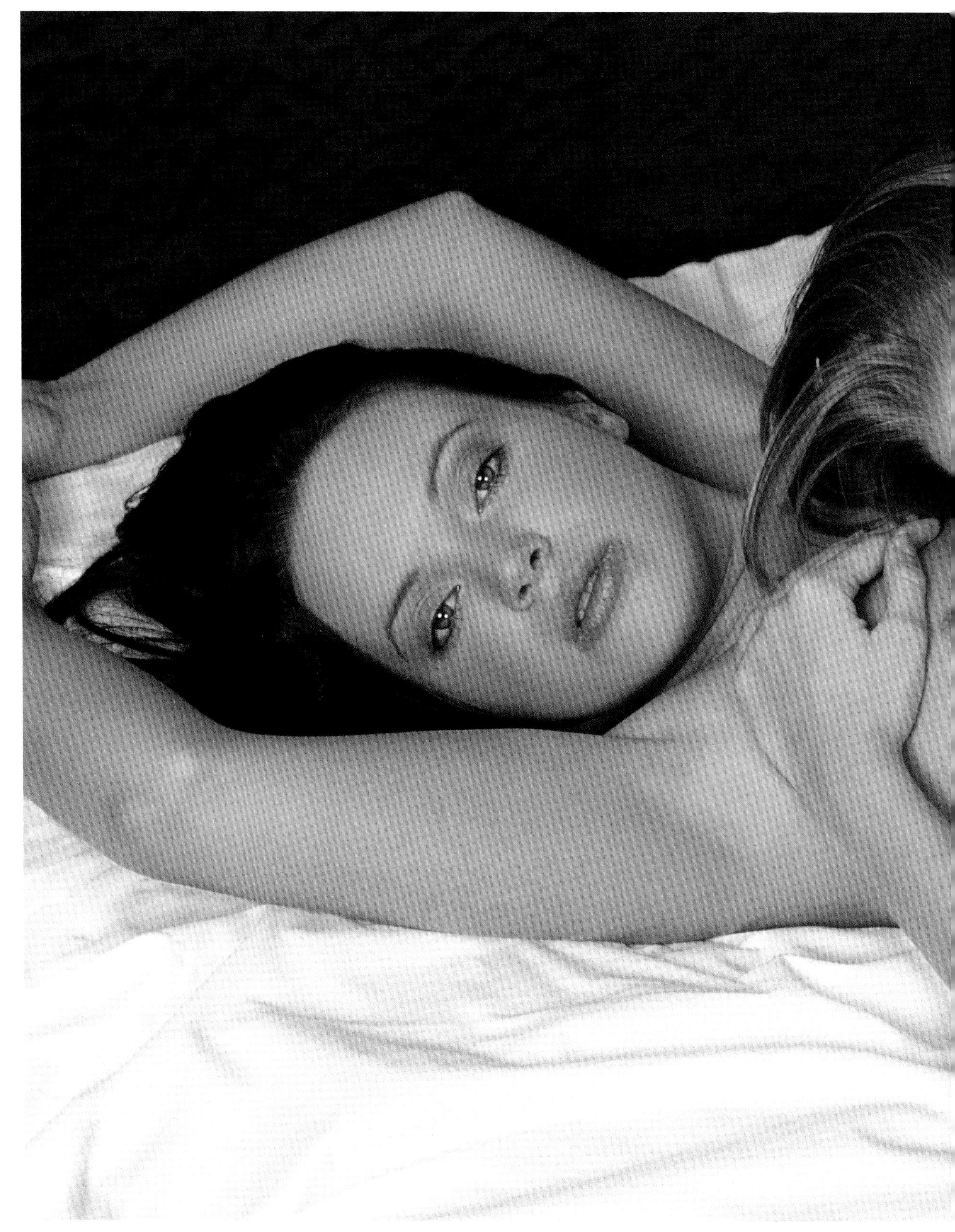

Eva and Anita

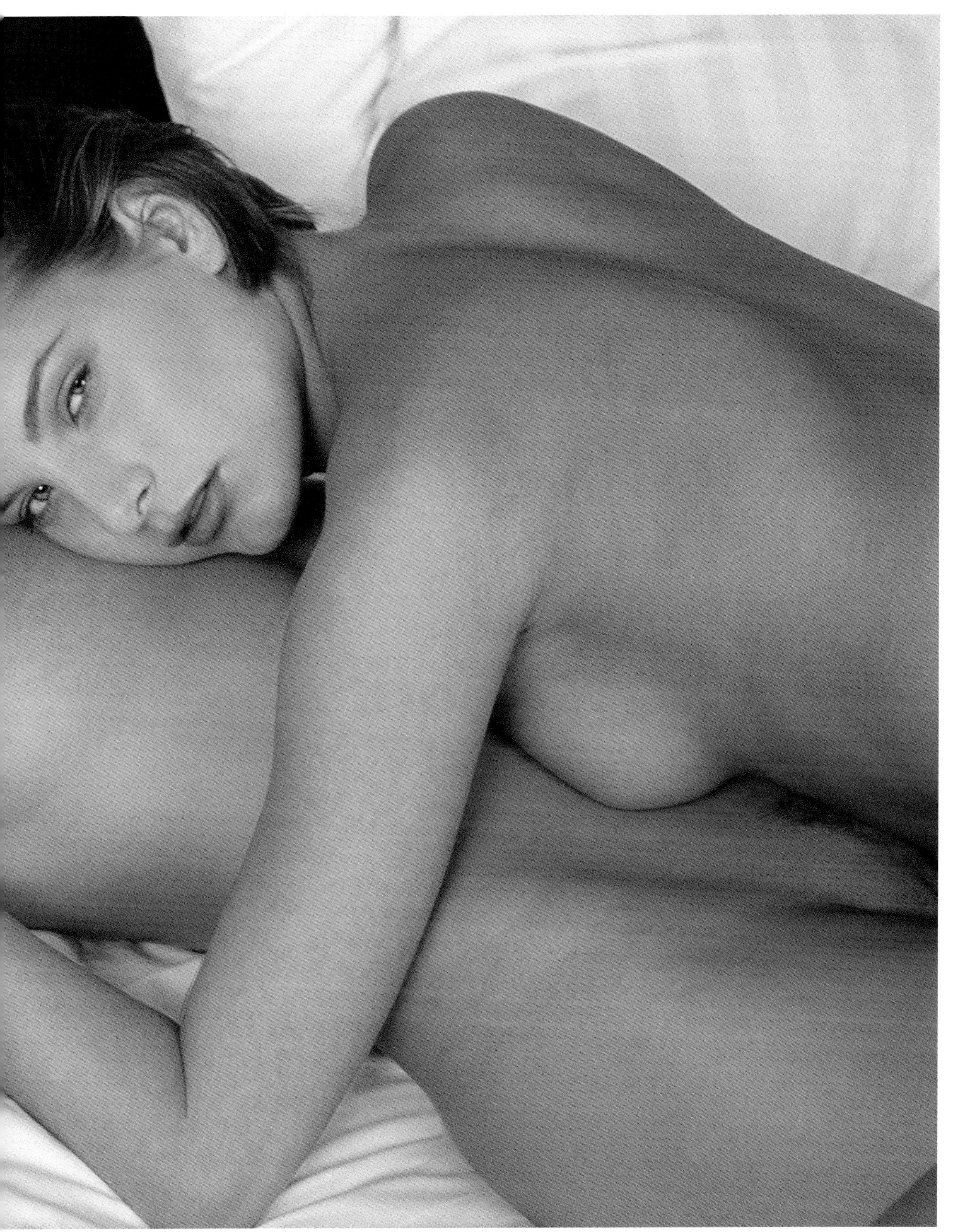

Eva and Anita

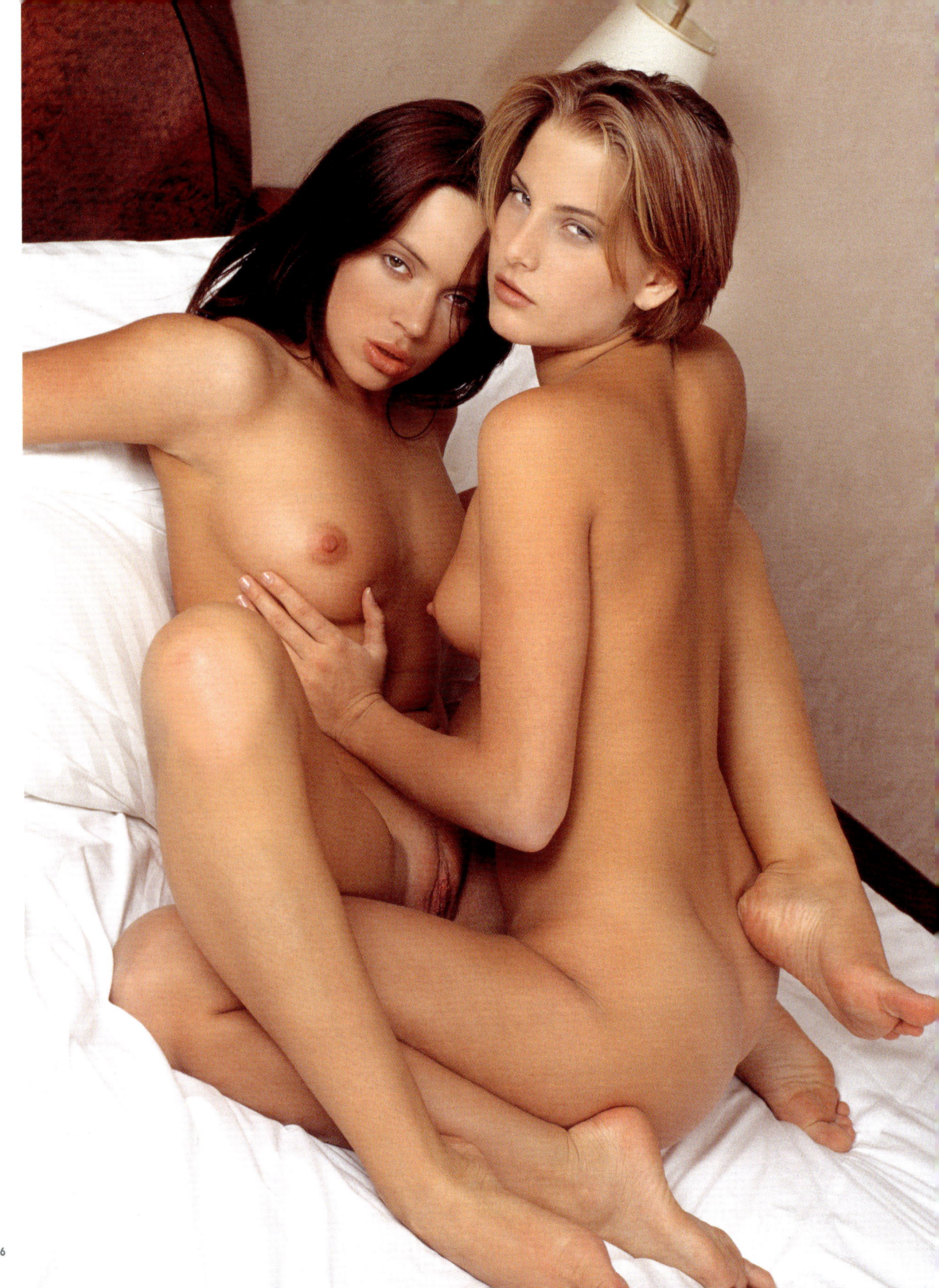

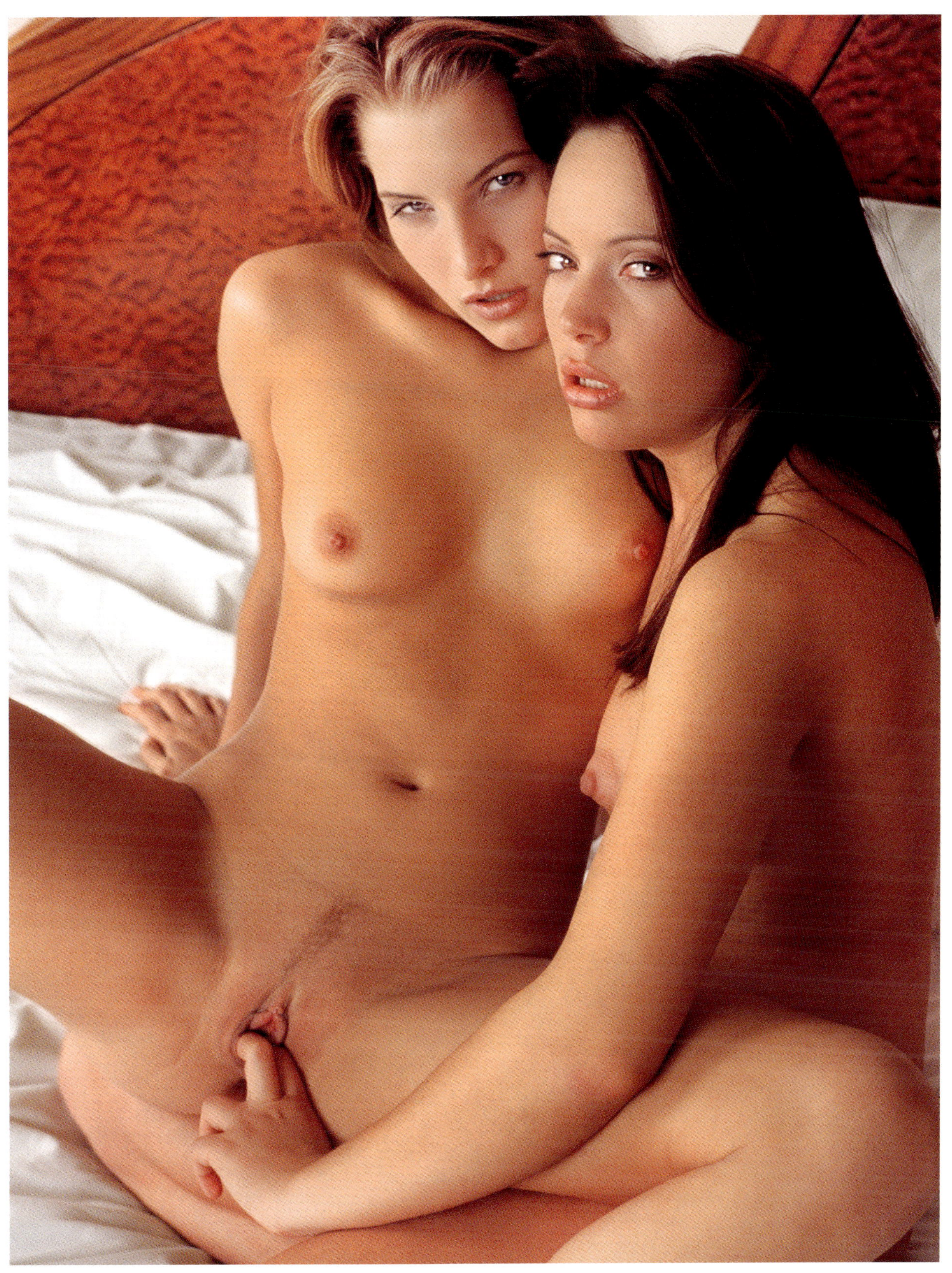

Eva and Anita

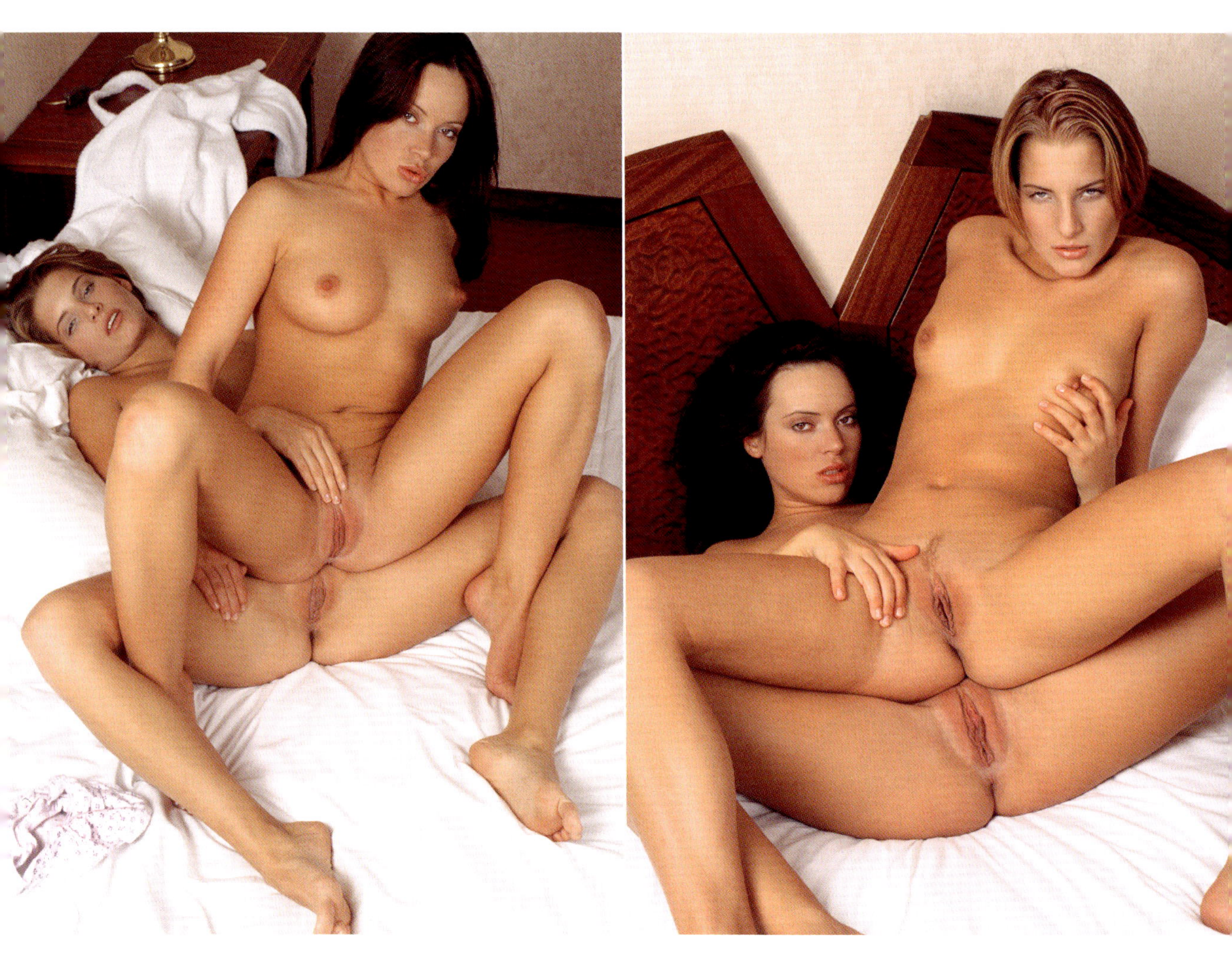

Eva and Anita

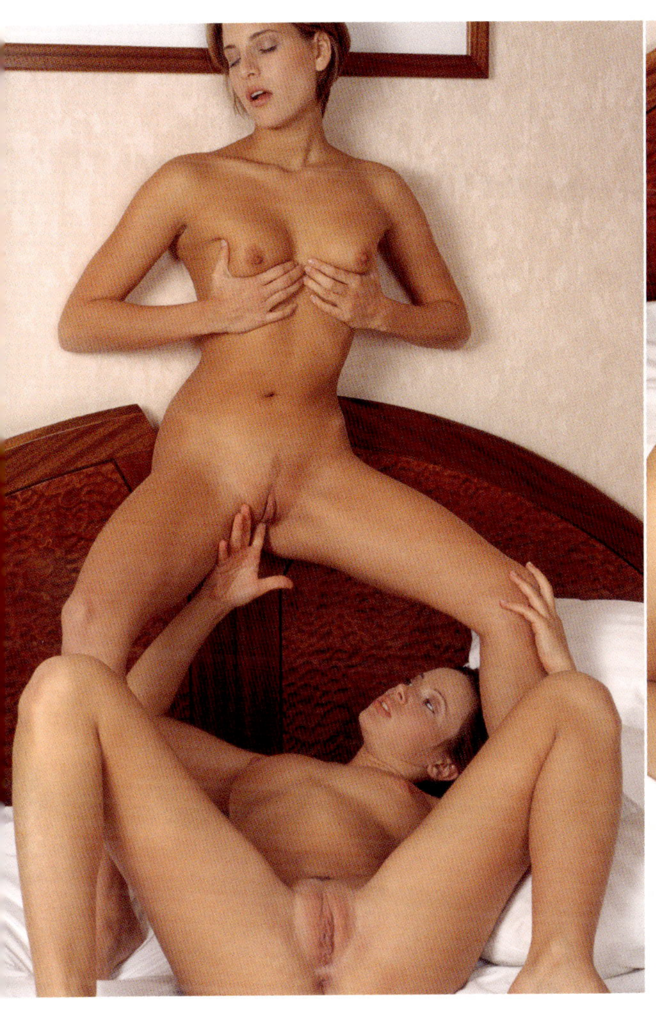

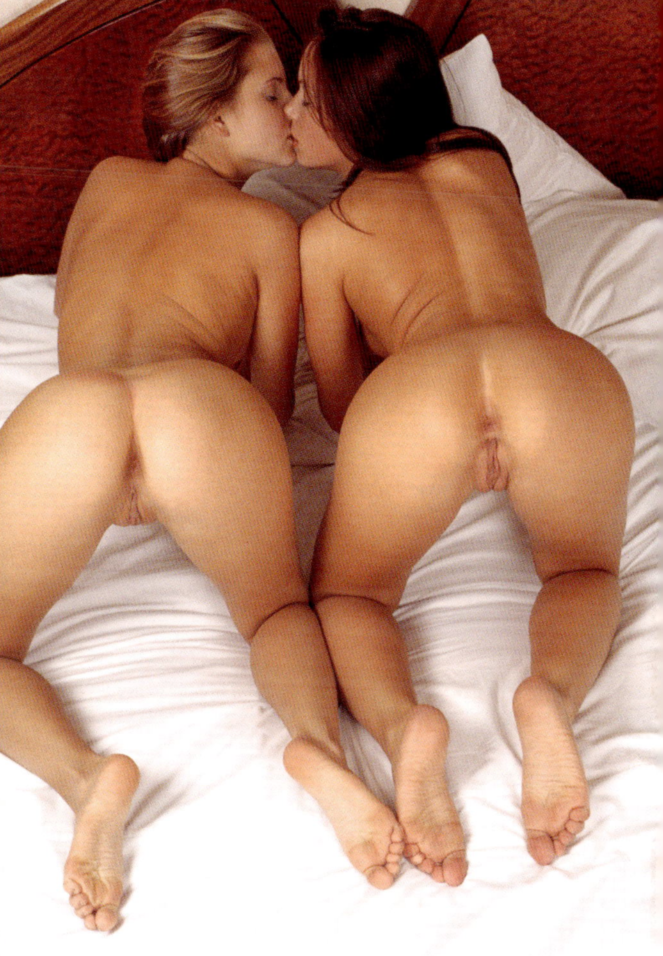

Eva and Anita

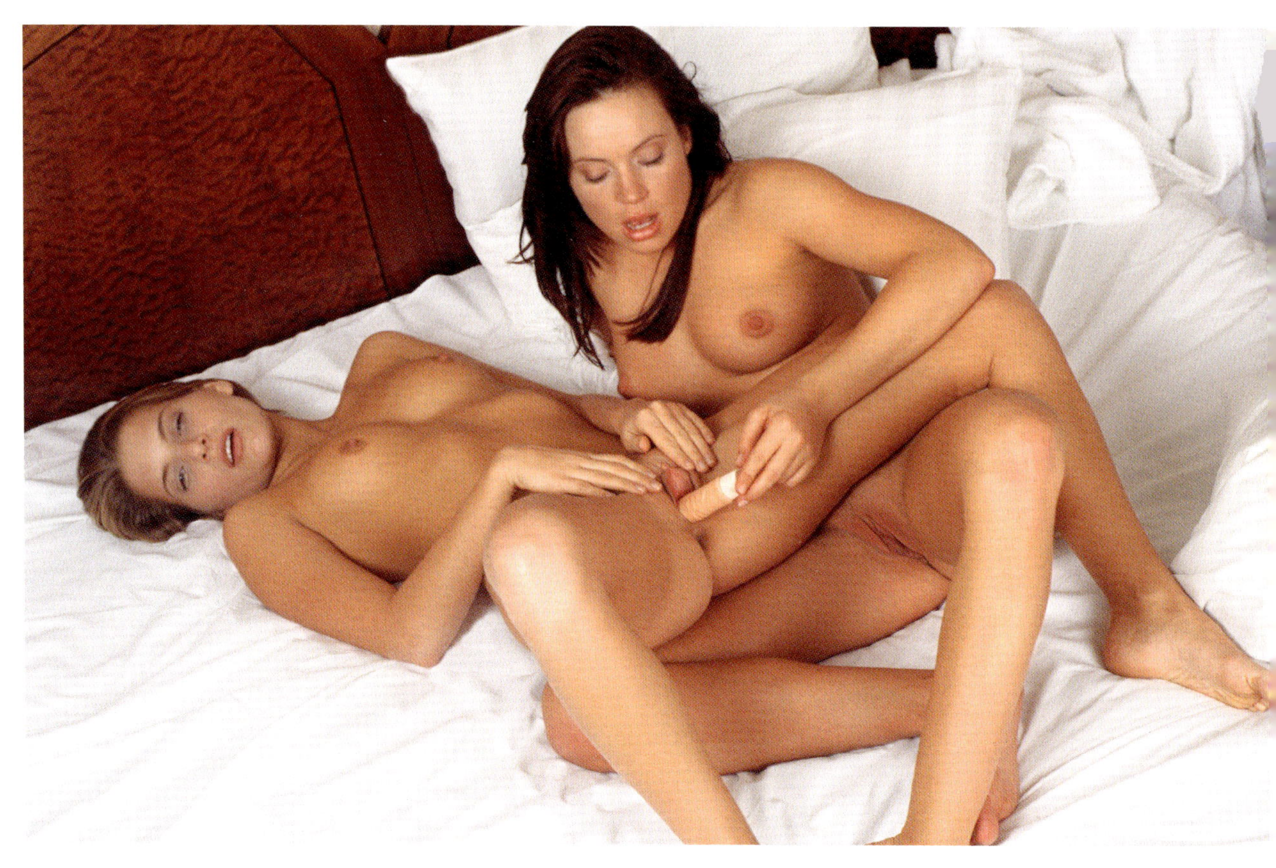

Eva and Anita

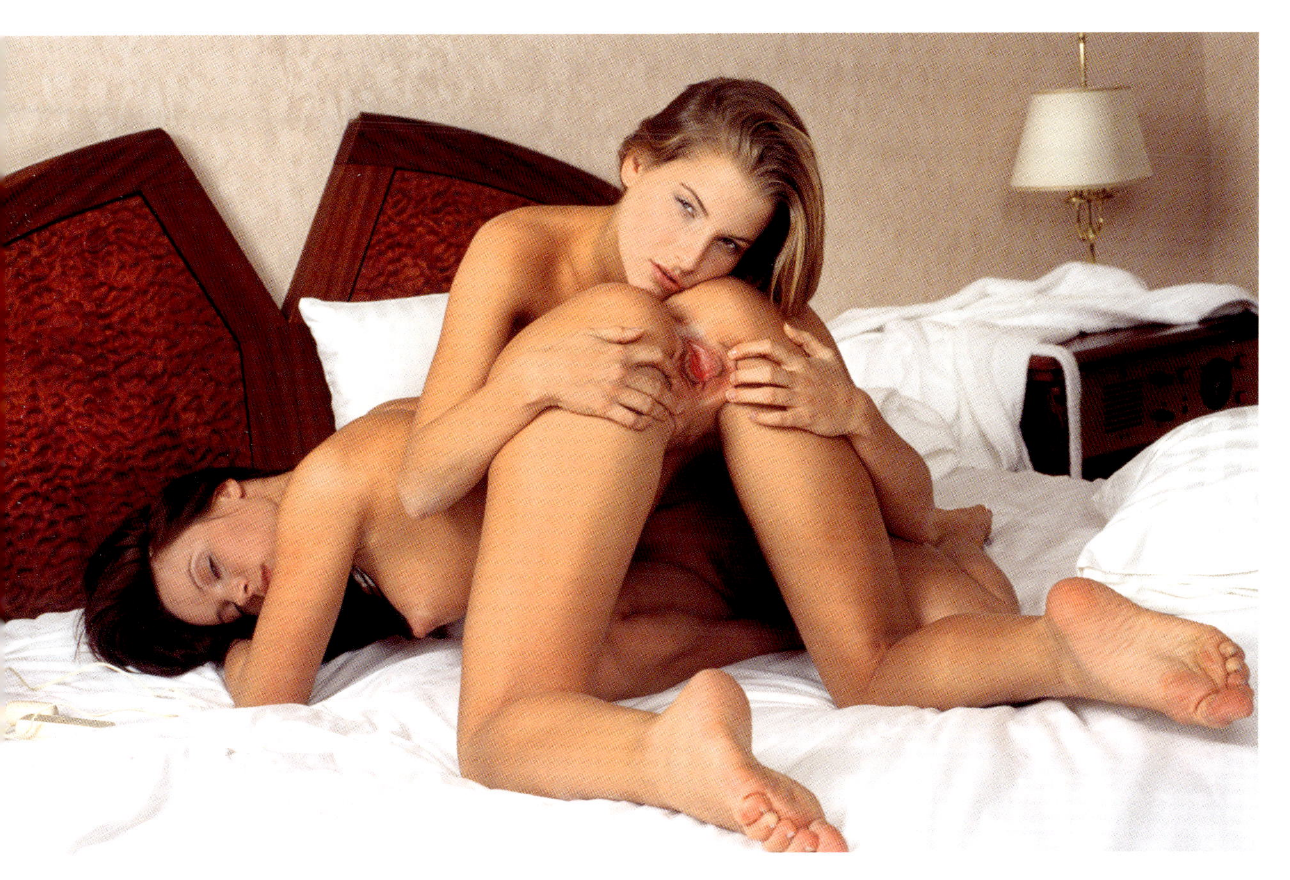

Eva and Anita

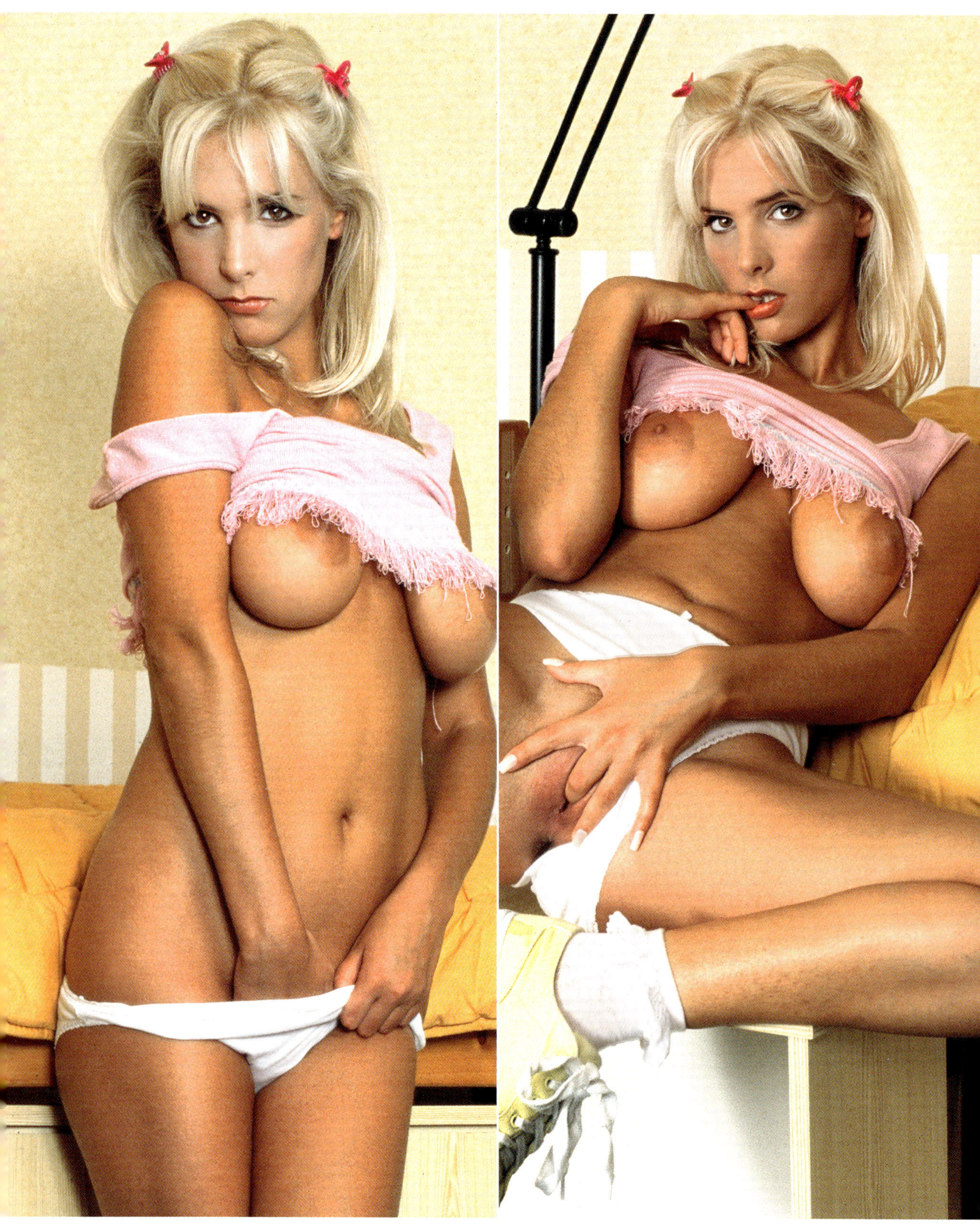



Katalin

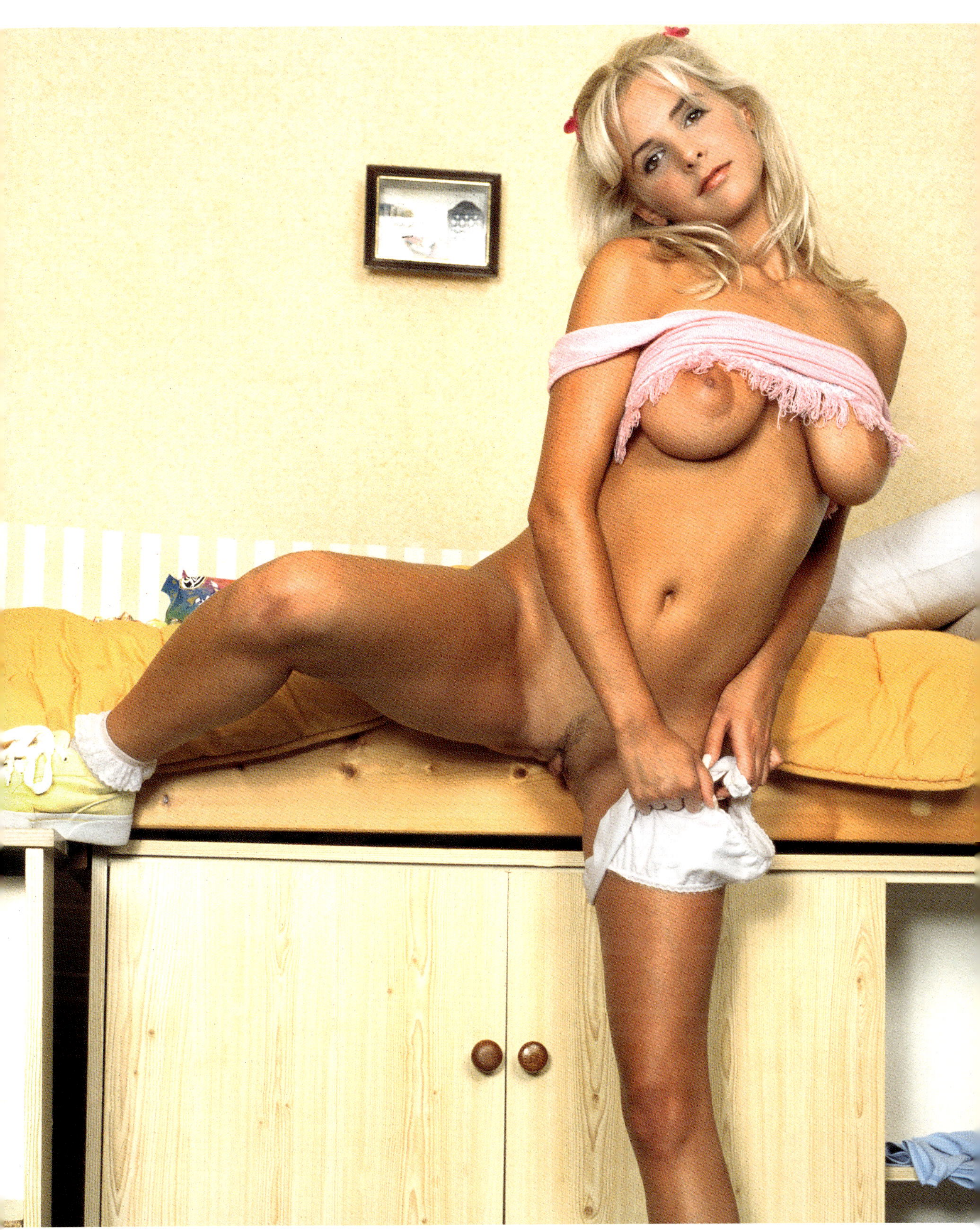

Katalin

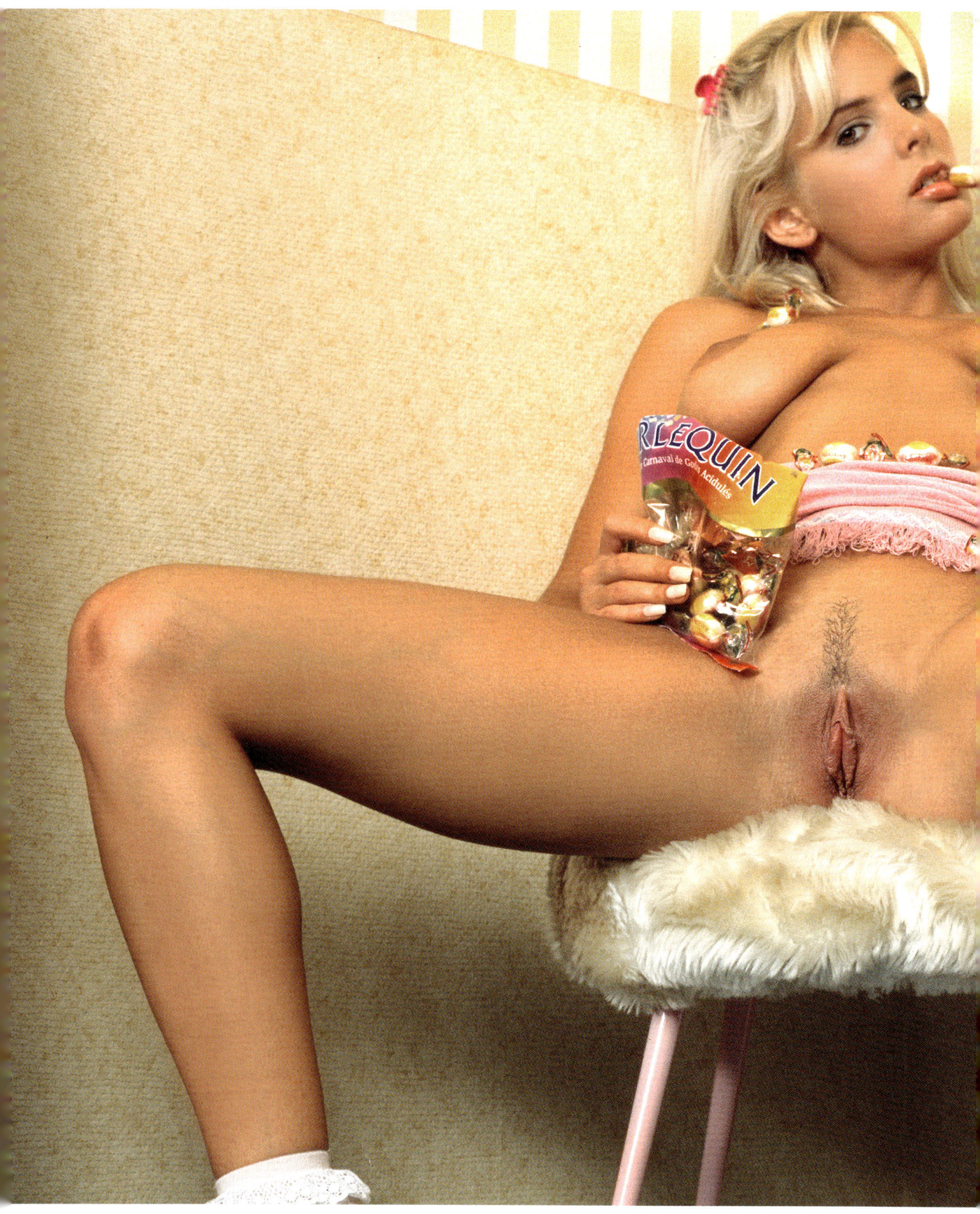


Katalin

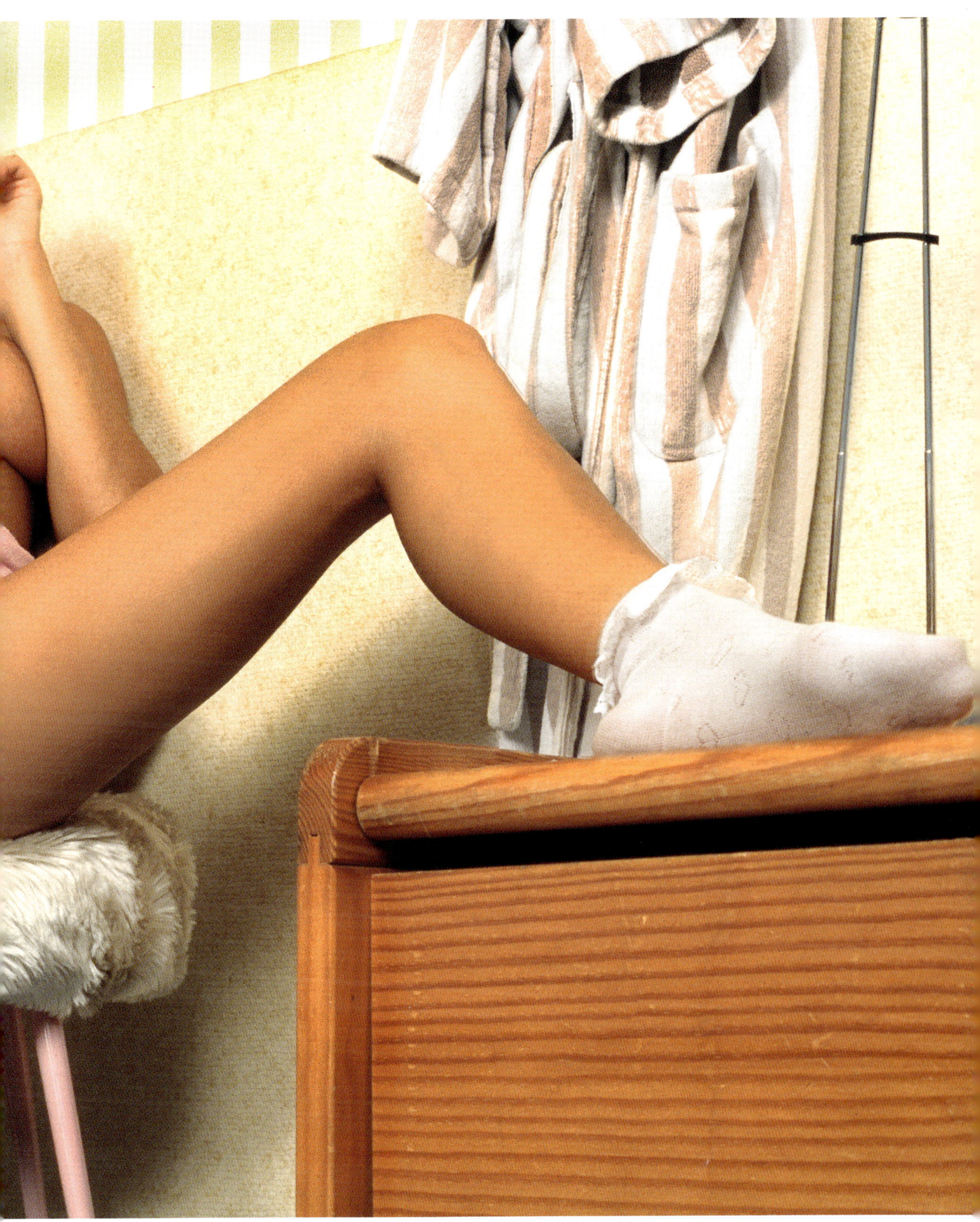

Katalin

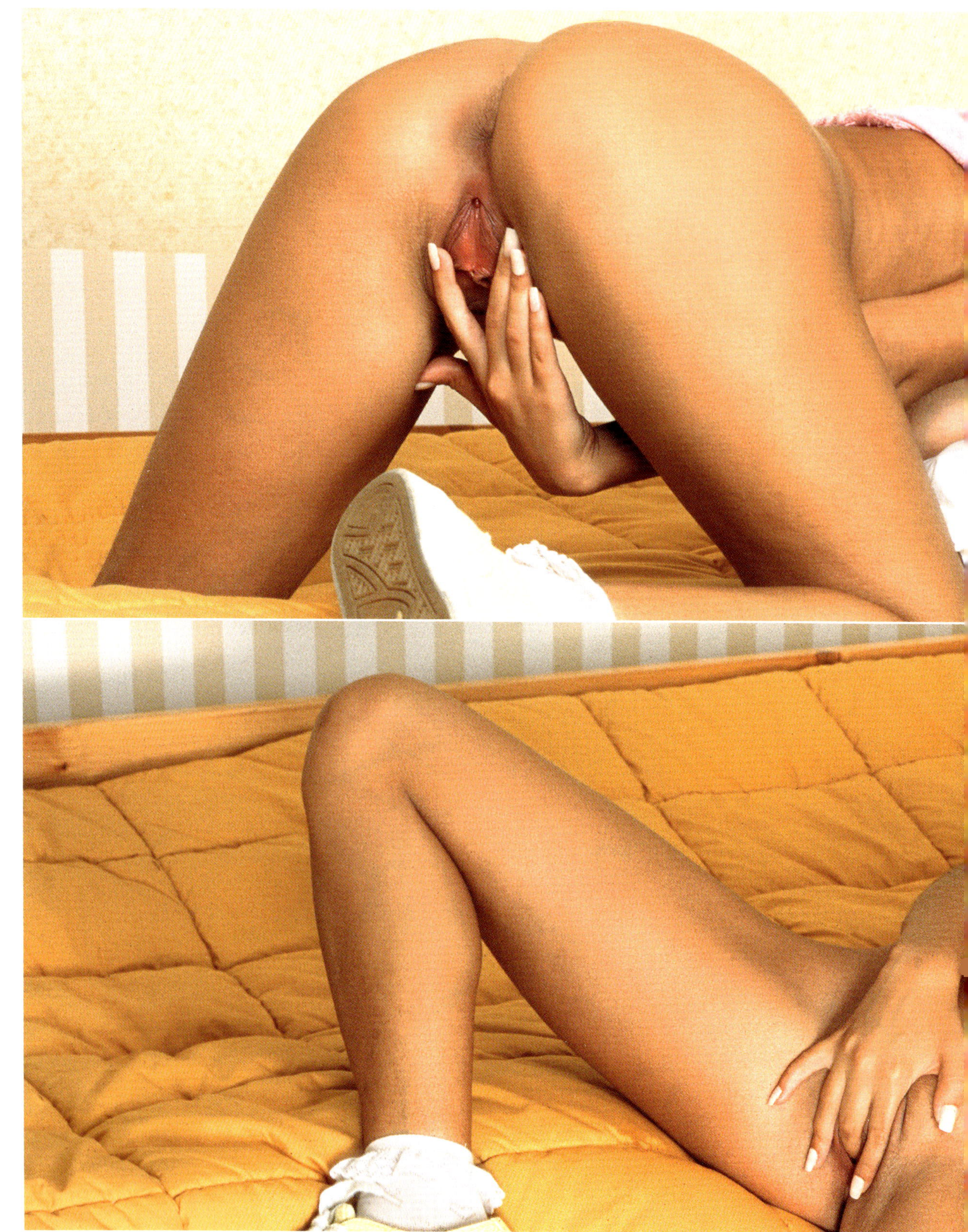

Katalin

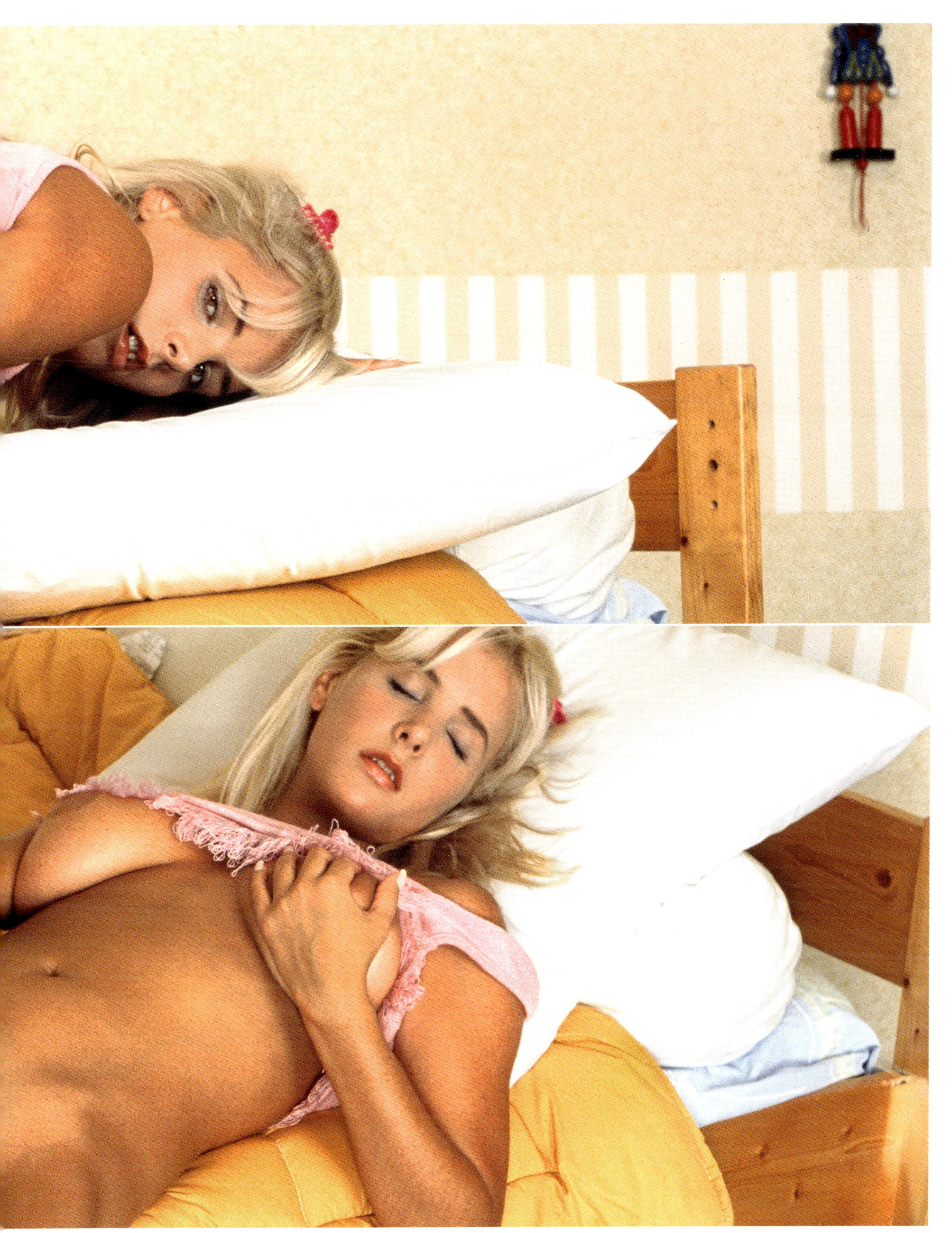

Katalin

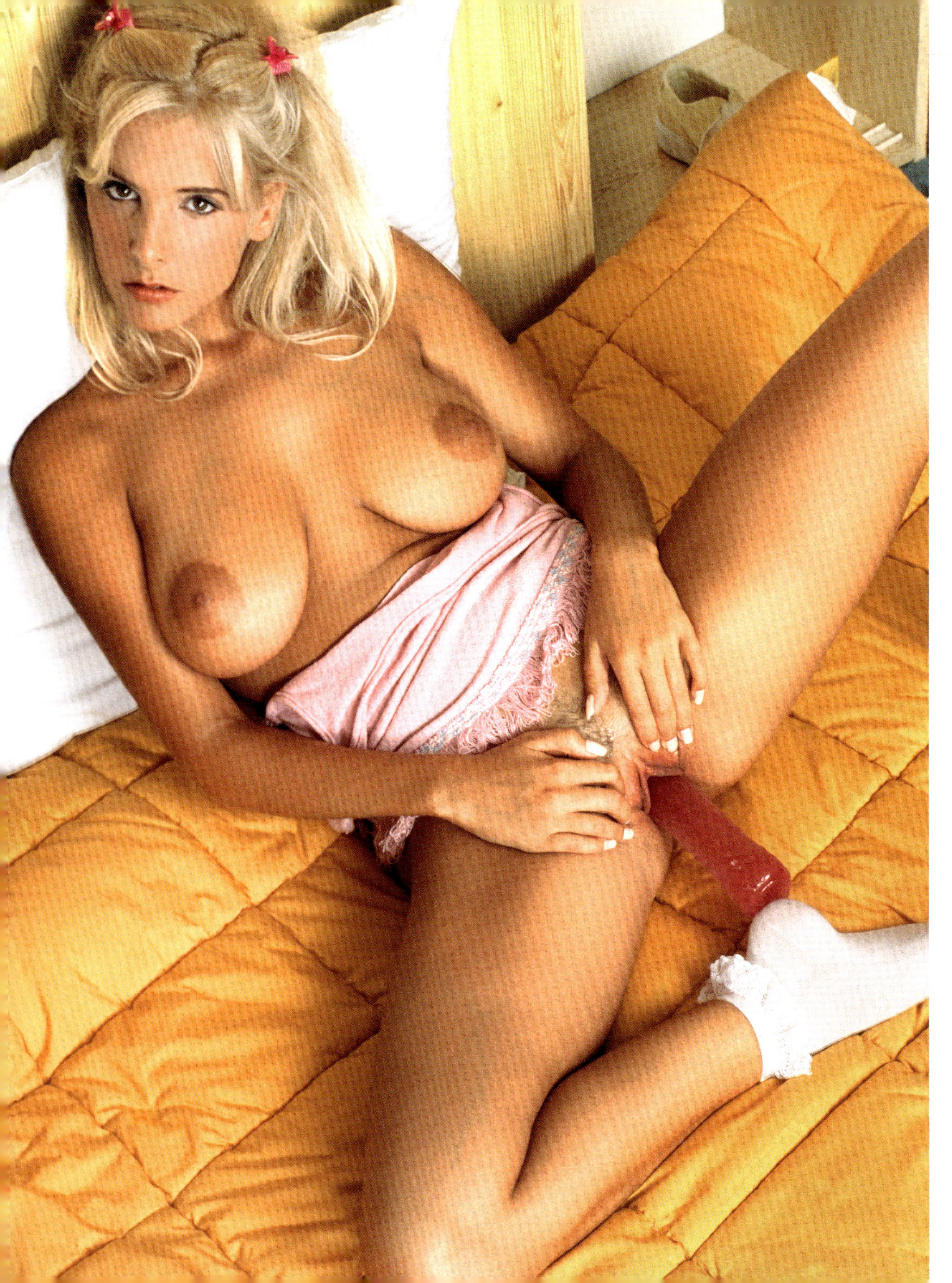

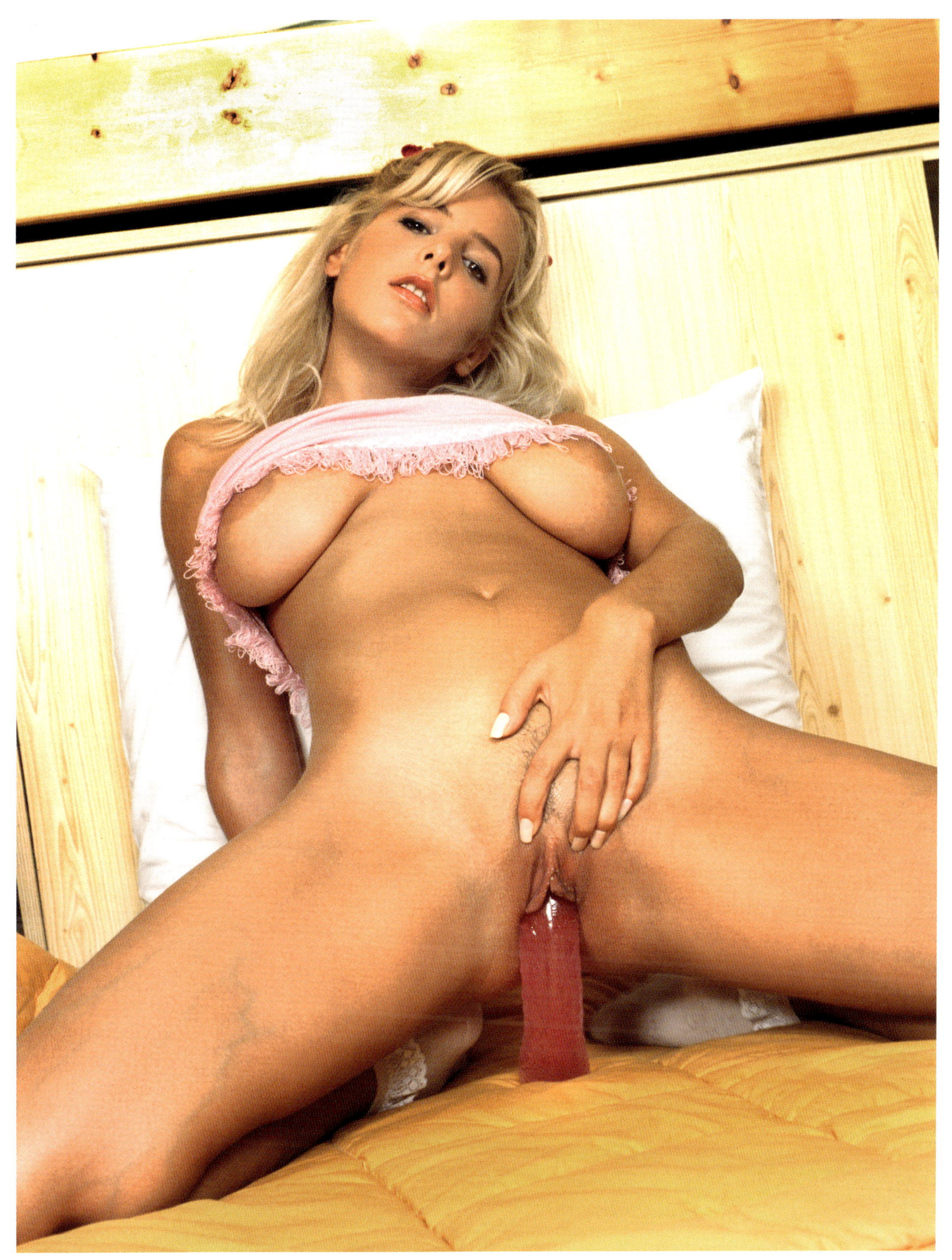

Katalin

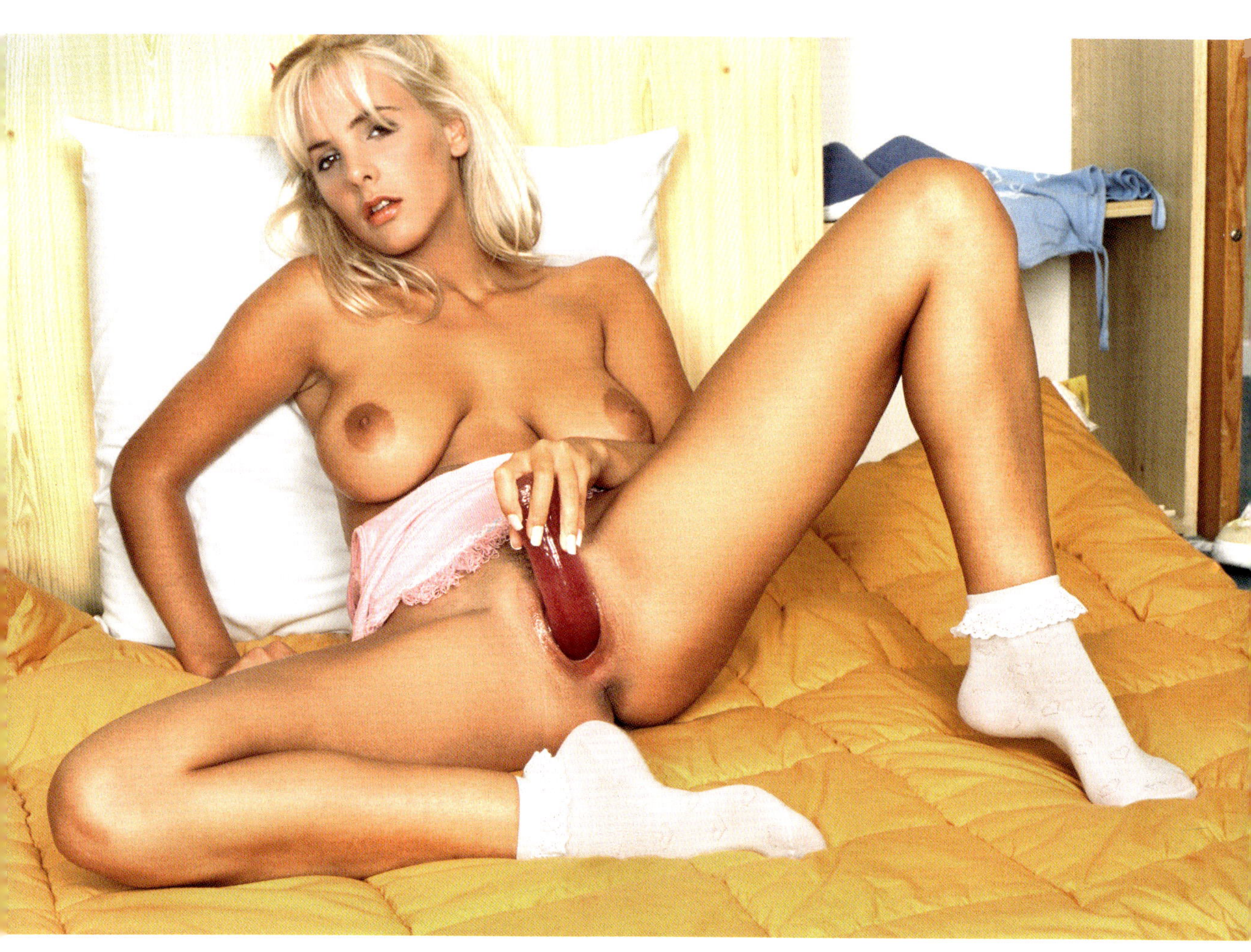



Katalin

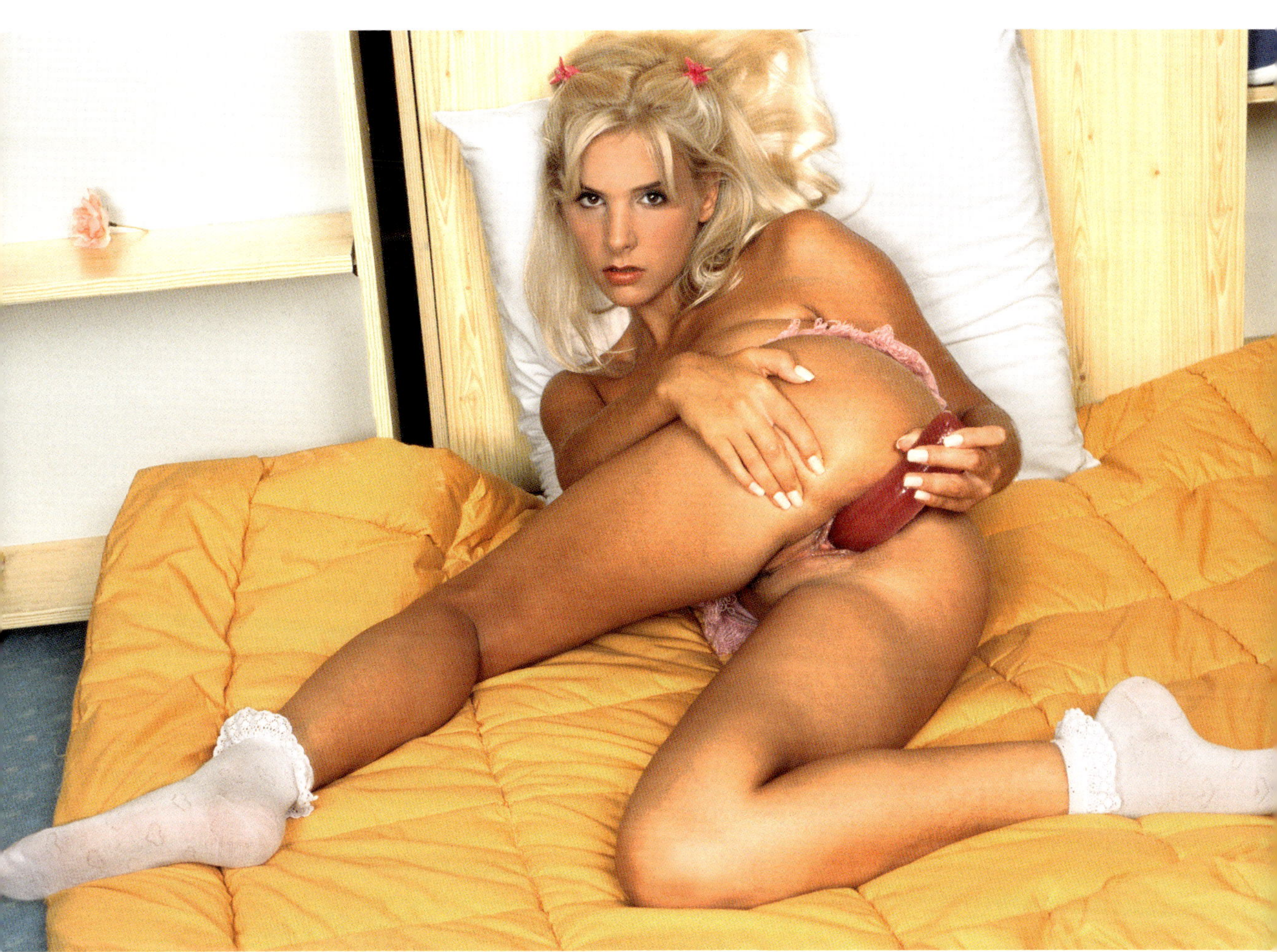

Katalin

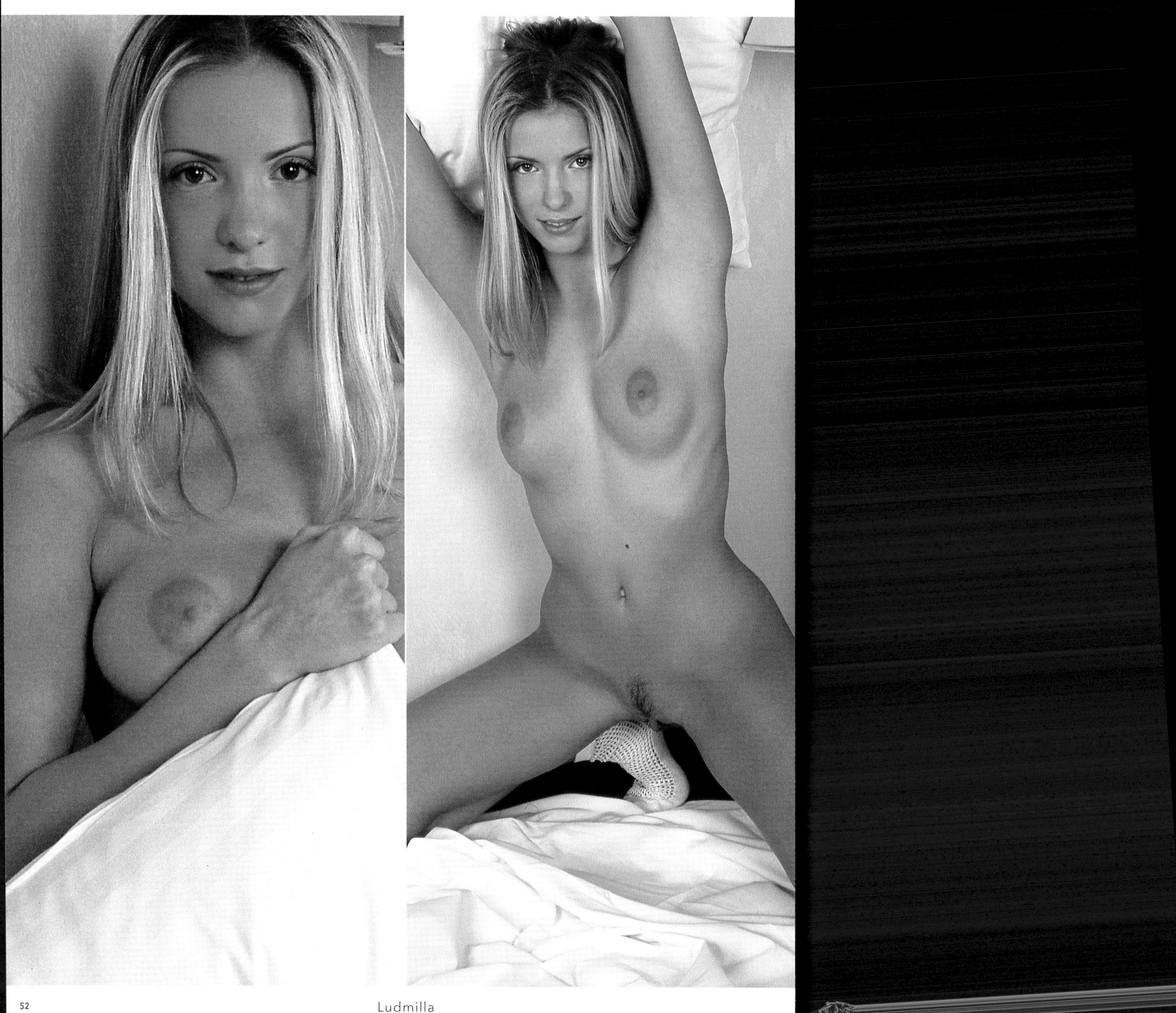



Ludmilla

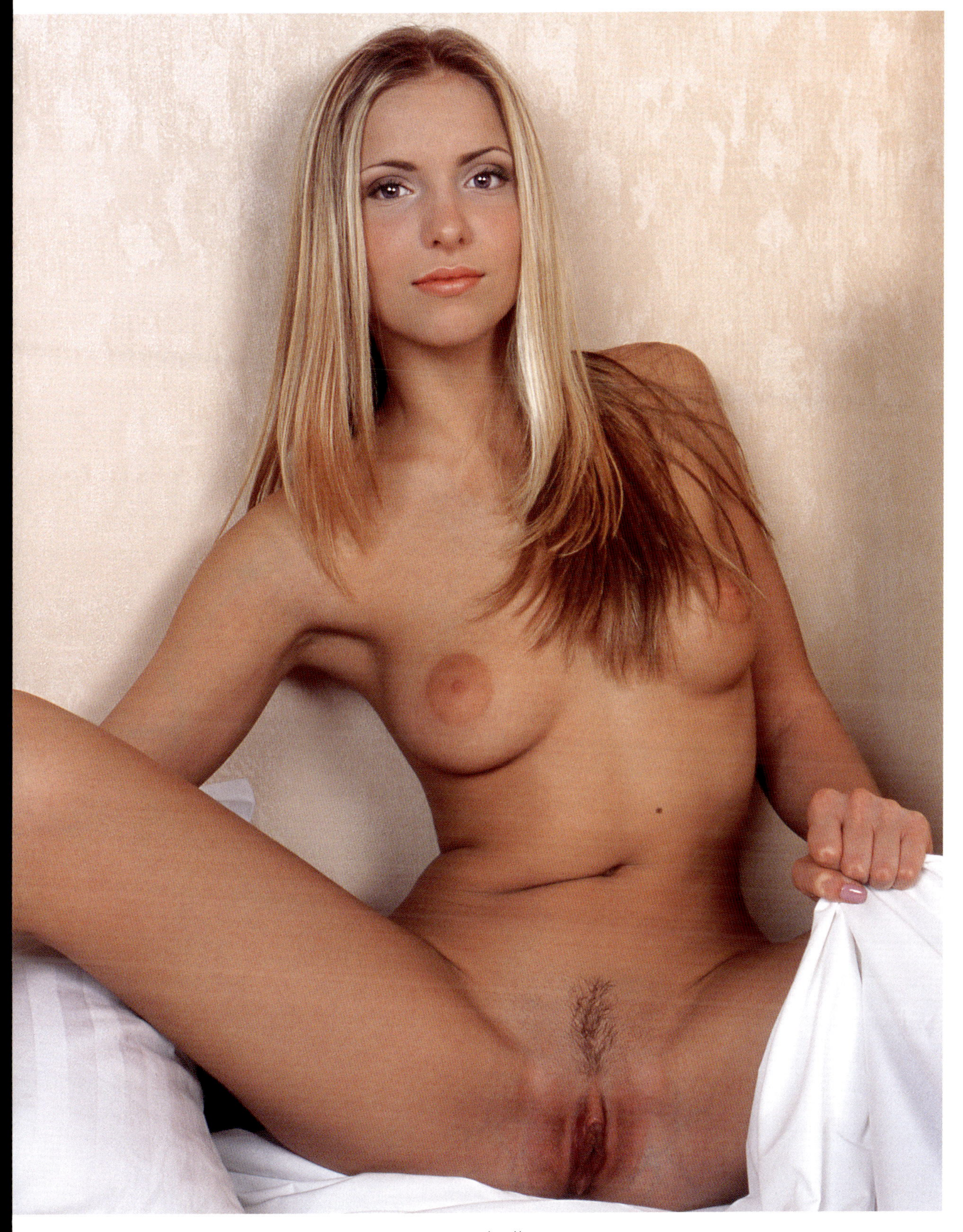

Ludmilla

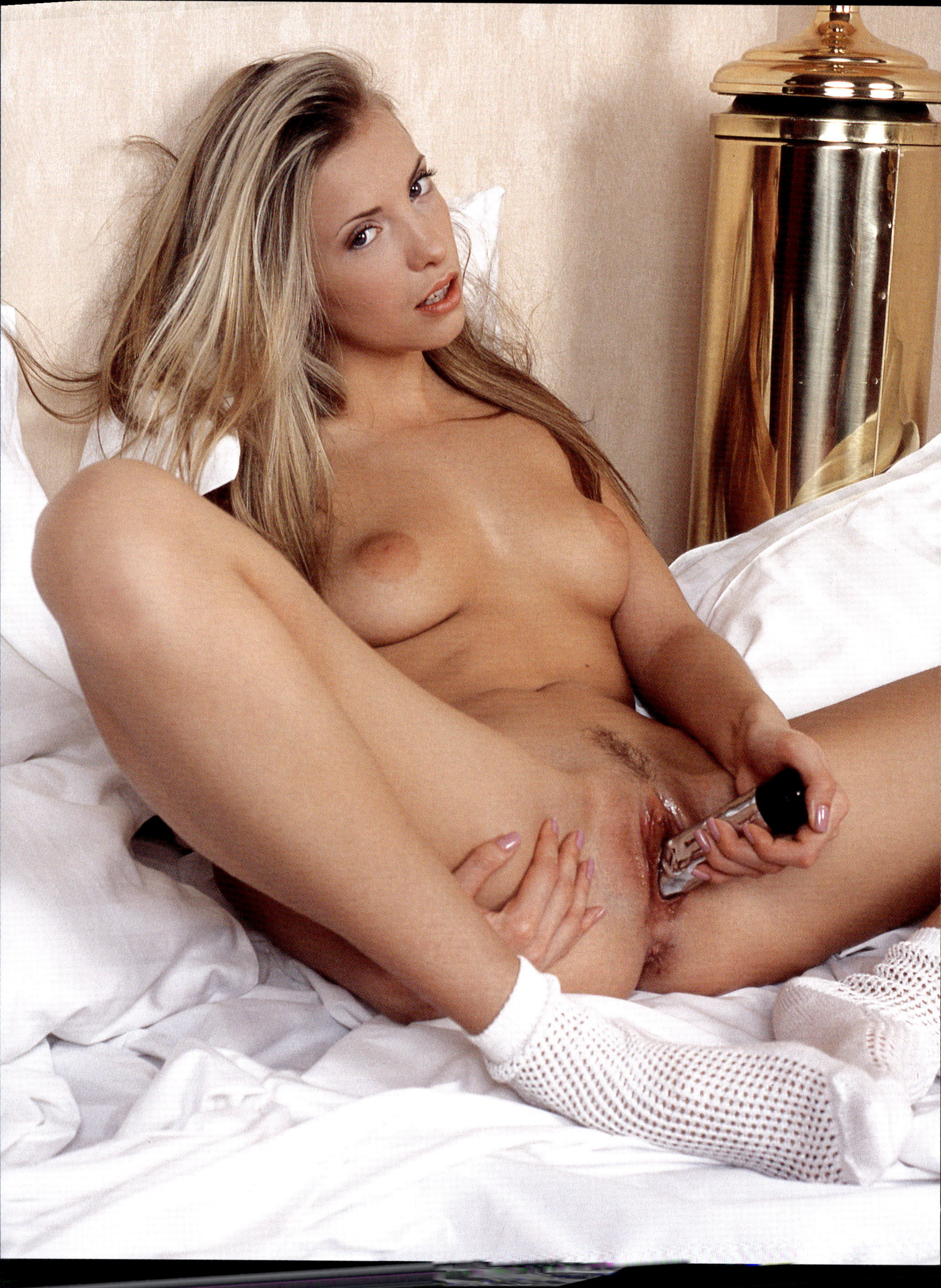

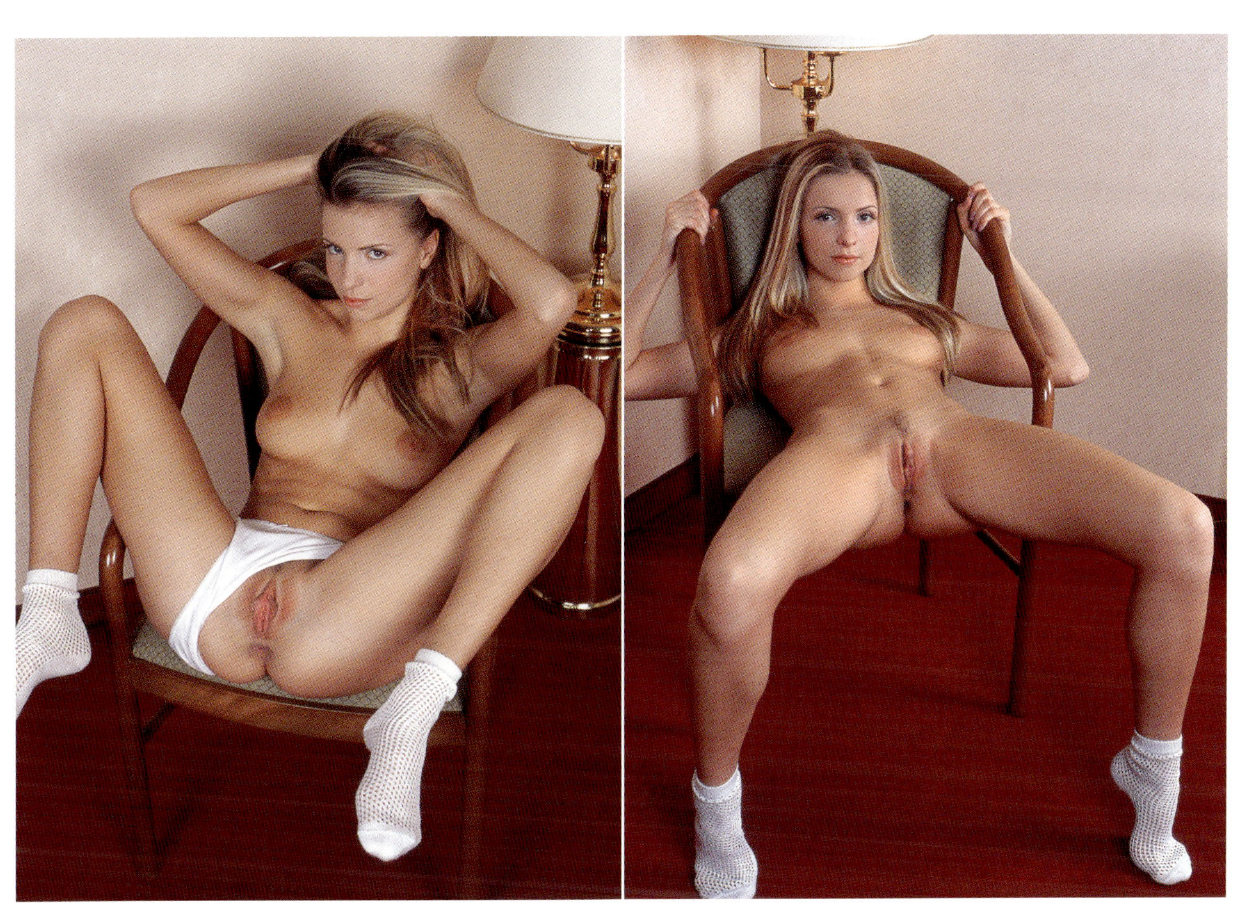

Ludmilla

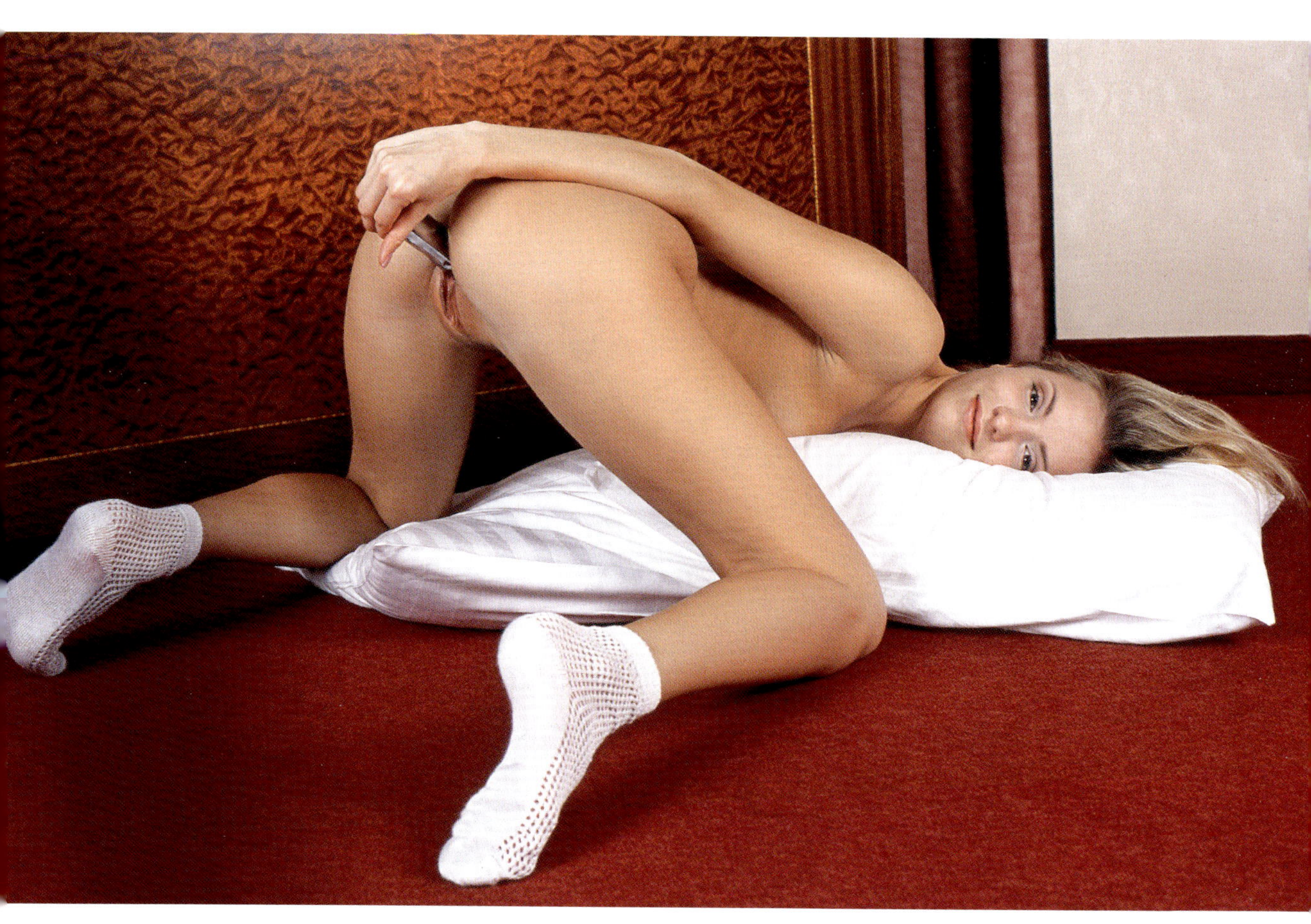



Ludmilla

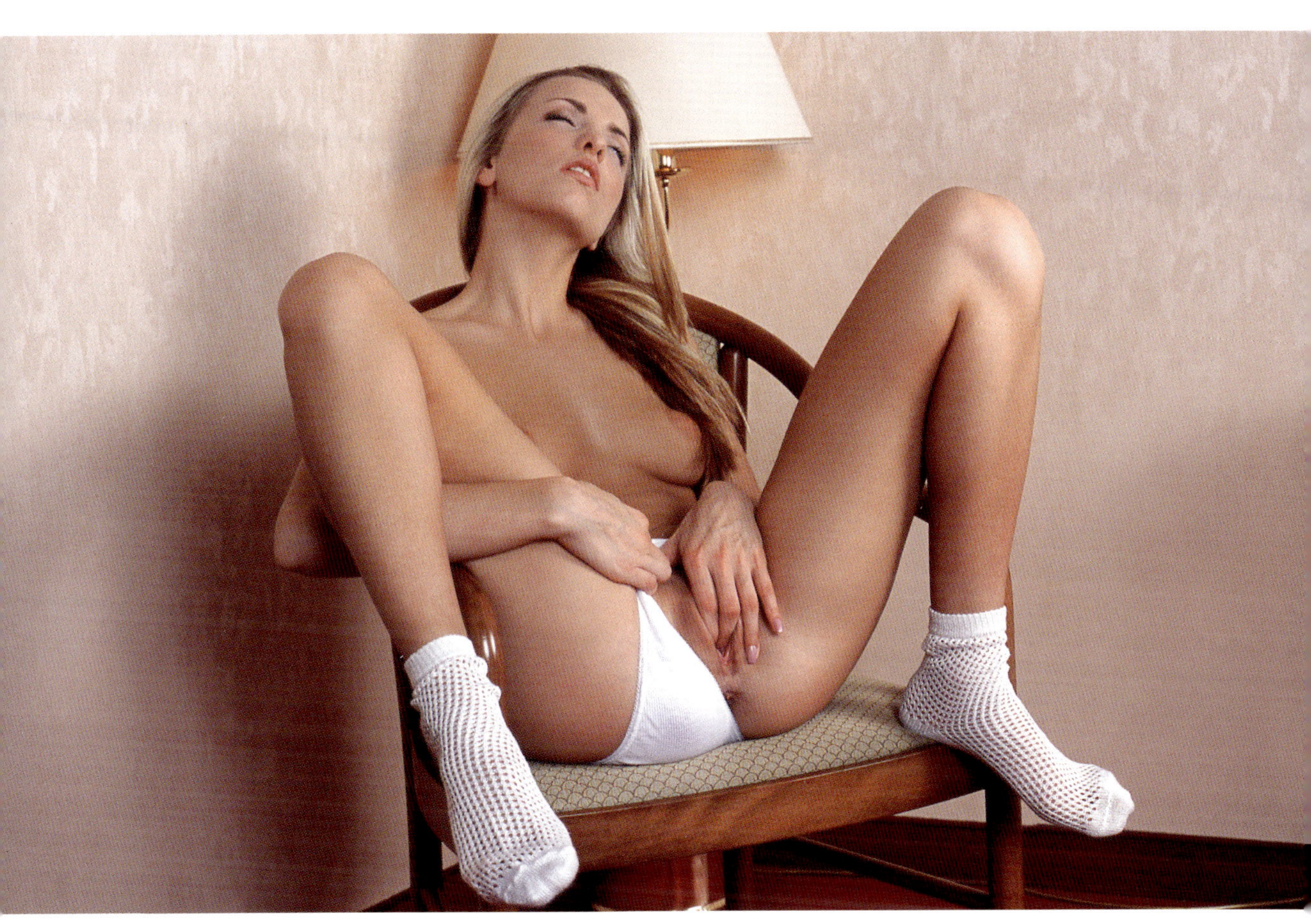

Ludmilla

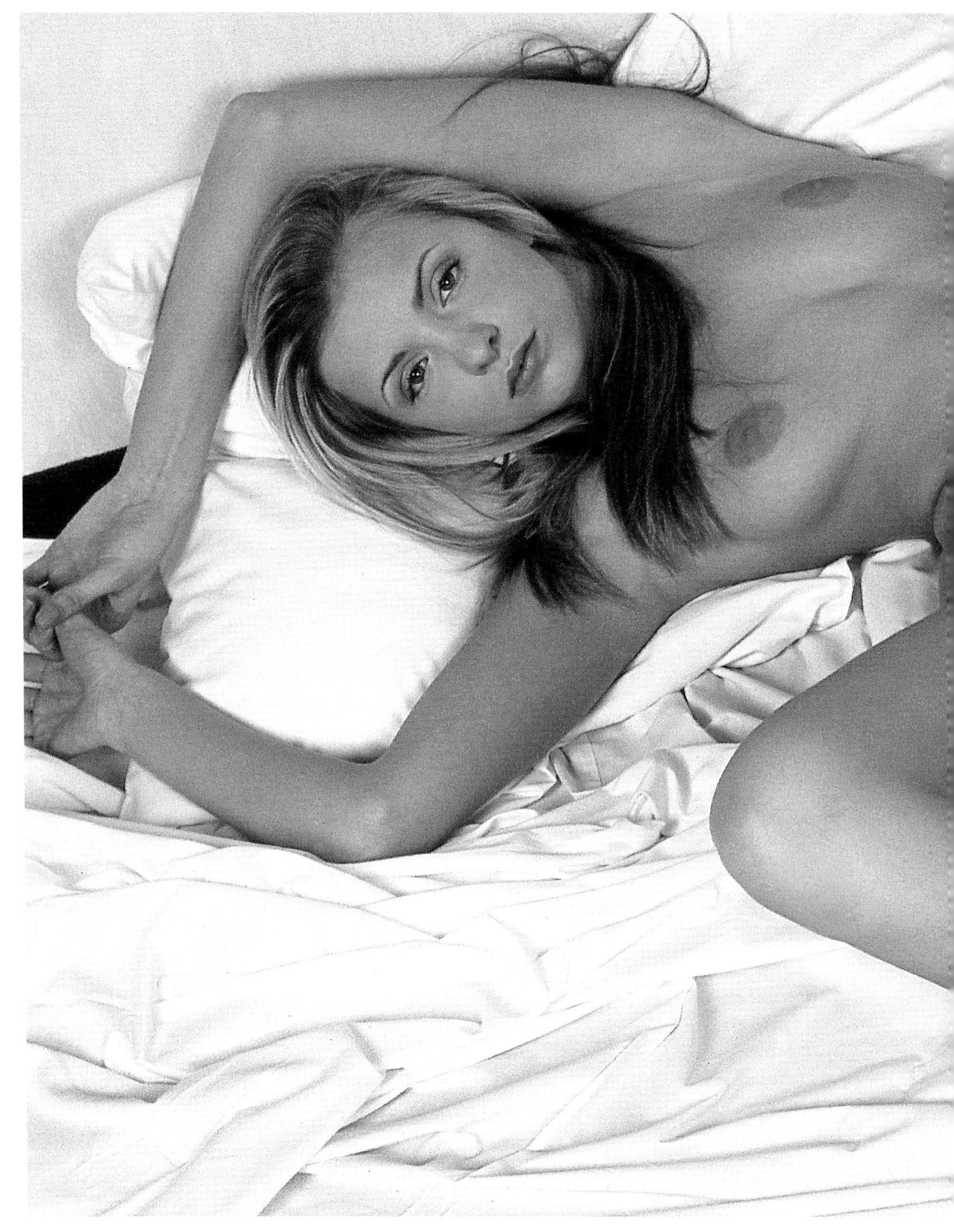

Ludmilla

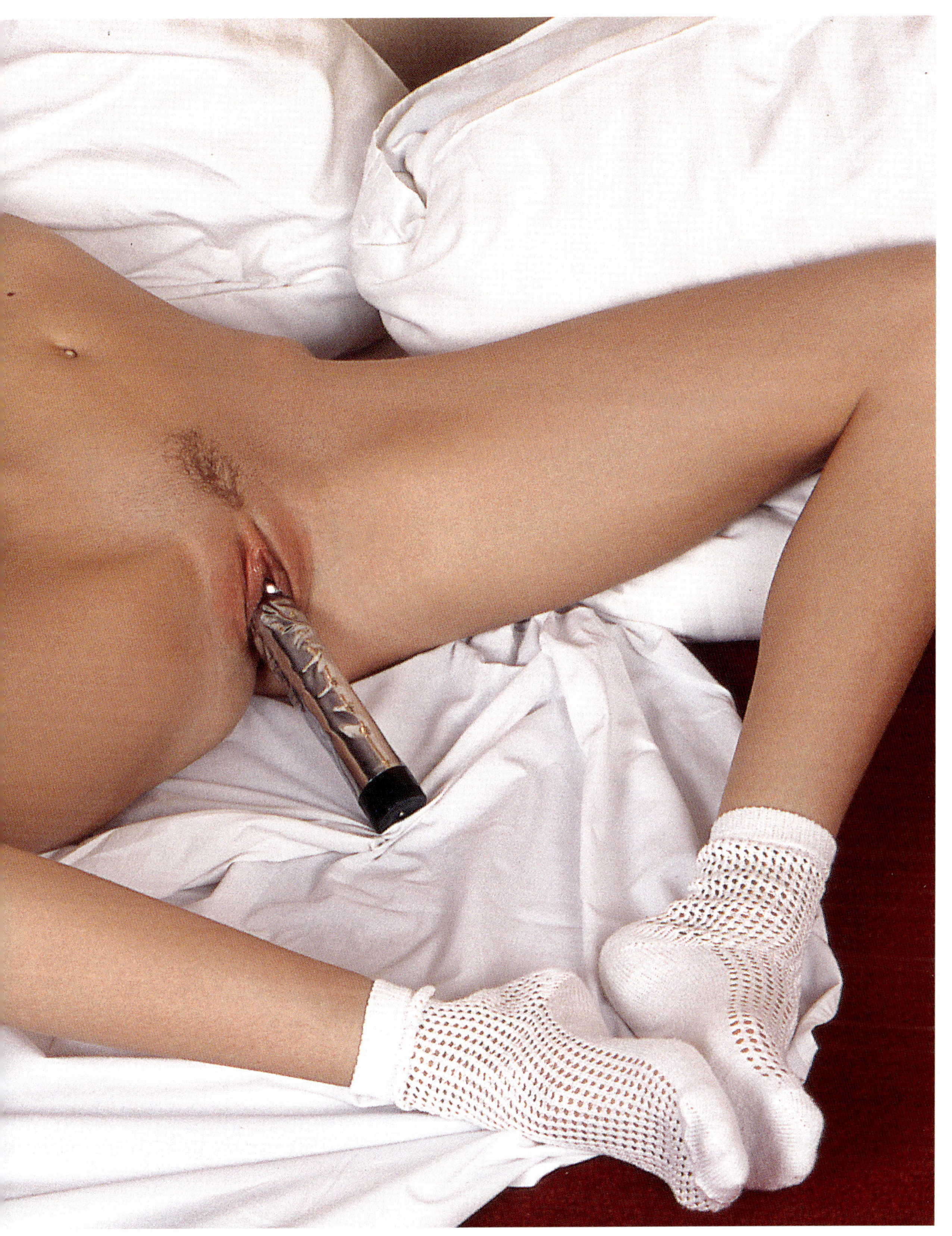

Ludmilla

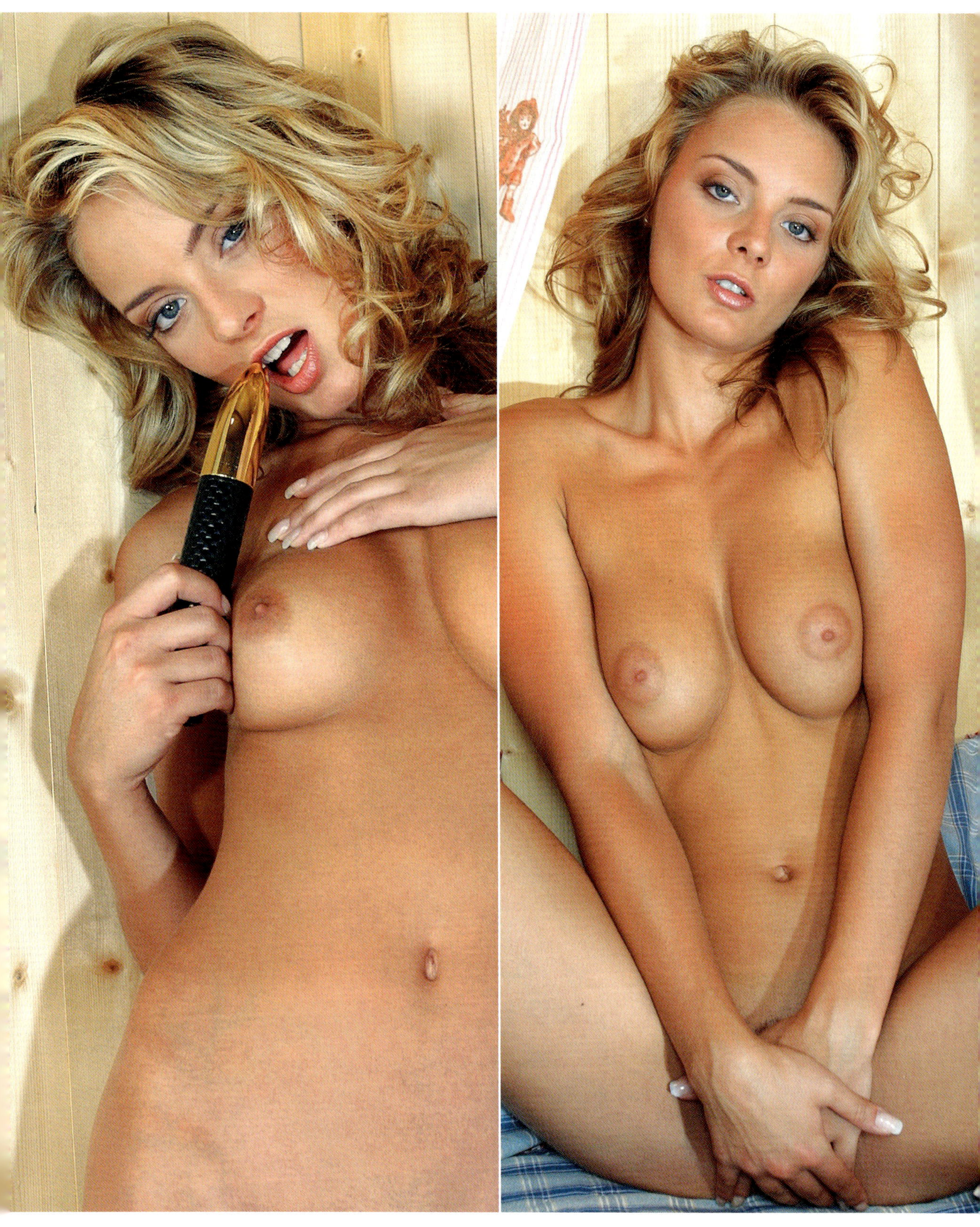

Mariann

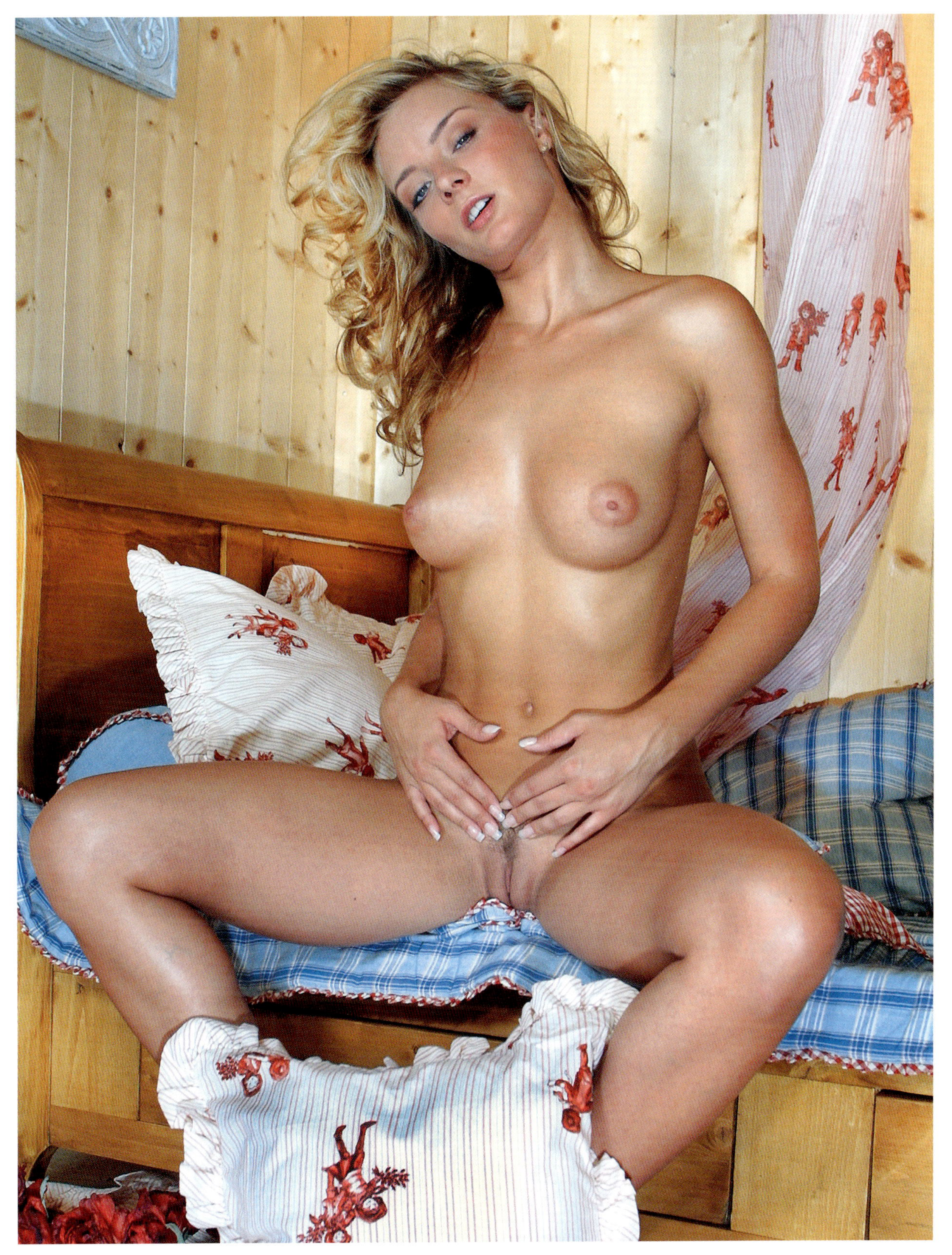

Mariann

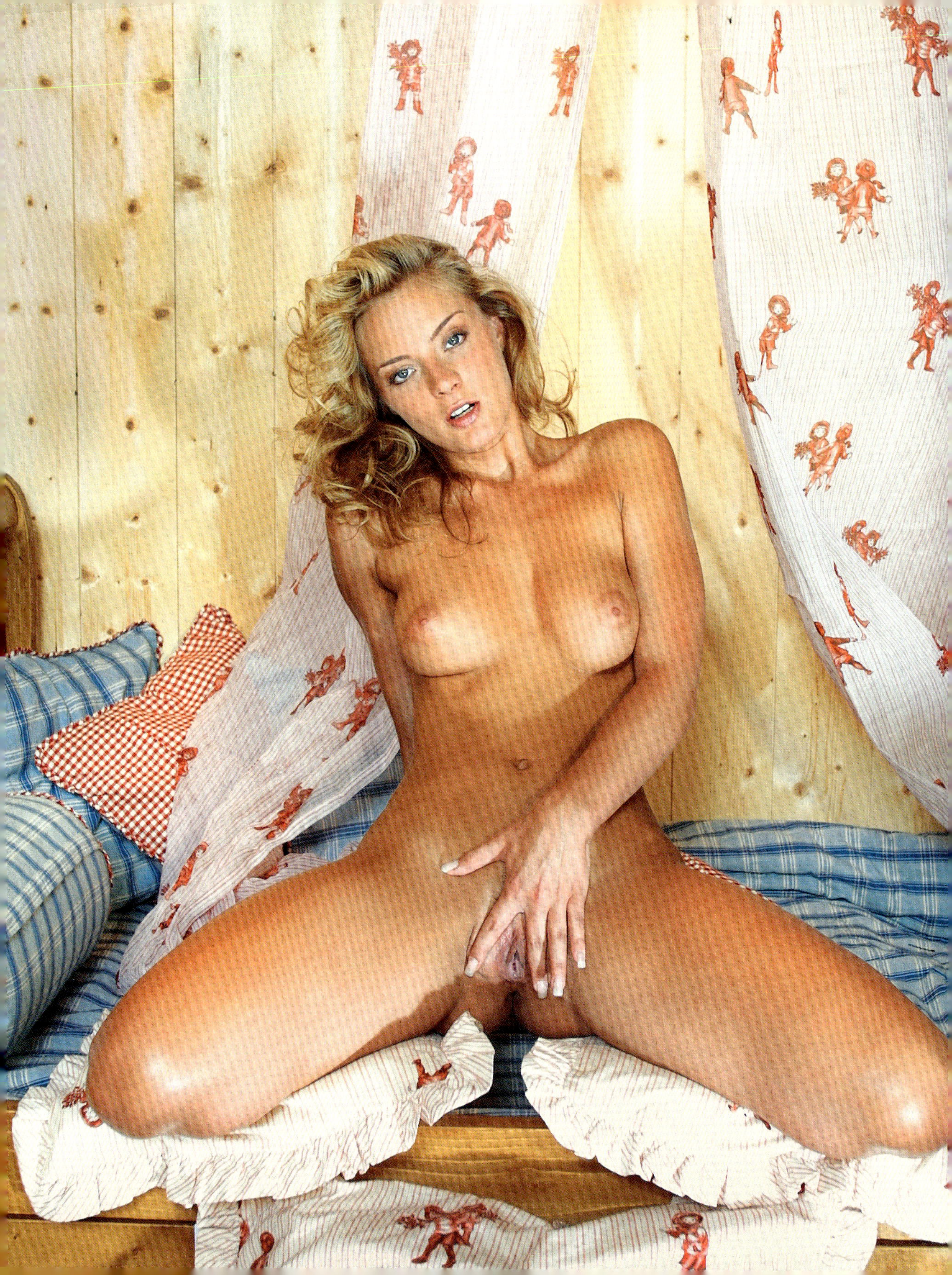

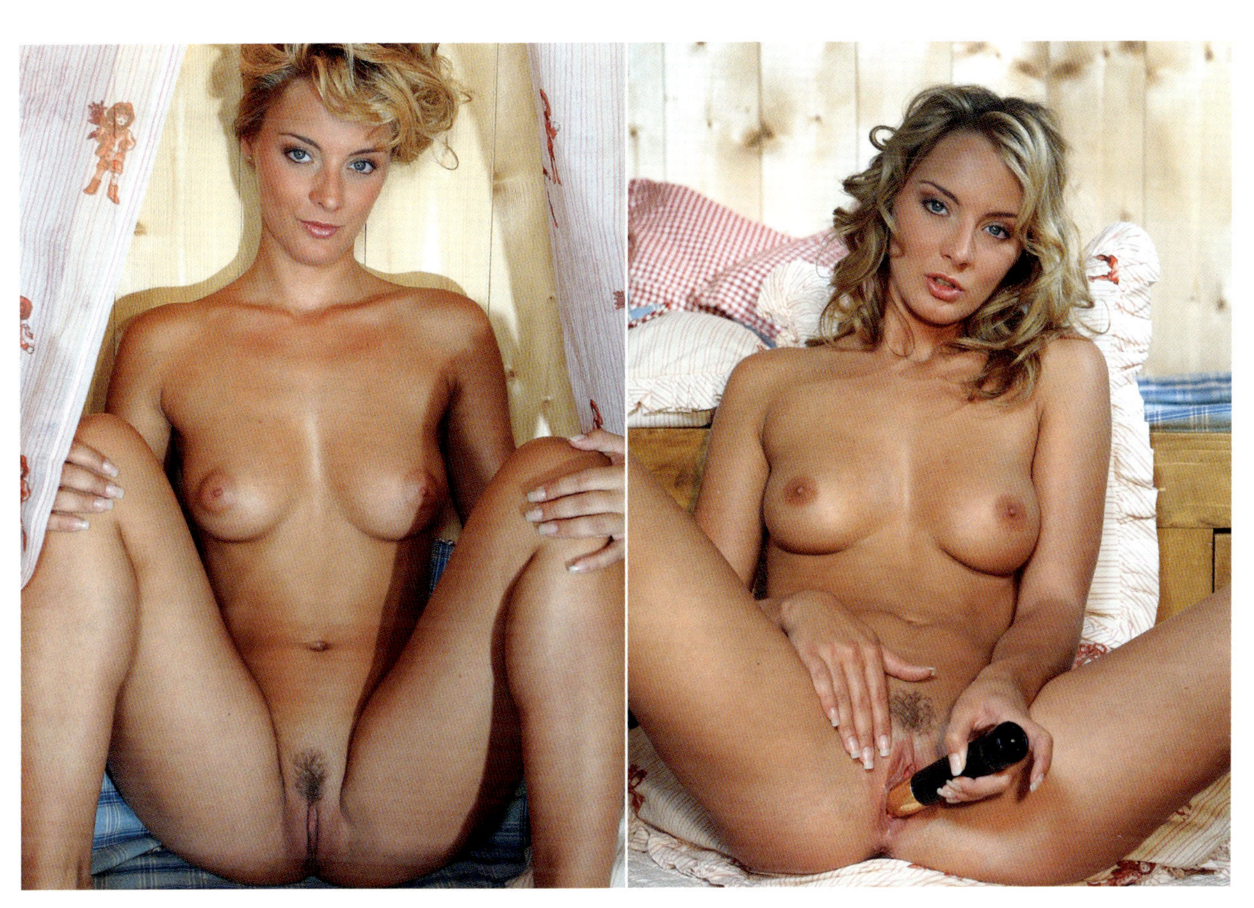

Mariann

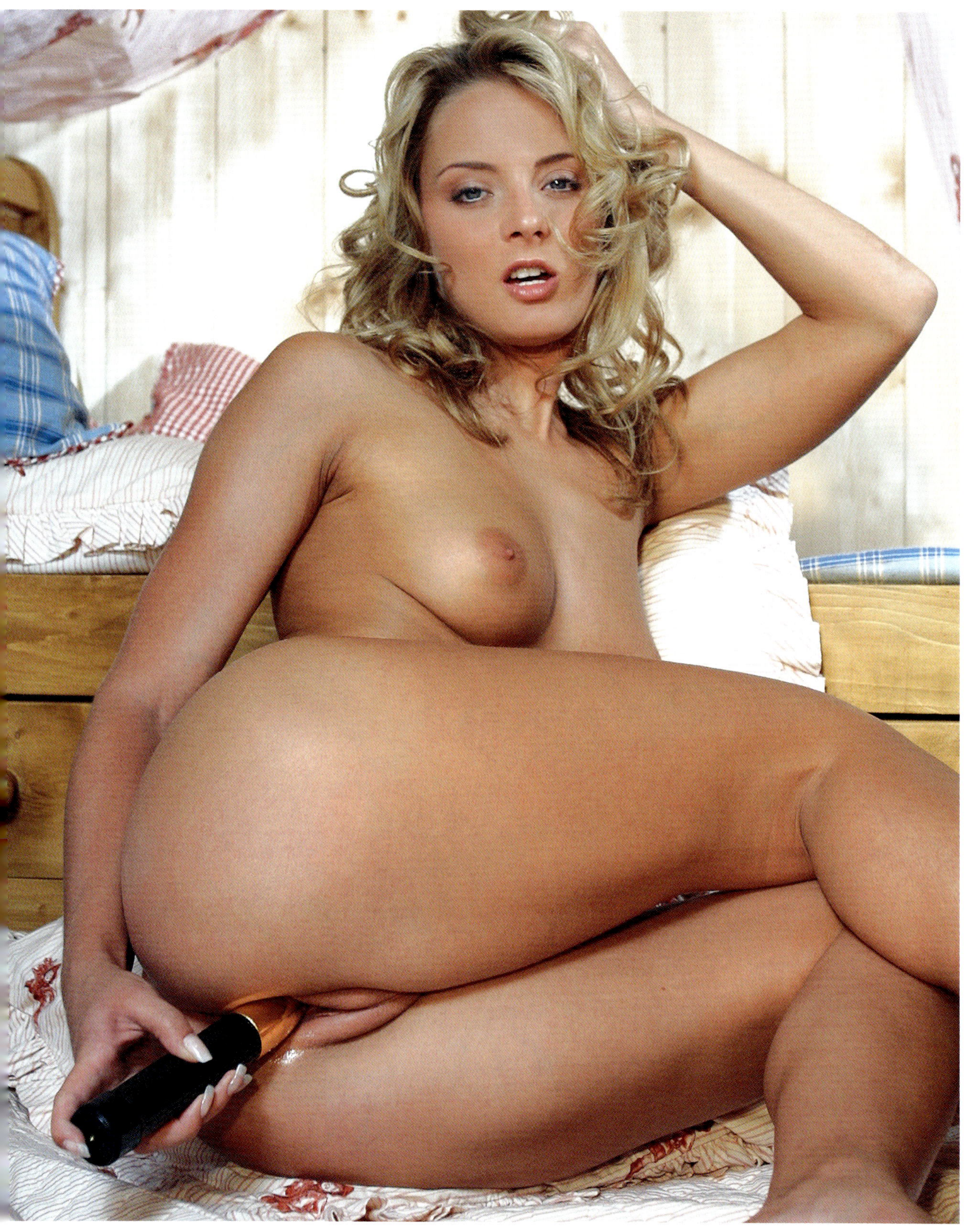

Mariann

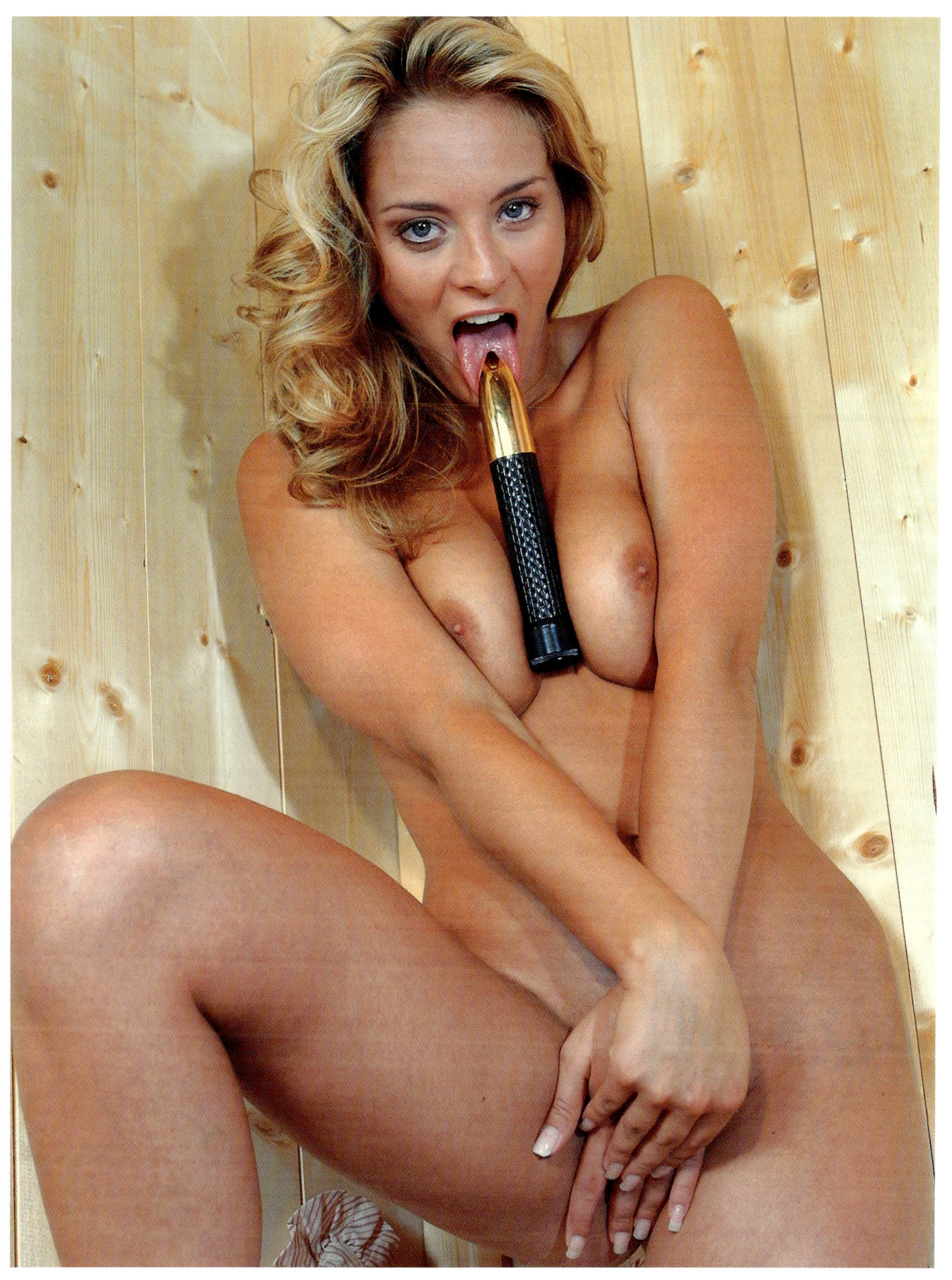

Mariann

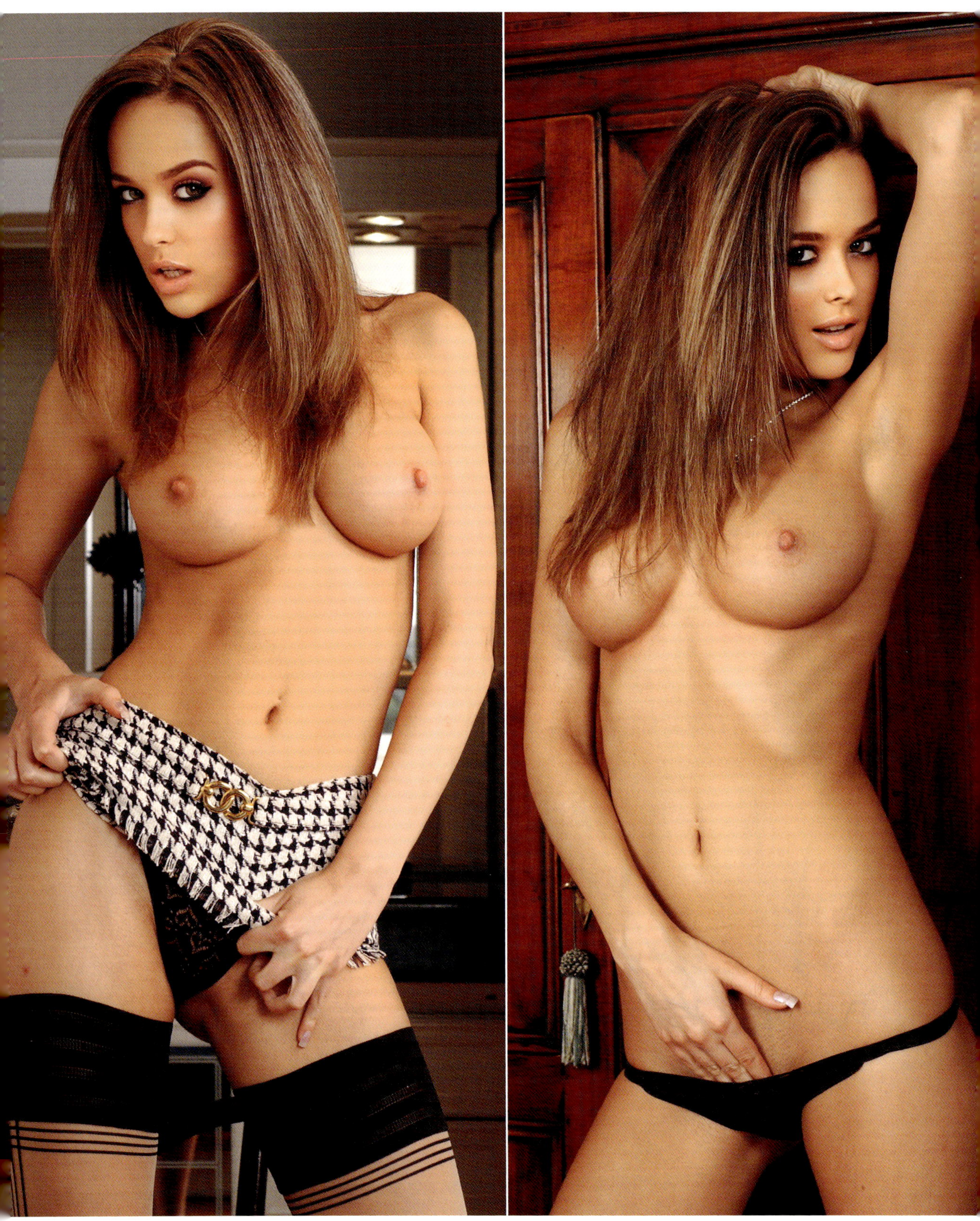

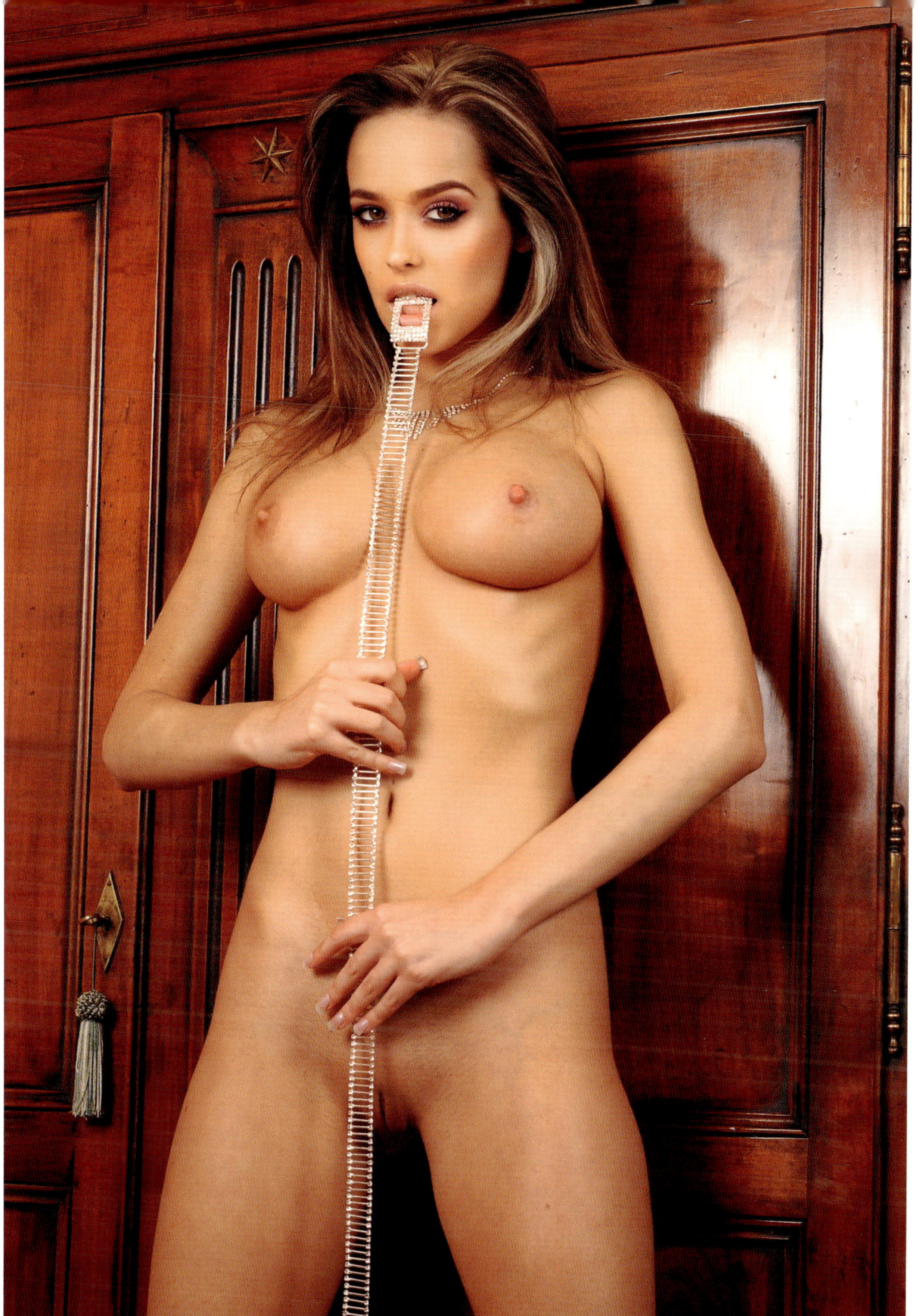

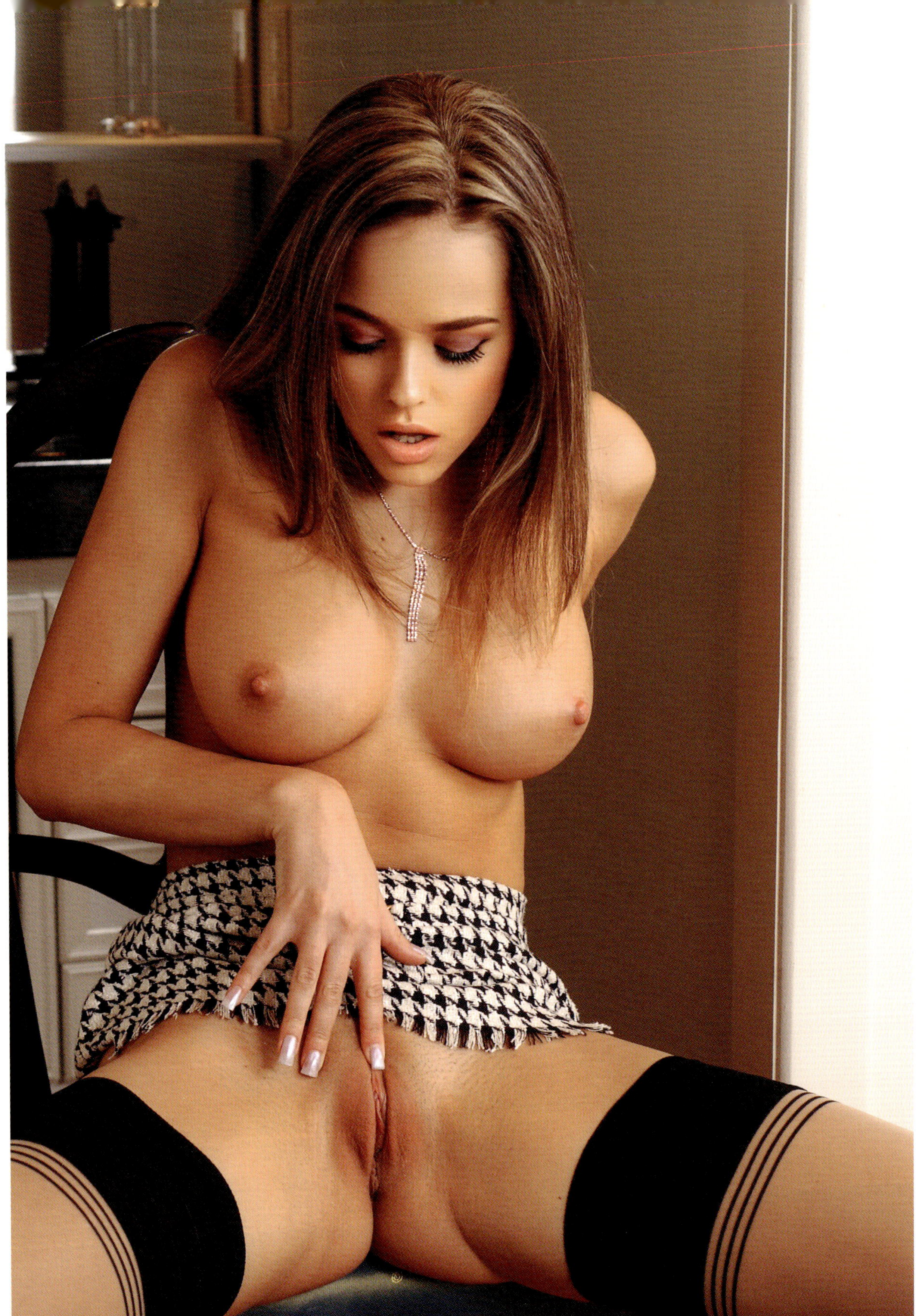

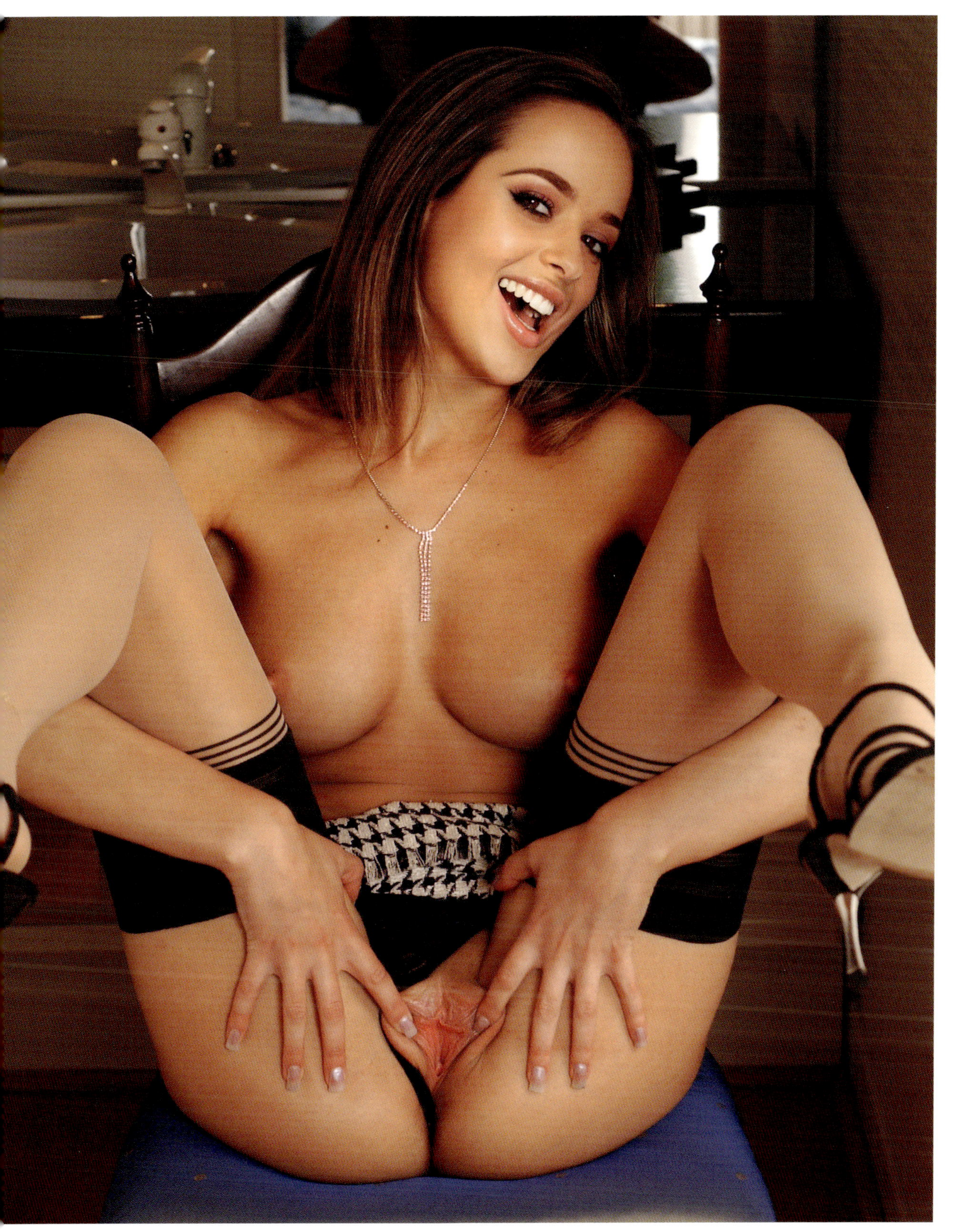

Claudia

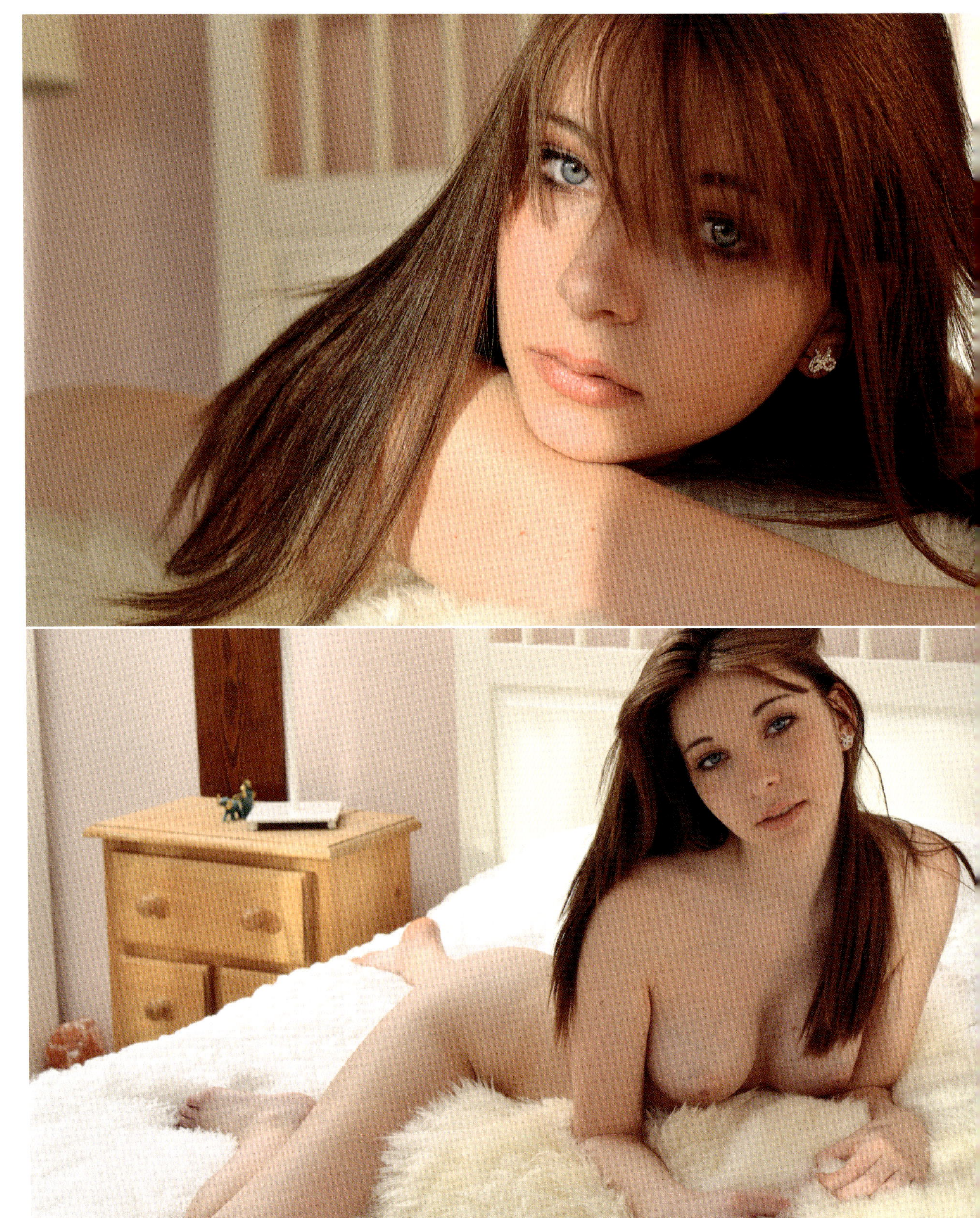



Emmy

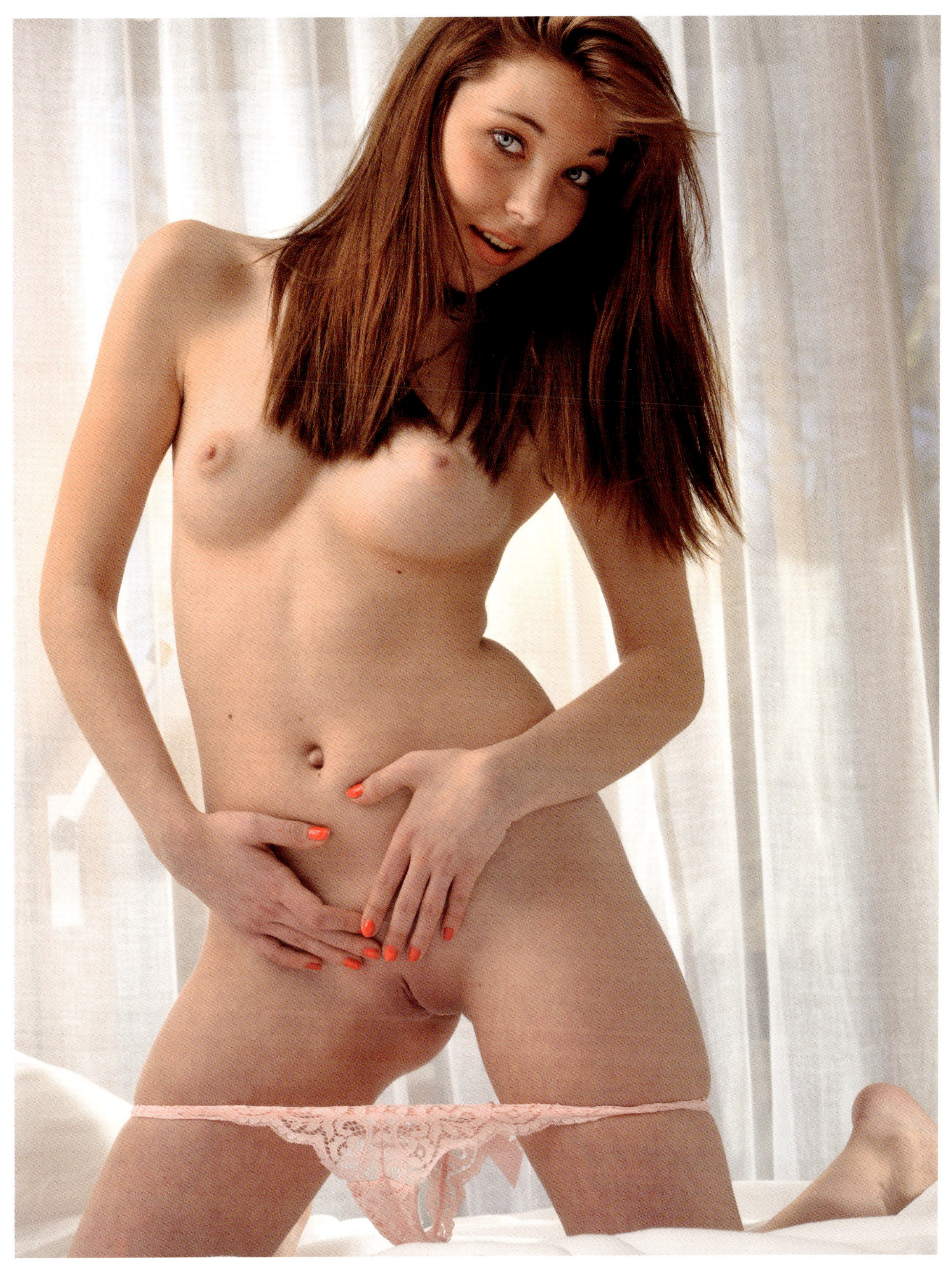

Emmy

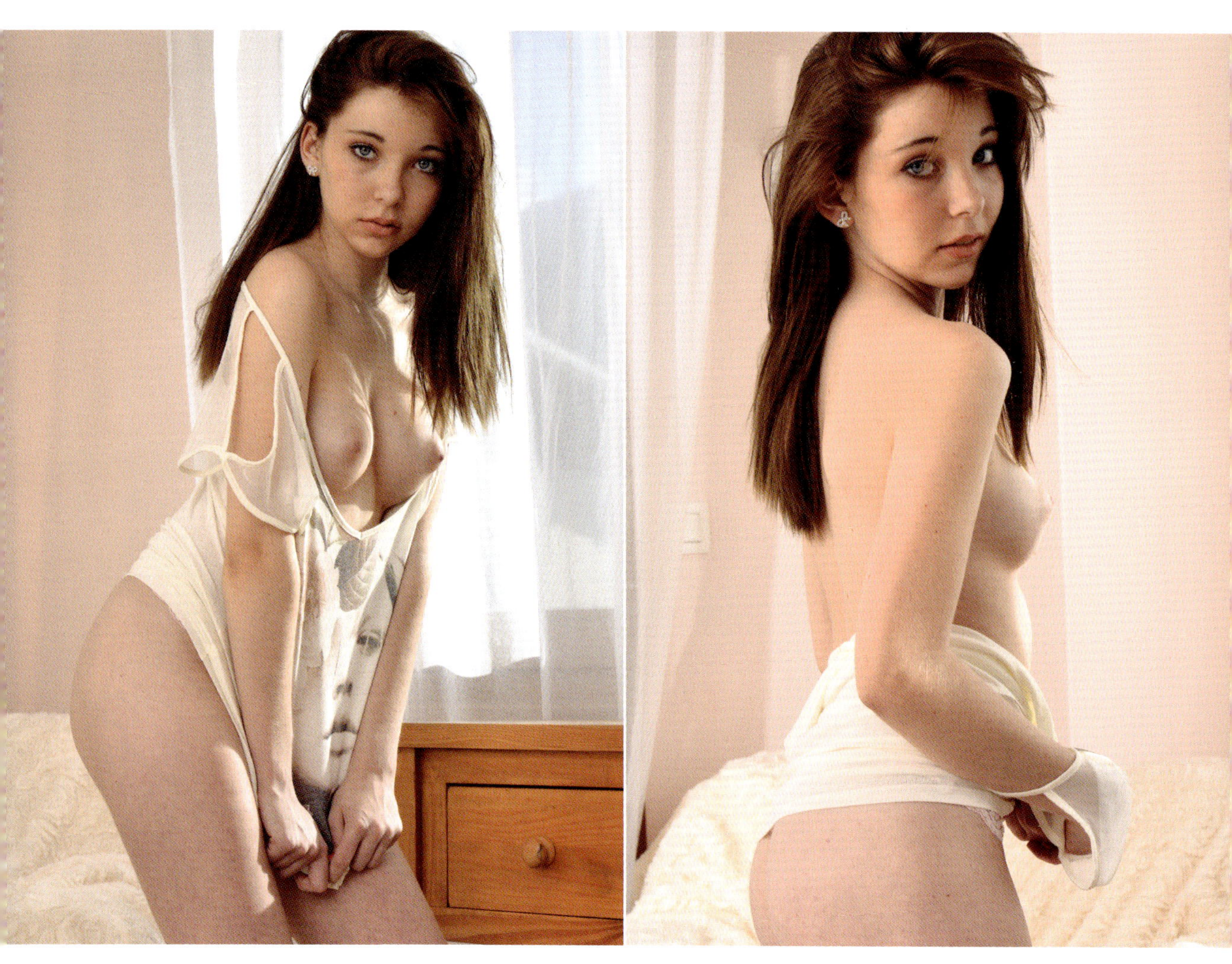

Emmy

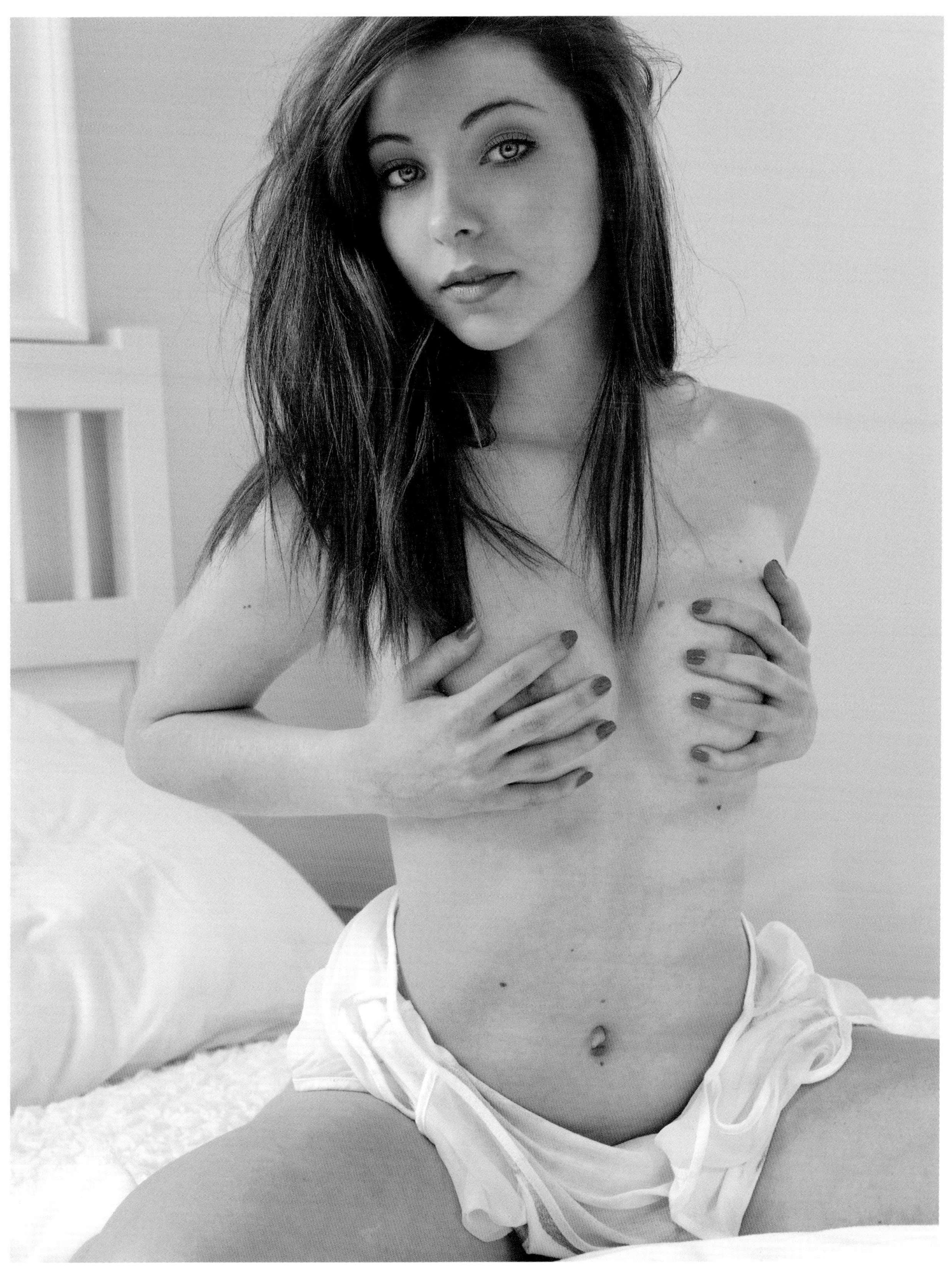

Emmy

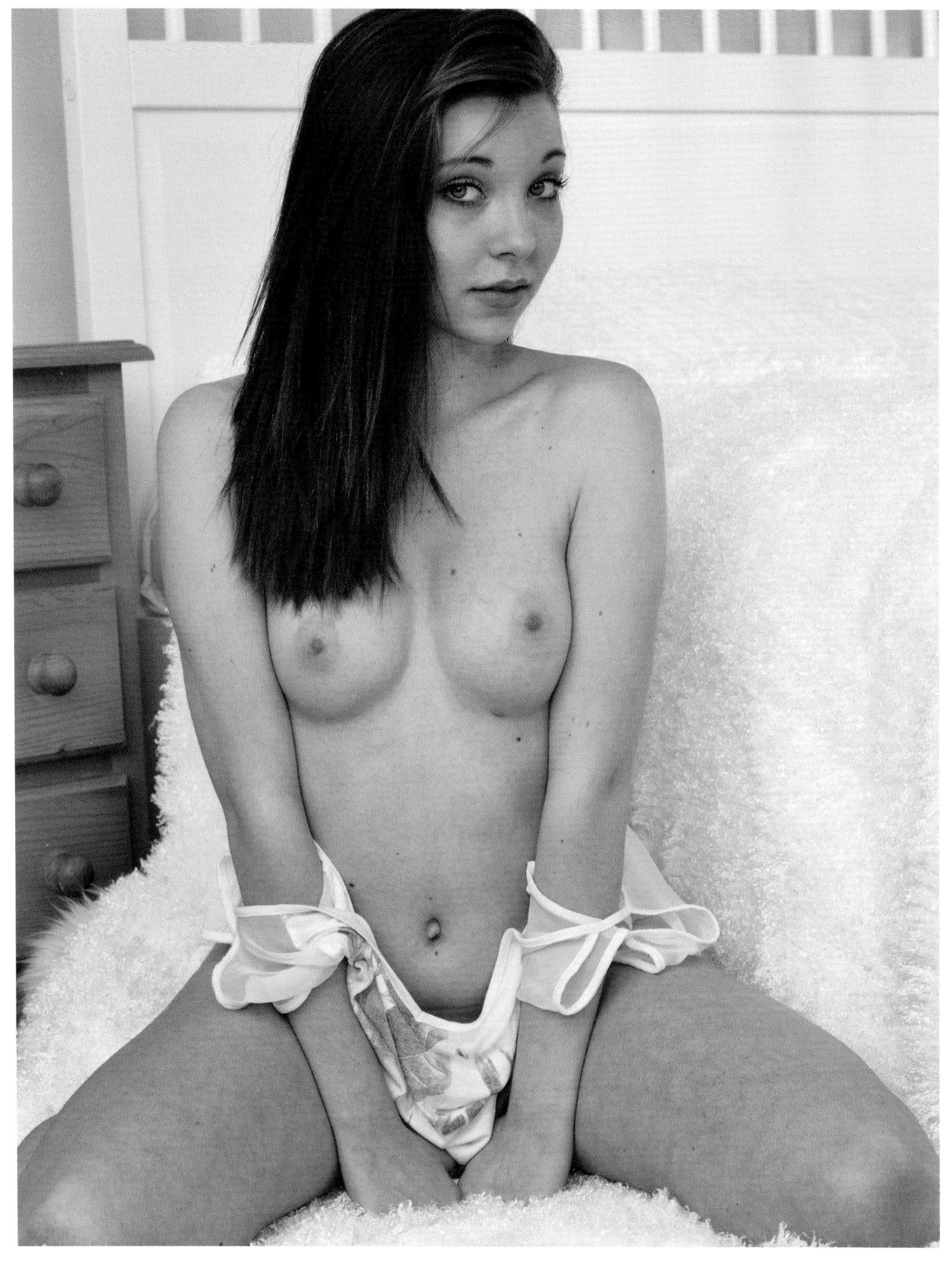

Emmy

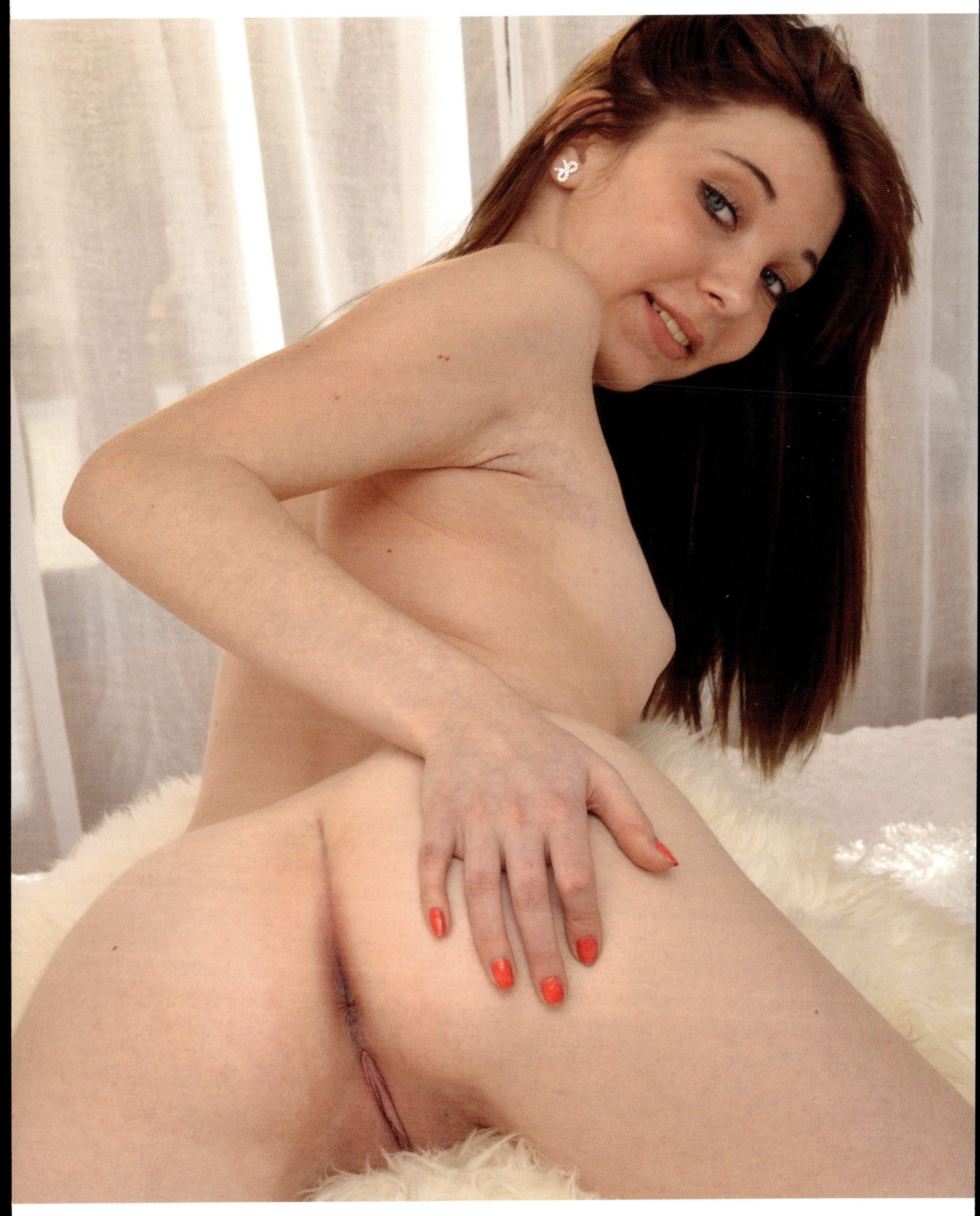

Emmy

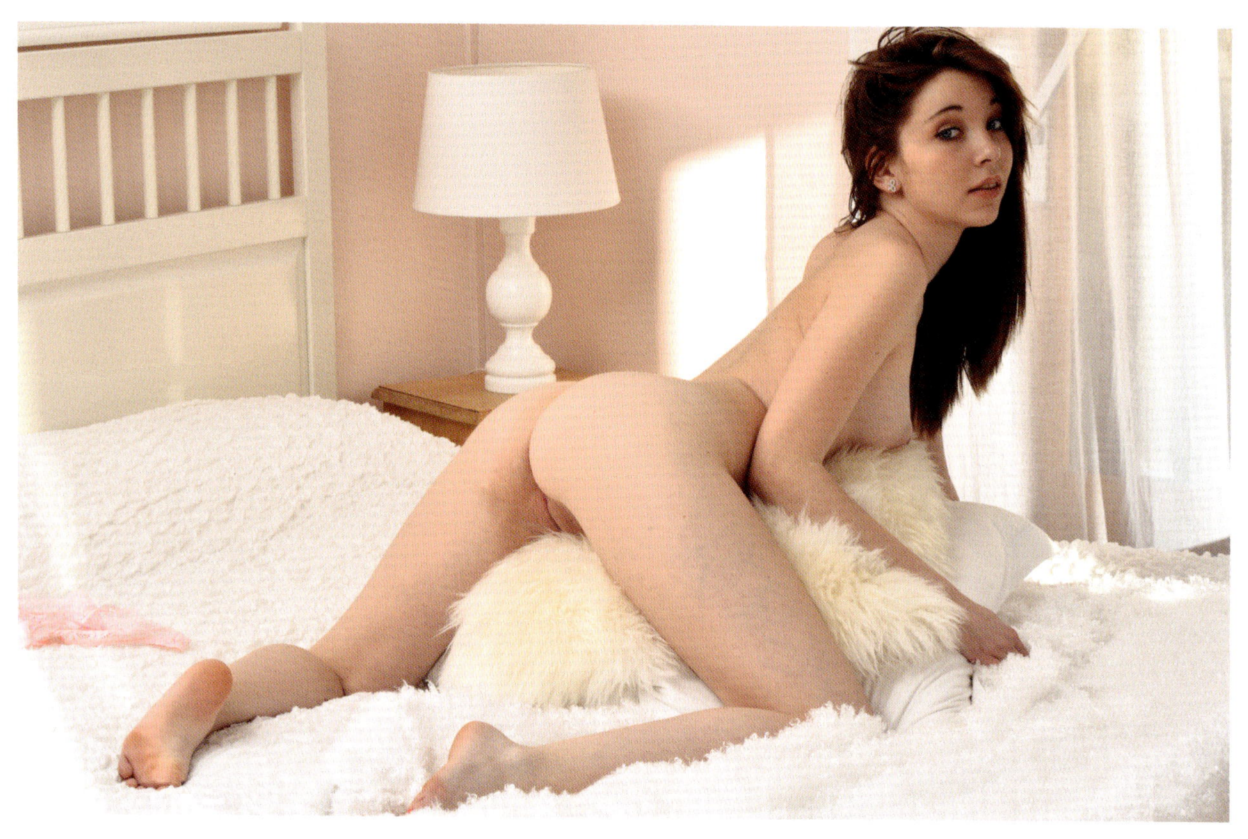



Emmy

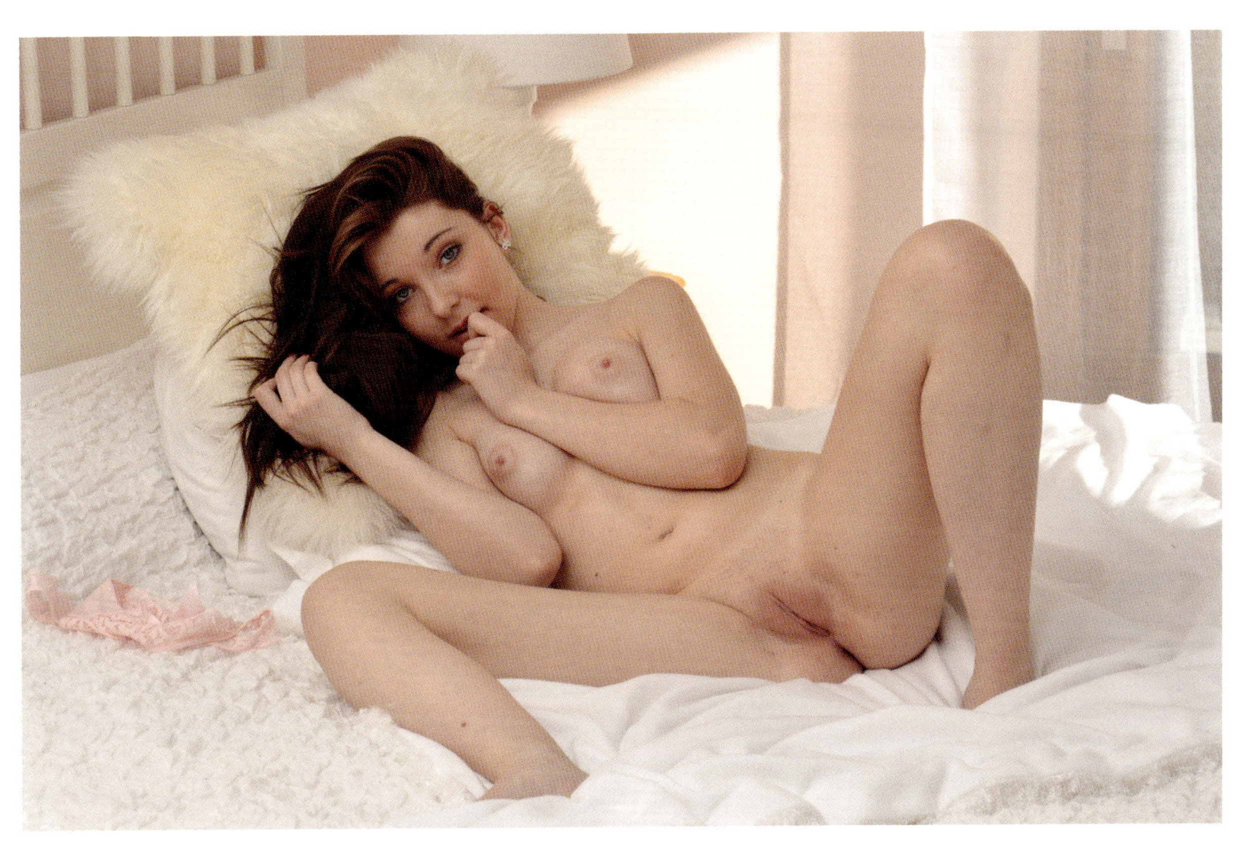

Emmy

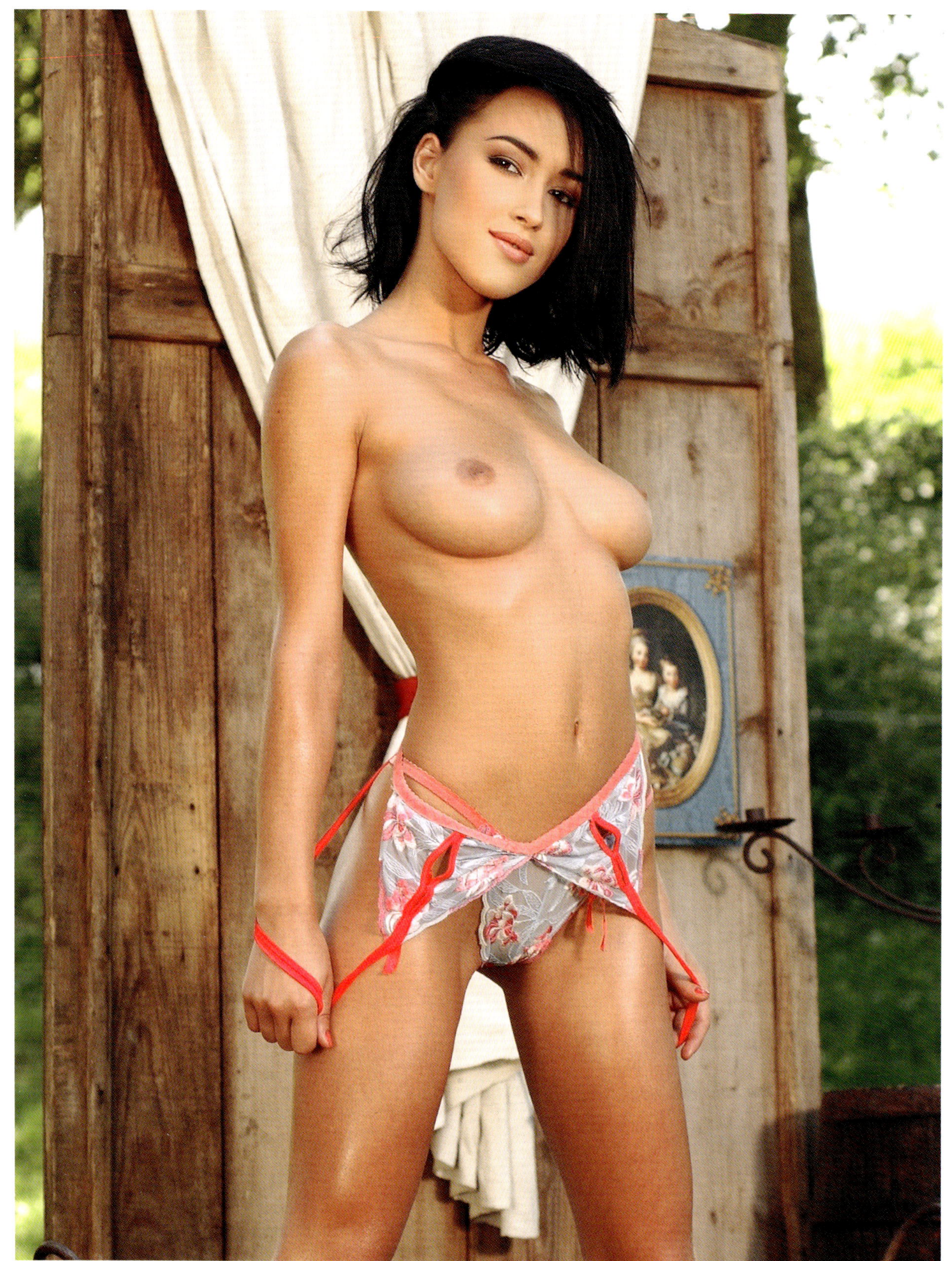

Mary

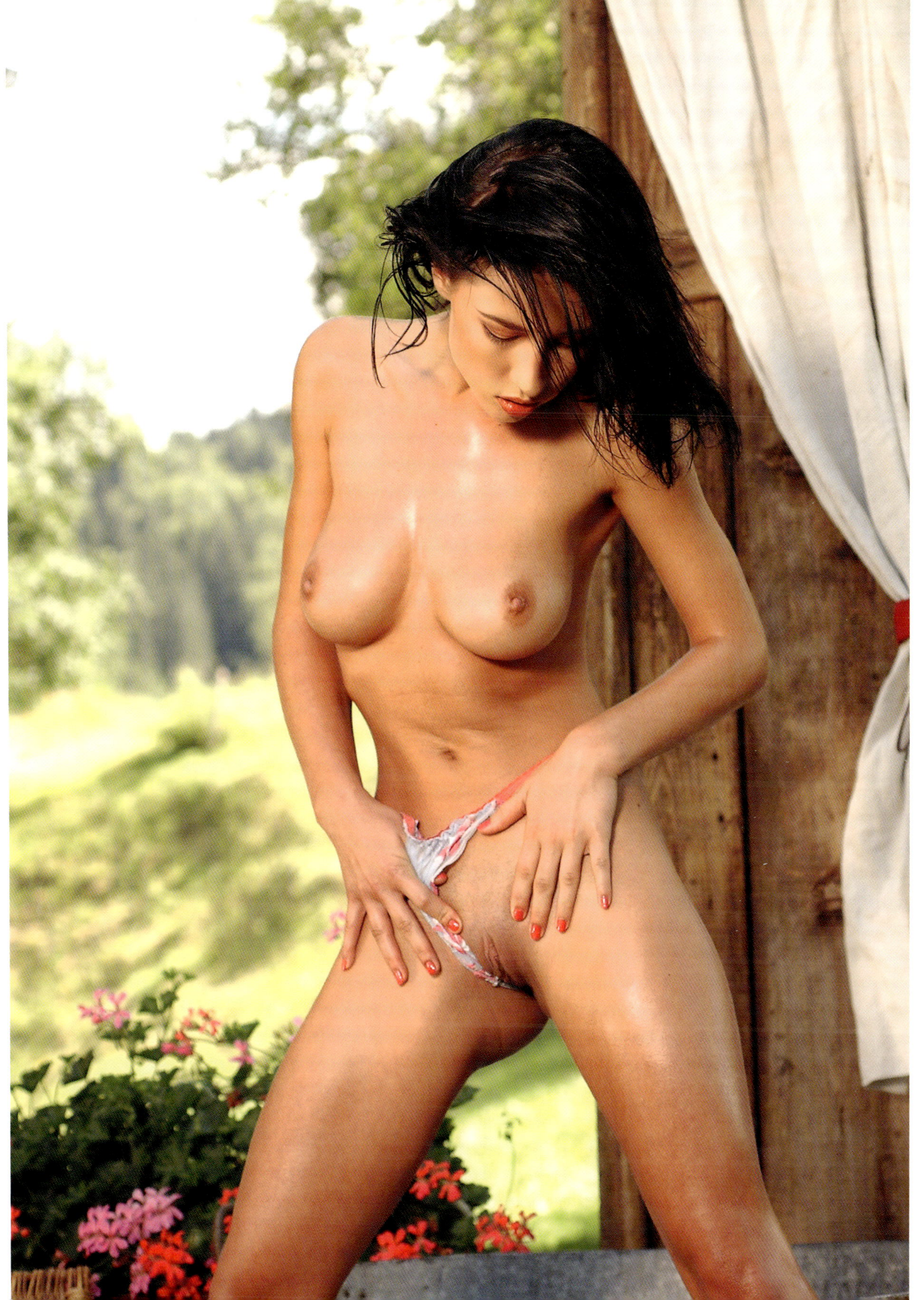

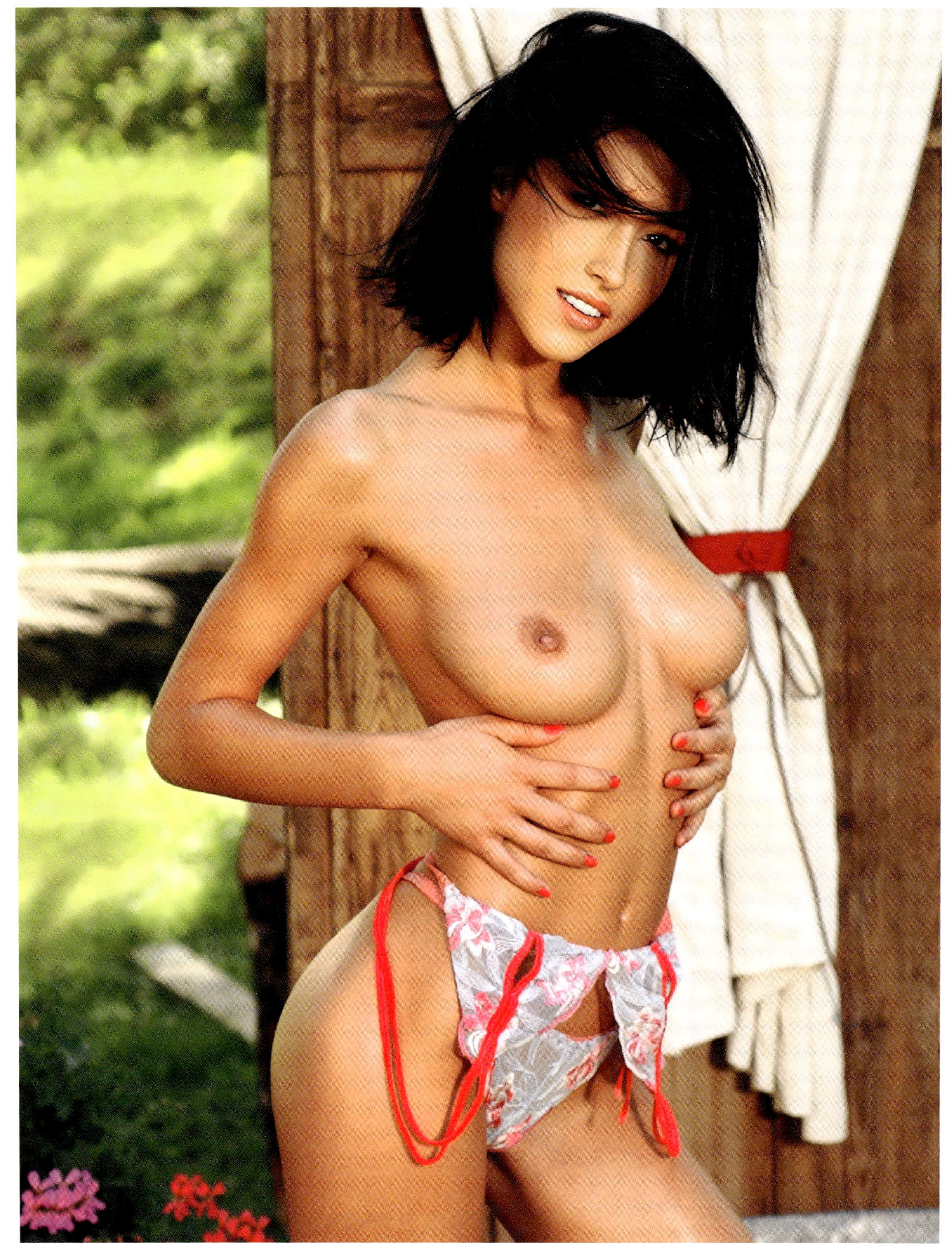

Mary

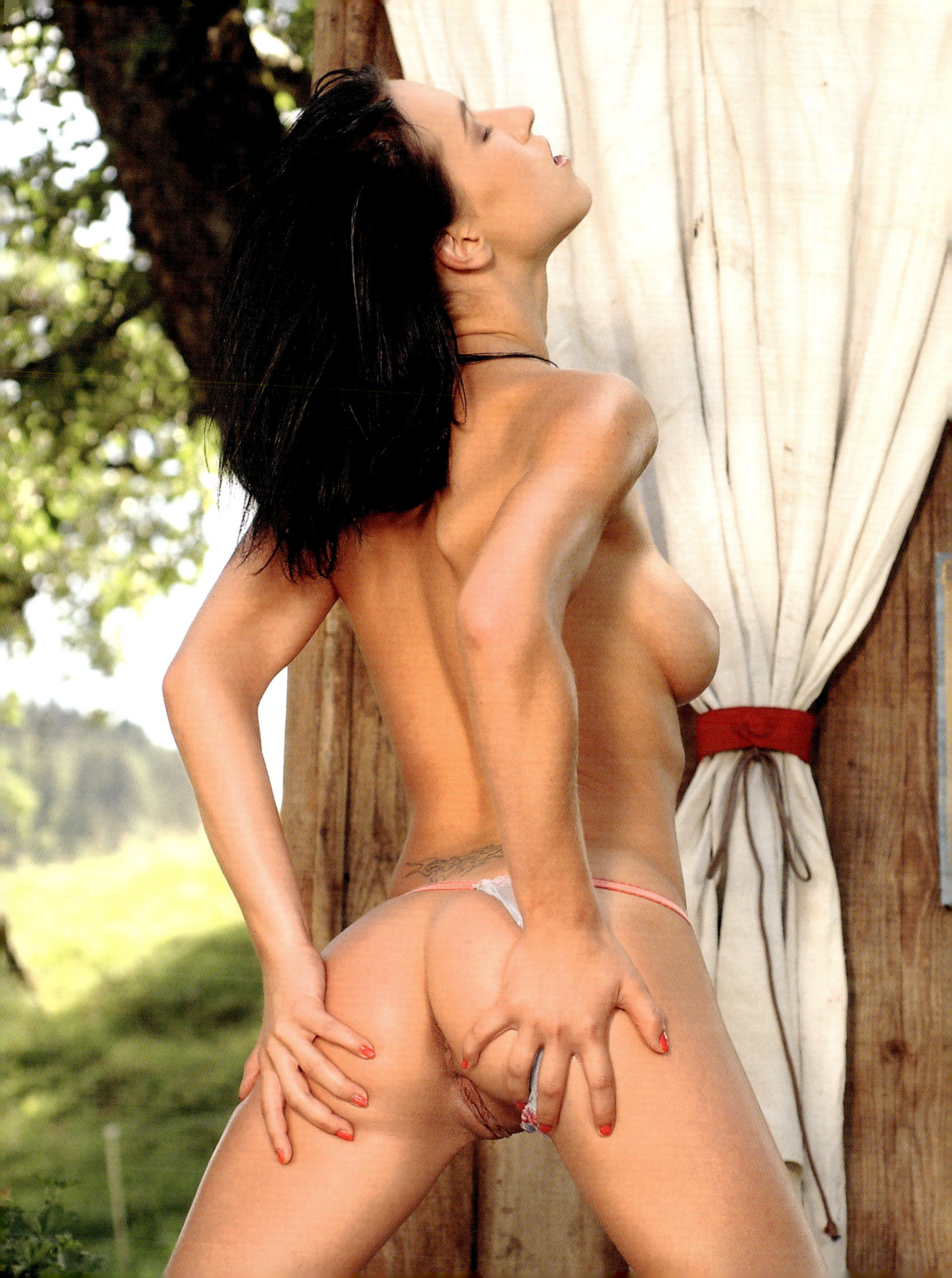

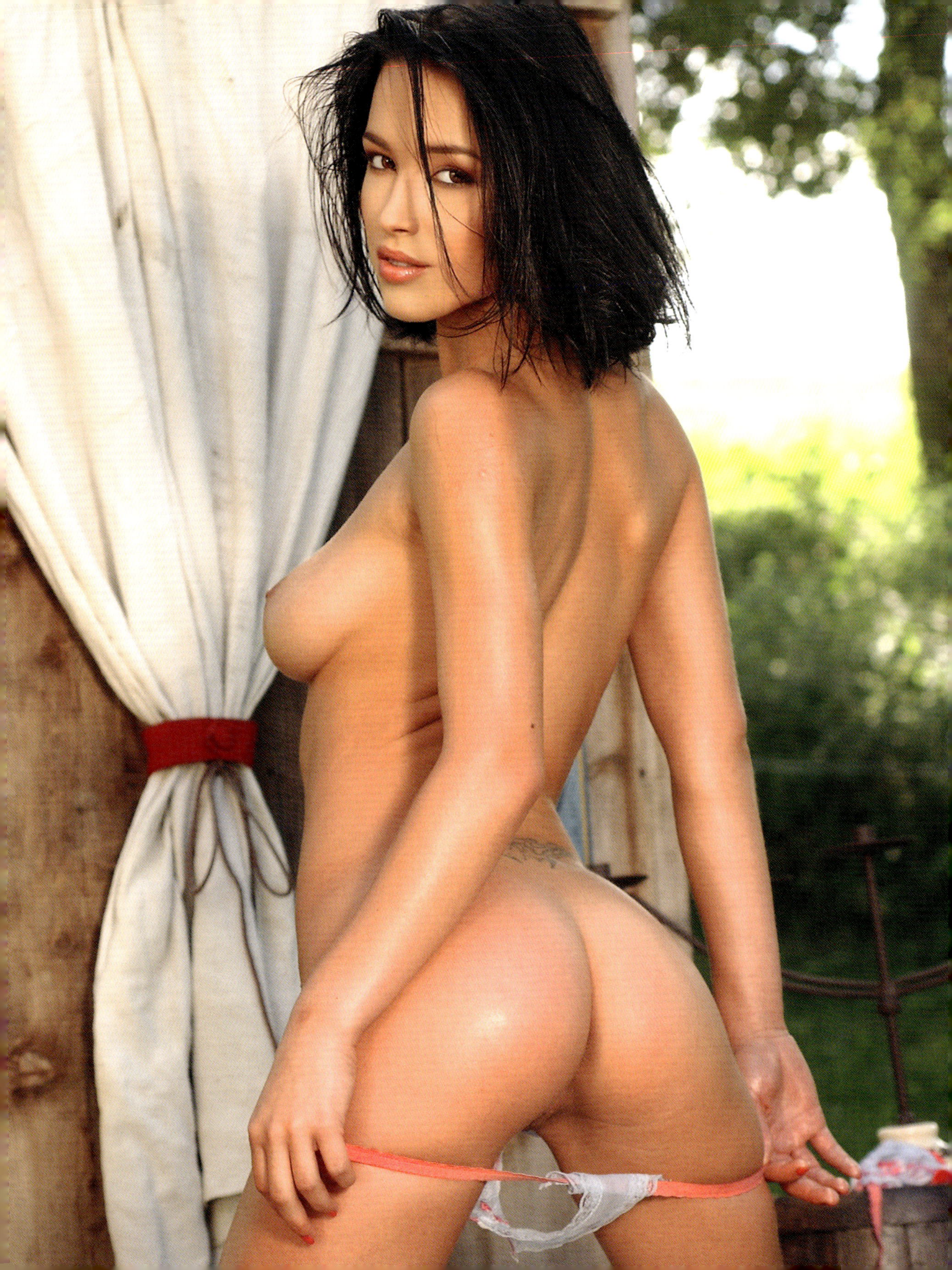

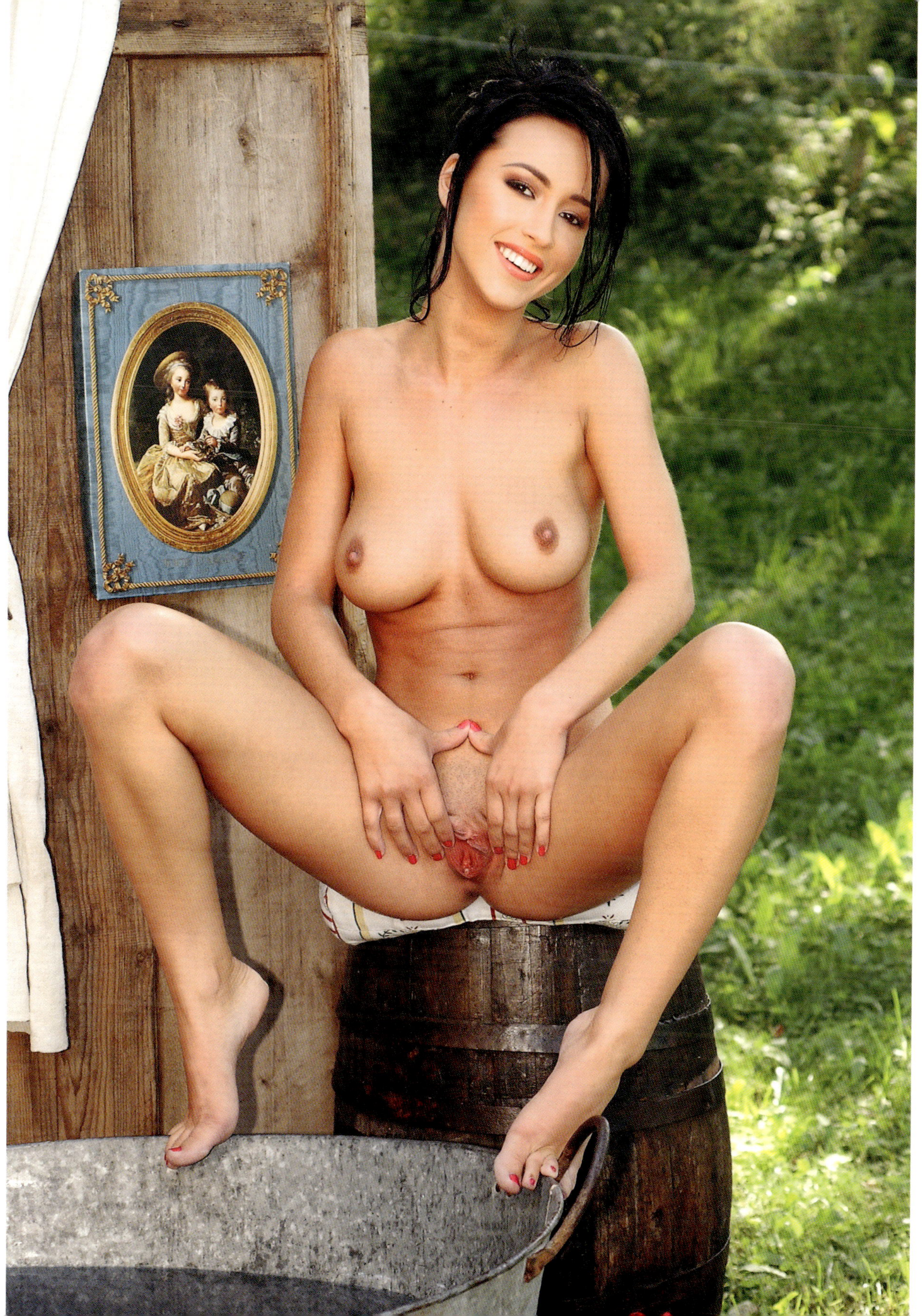

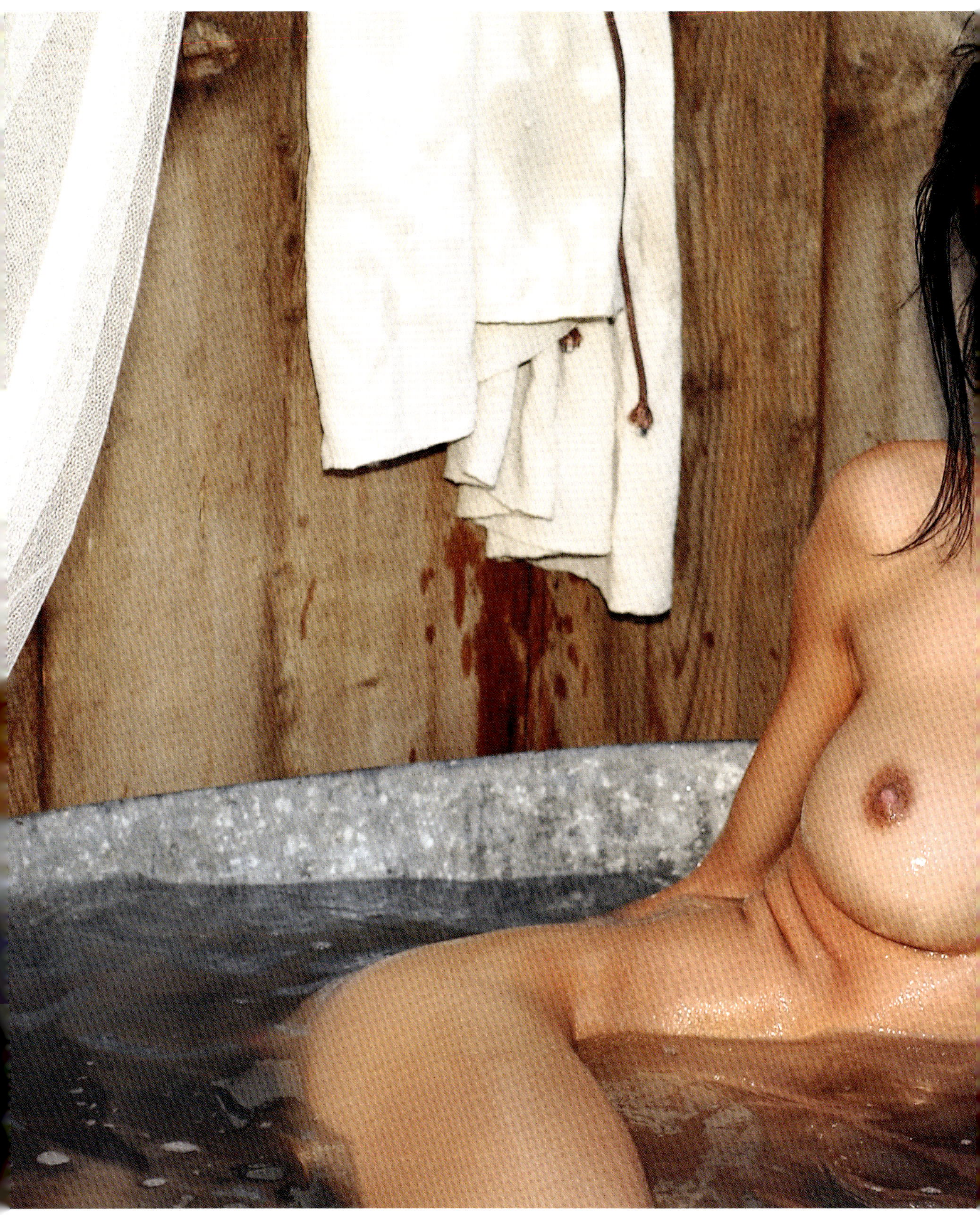



Mary

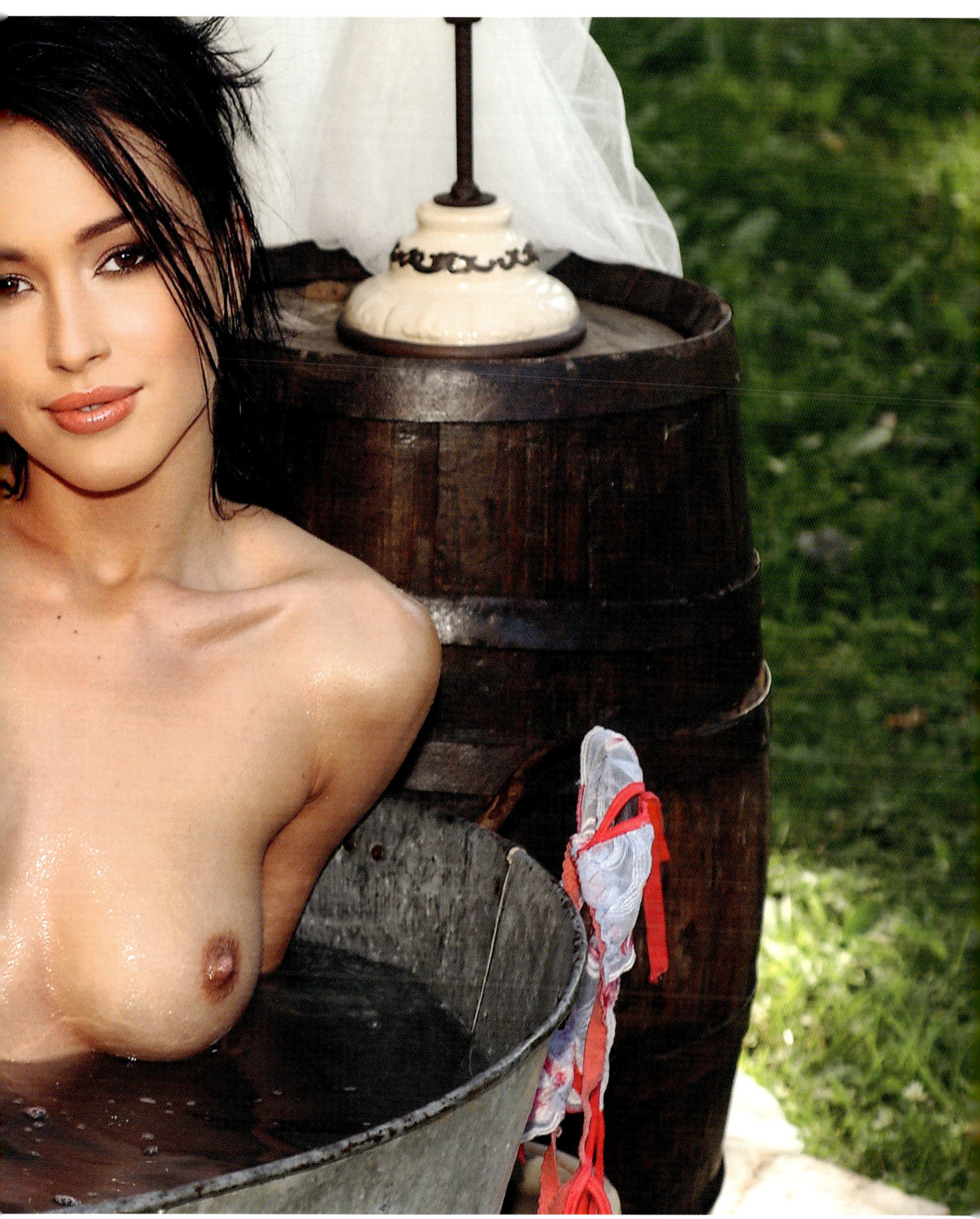

Mary

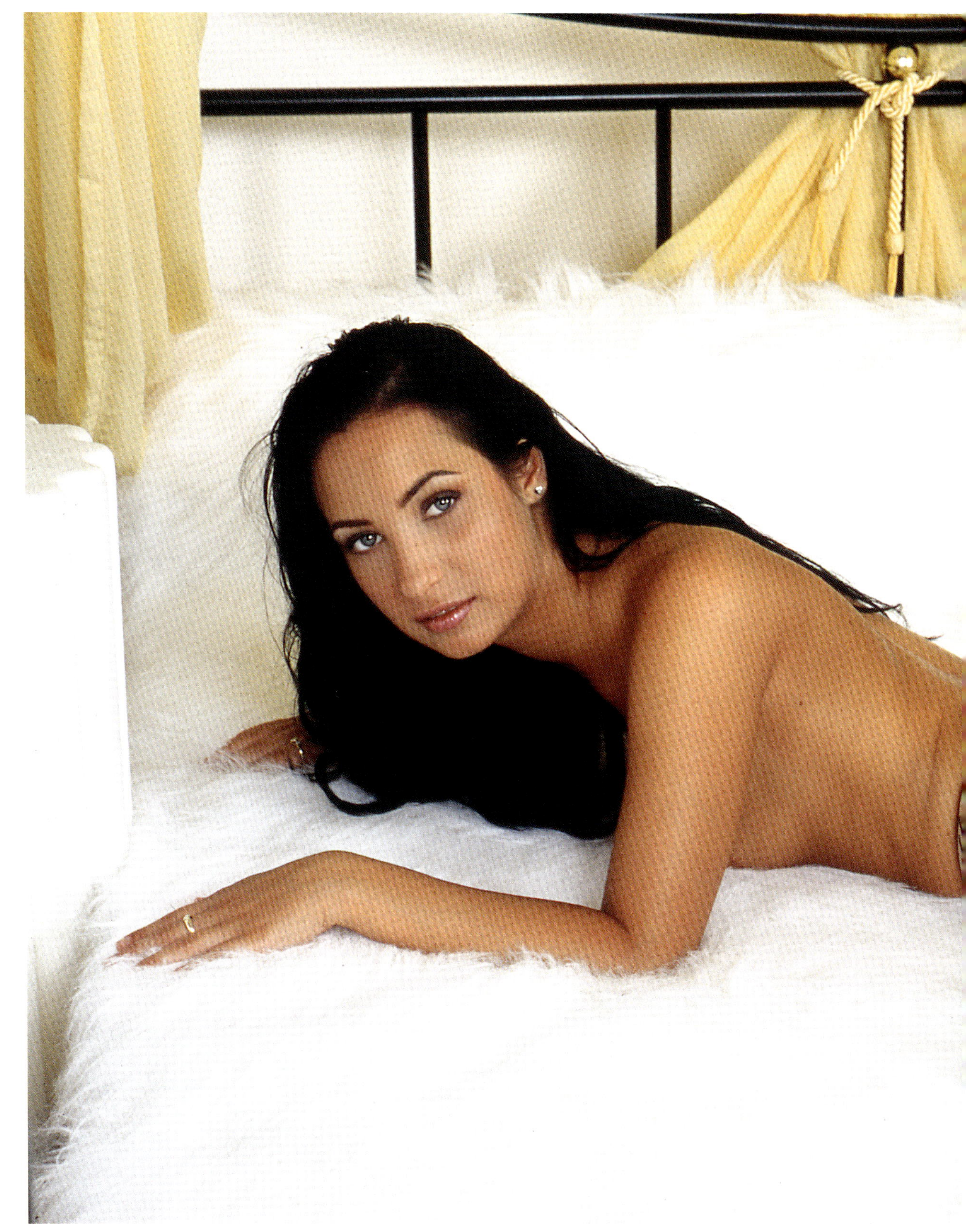

Sofia

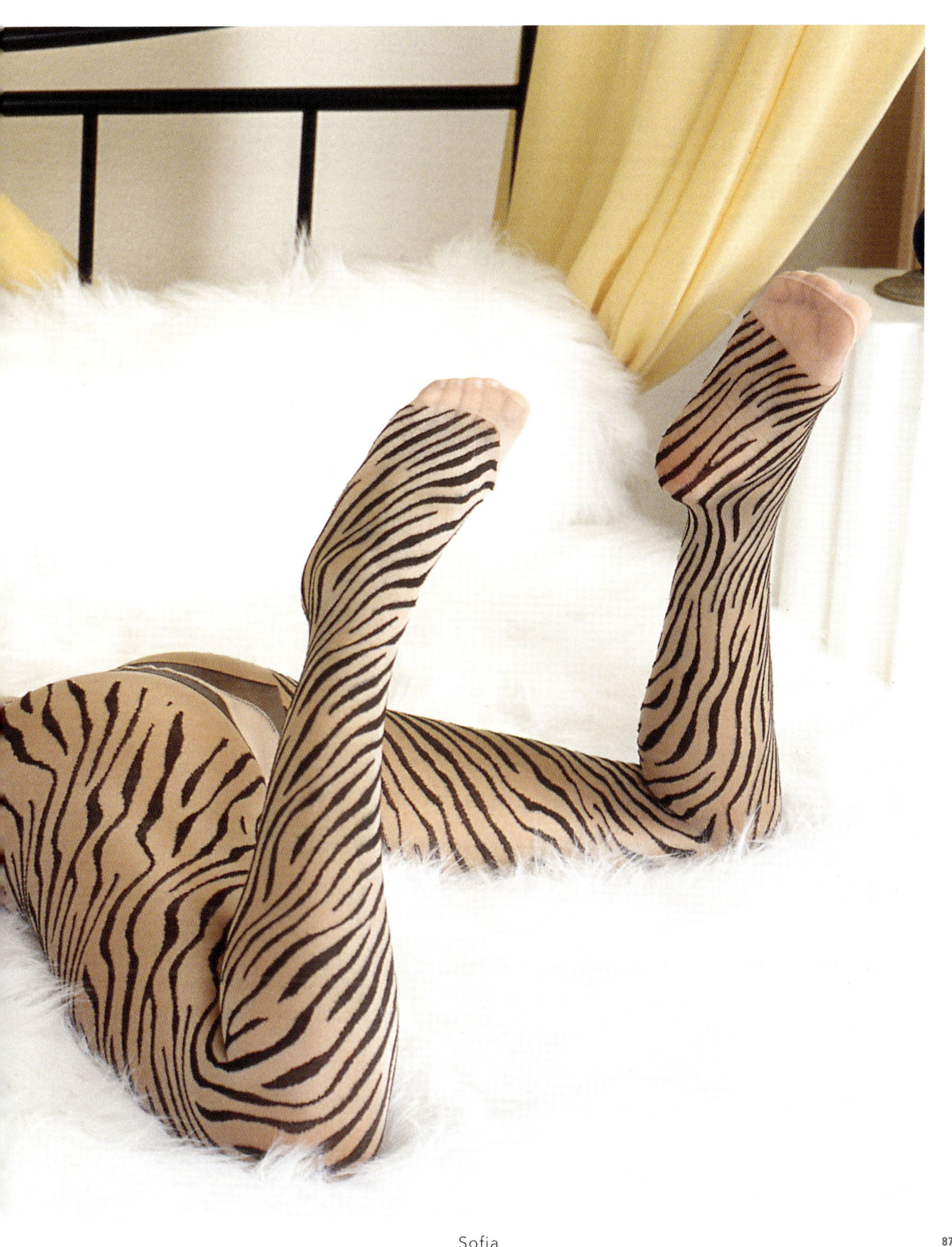

Sofia

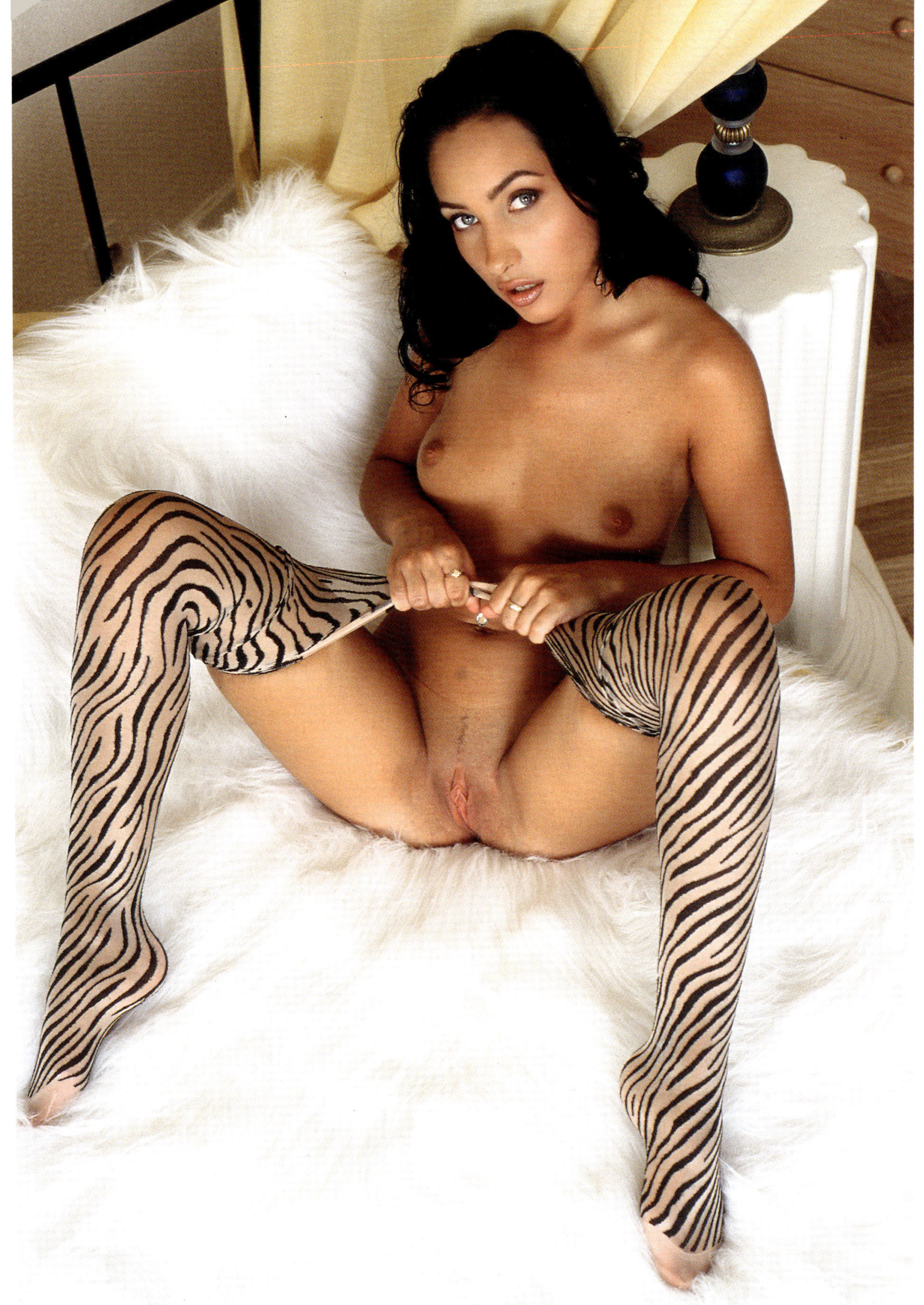

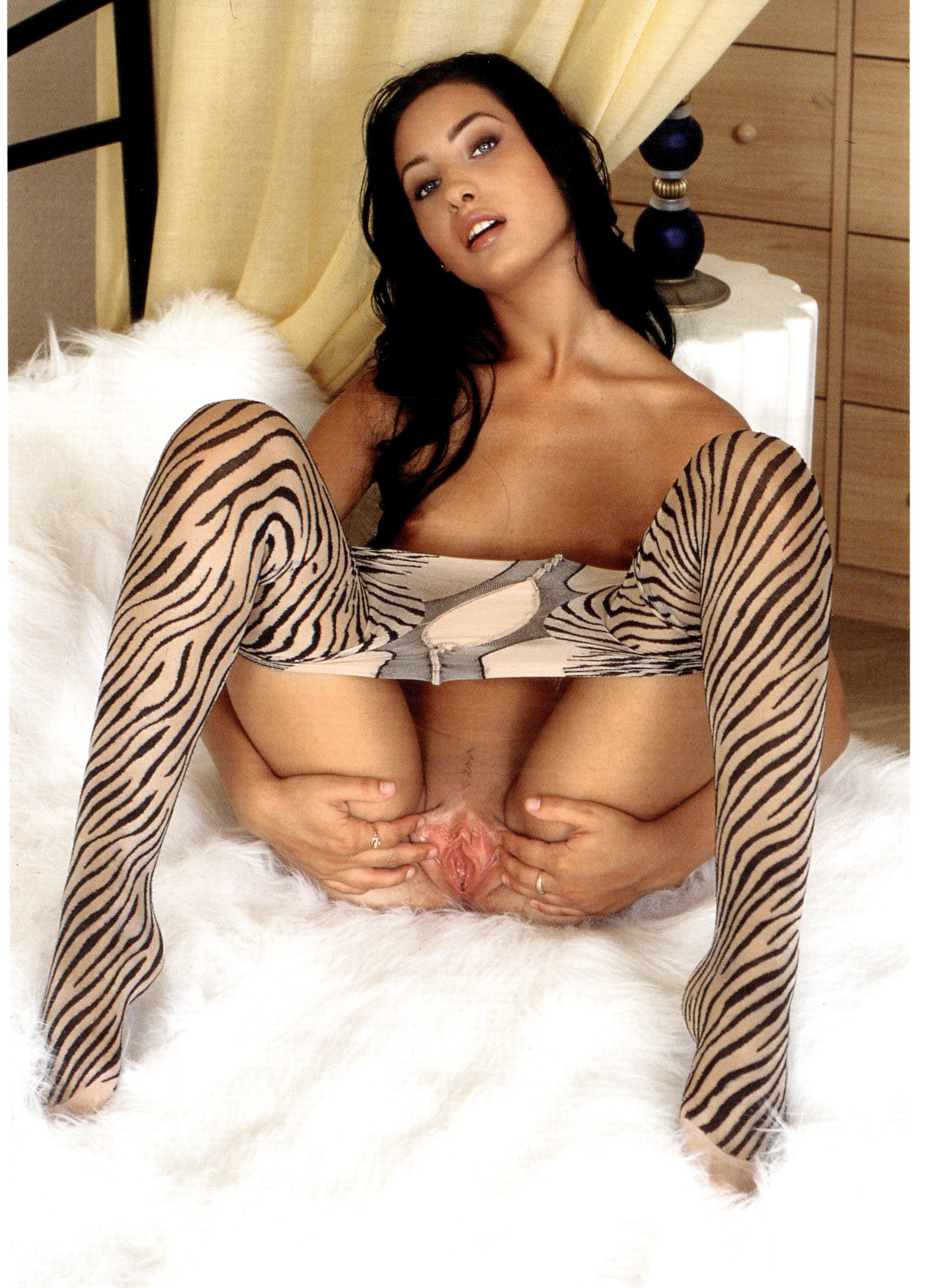

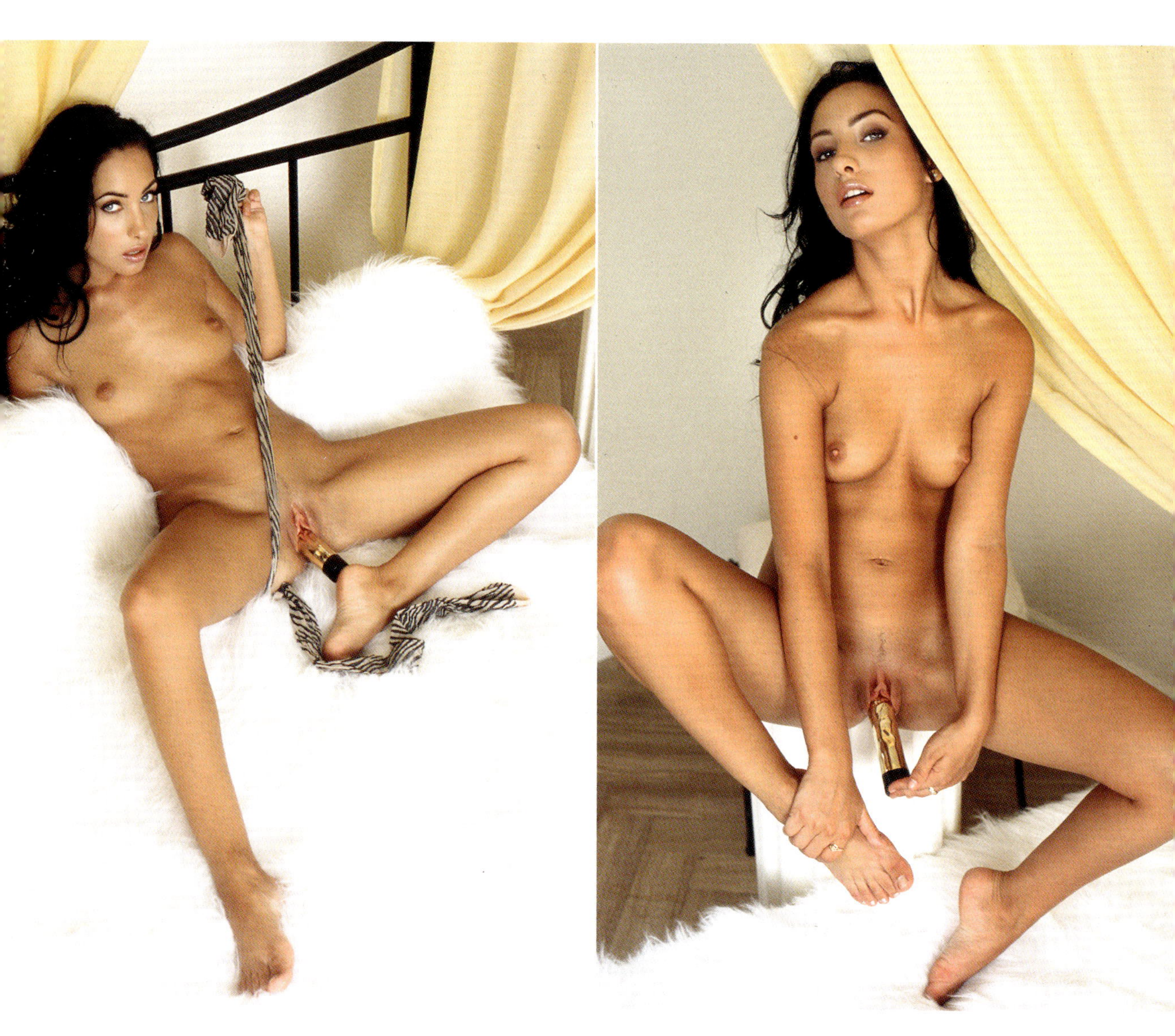



Sofia

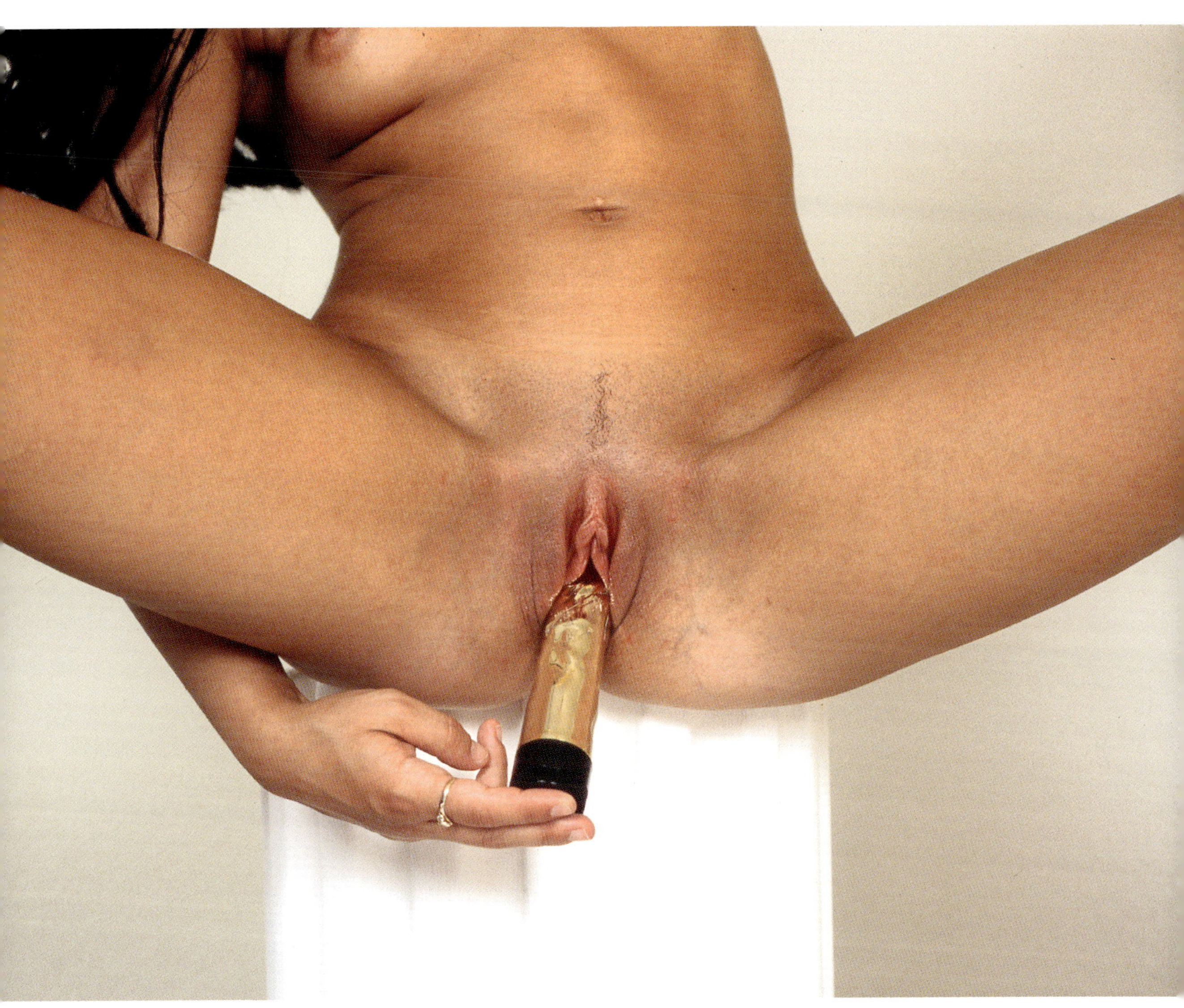

Sofia

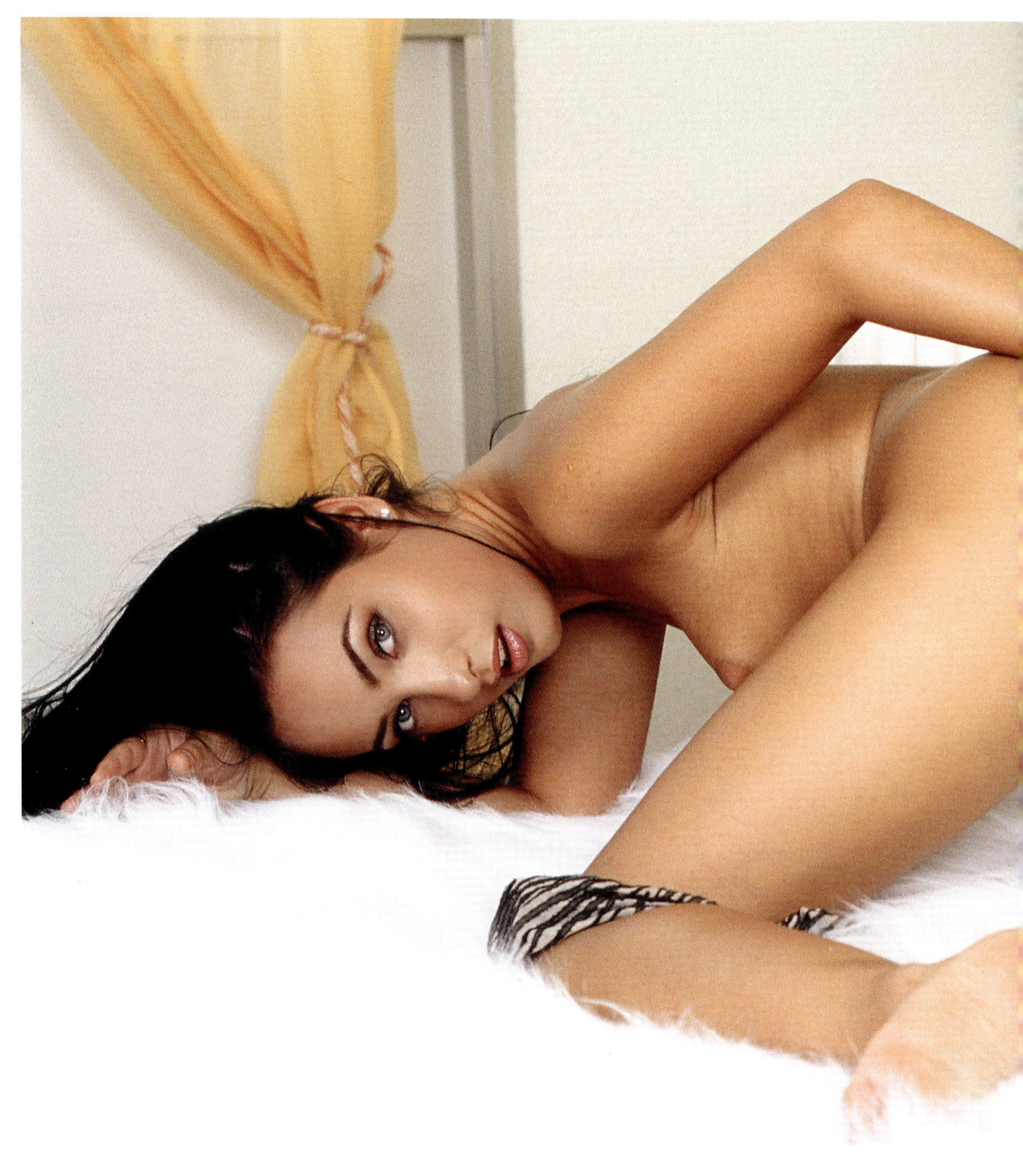

Sofia

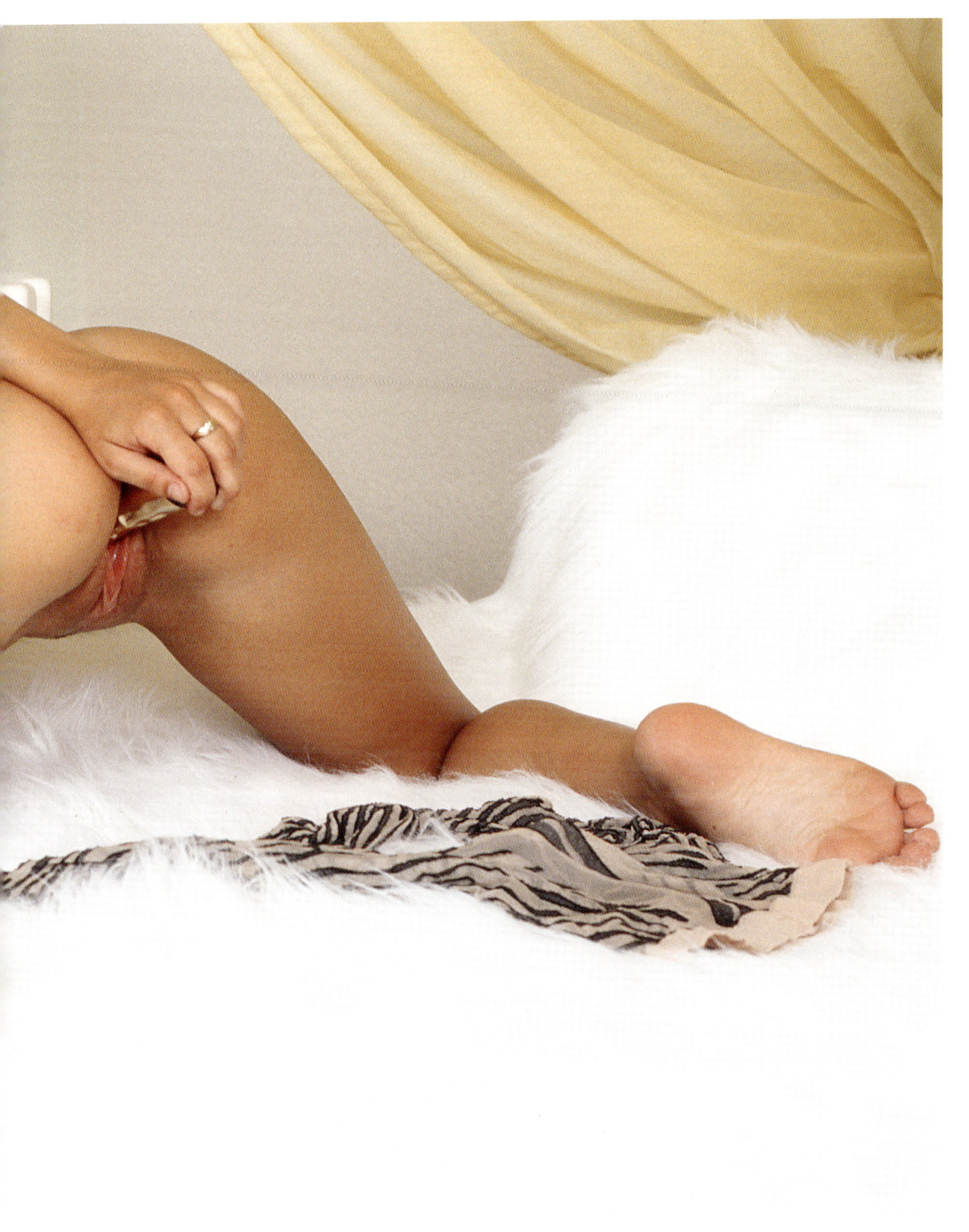

Sofia

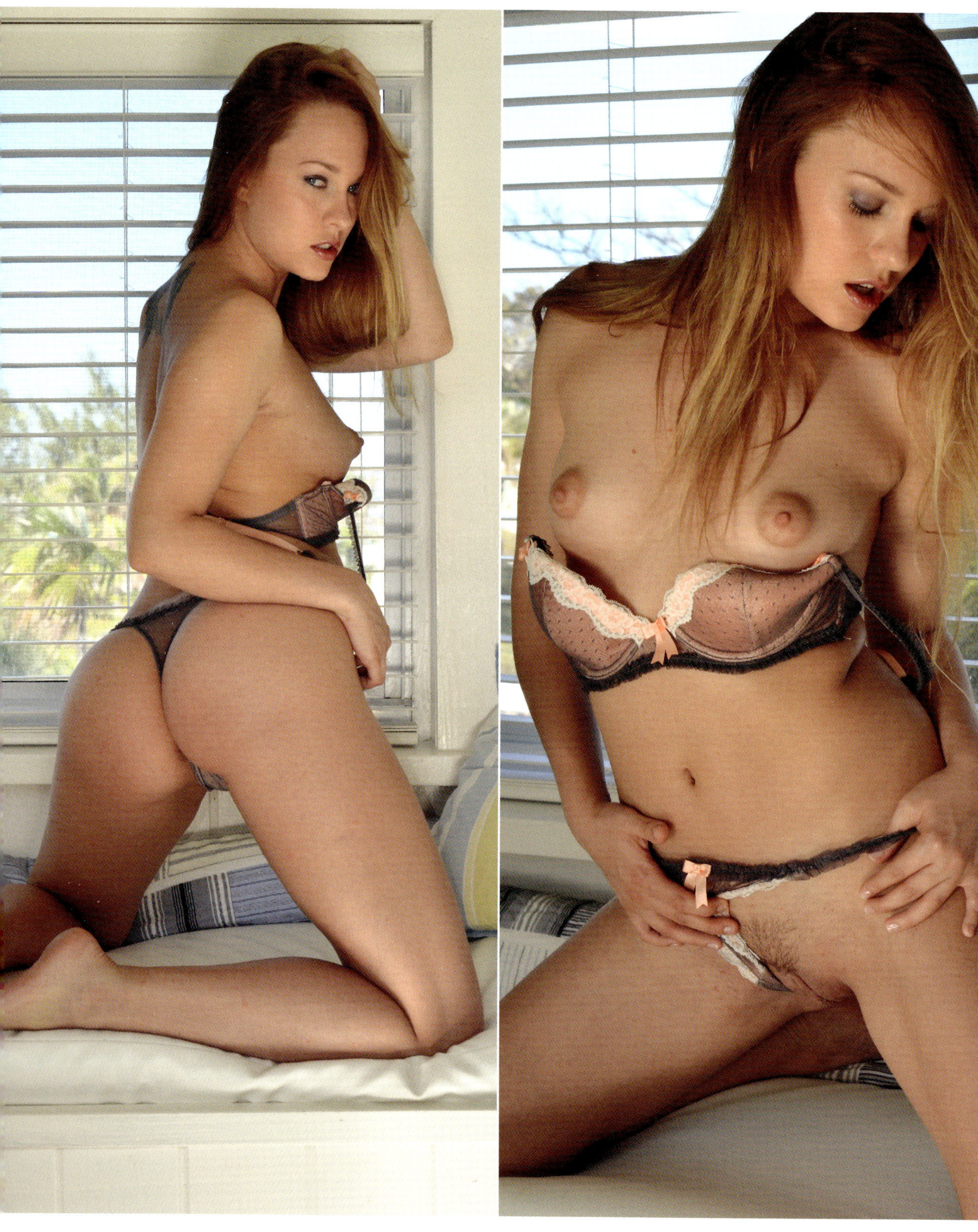

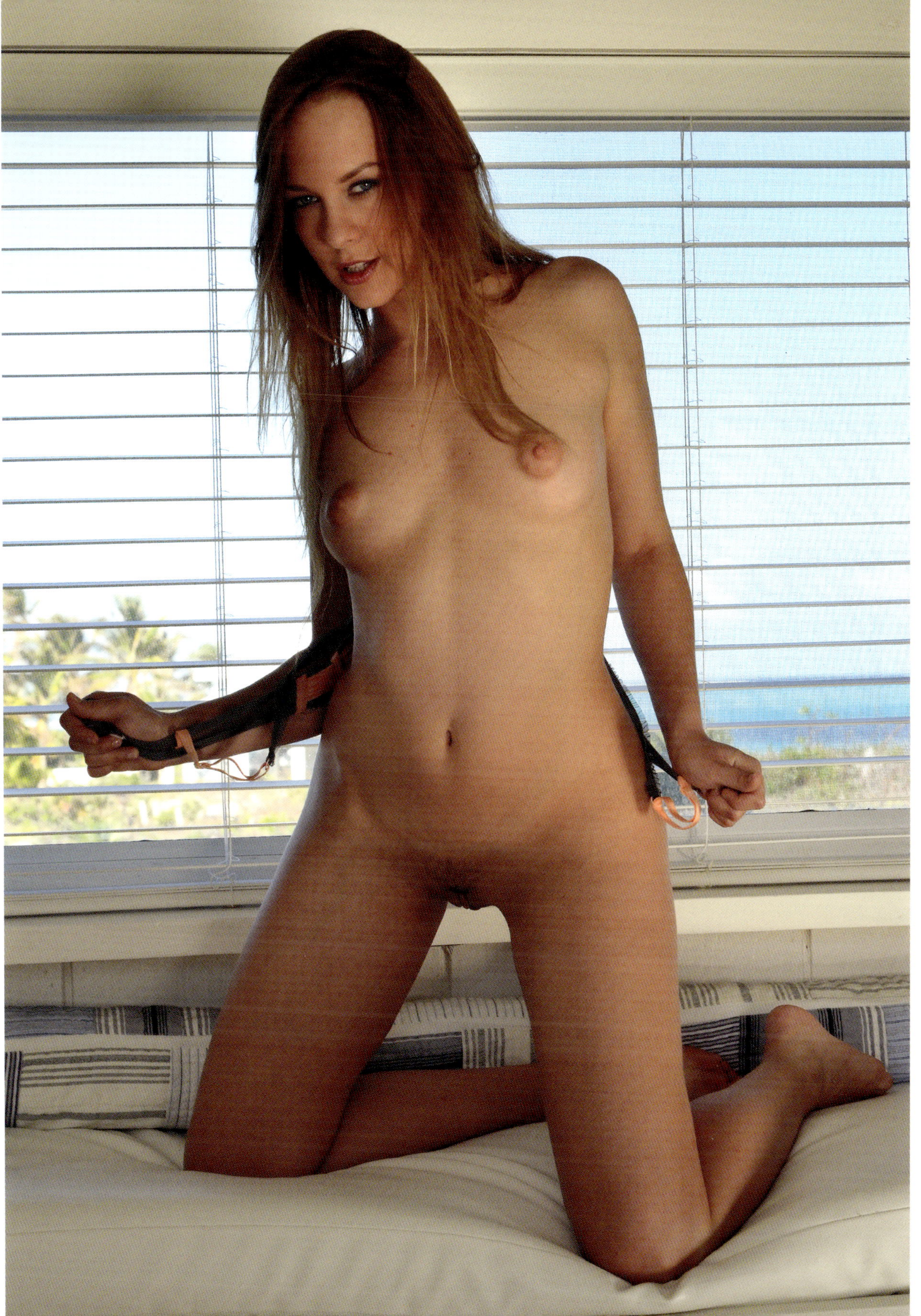

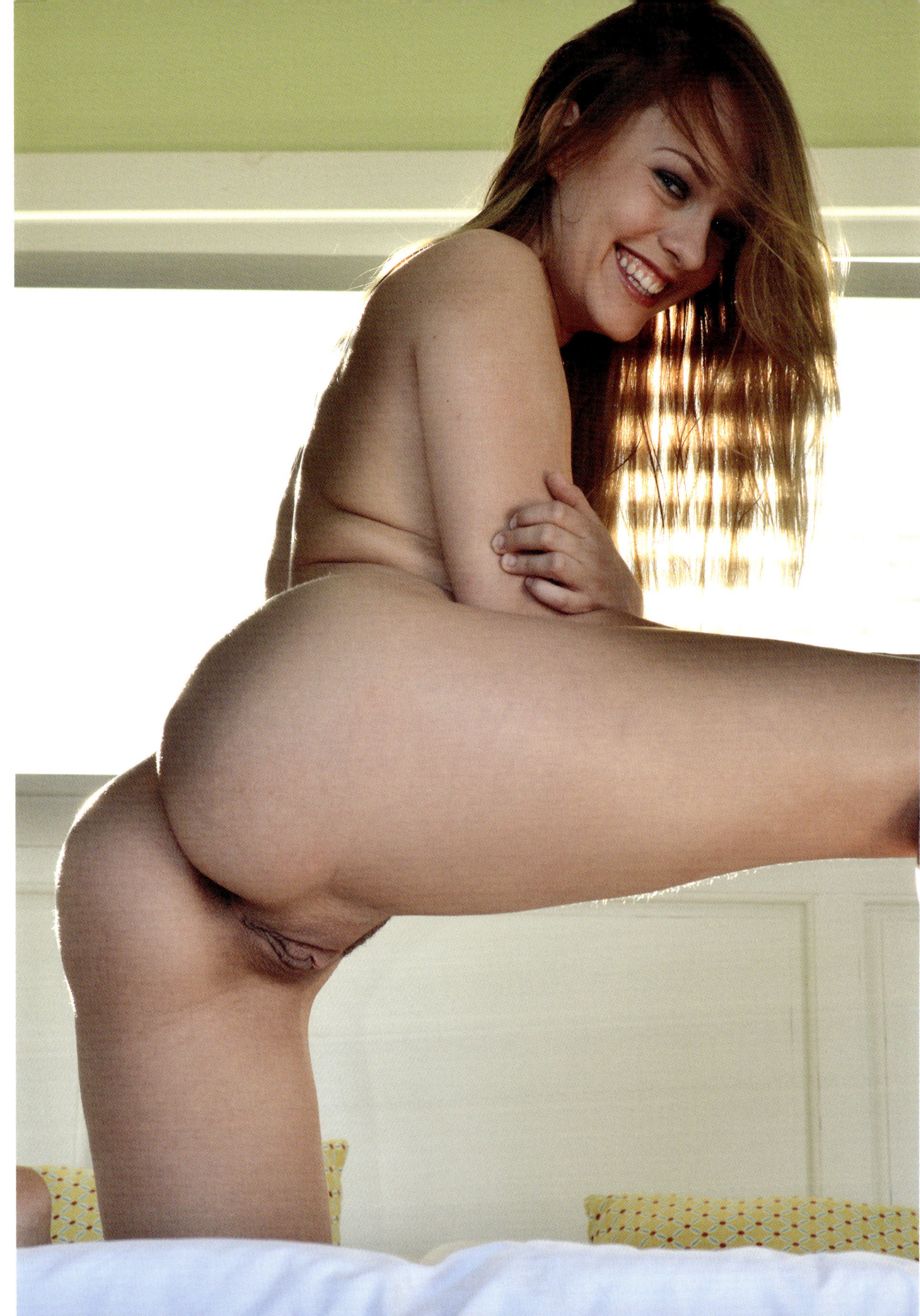

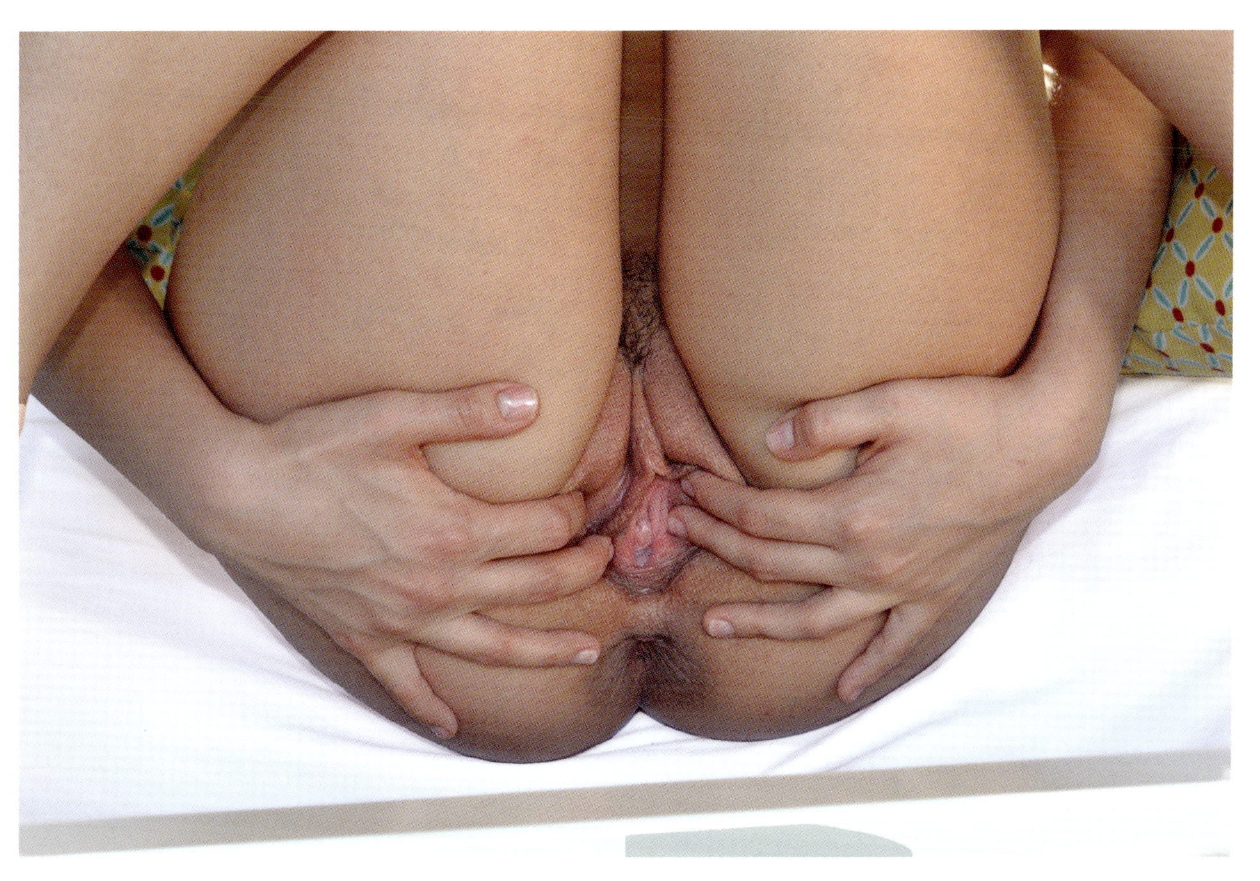

Vivien

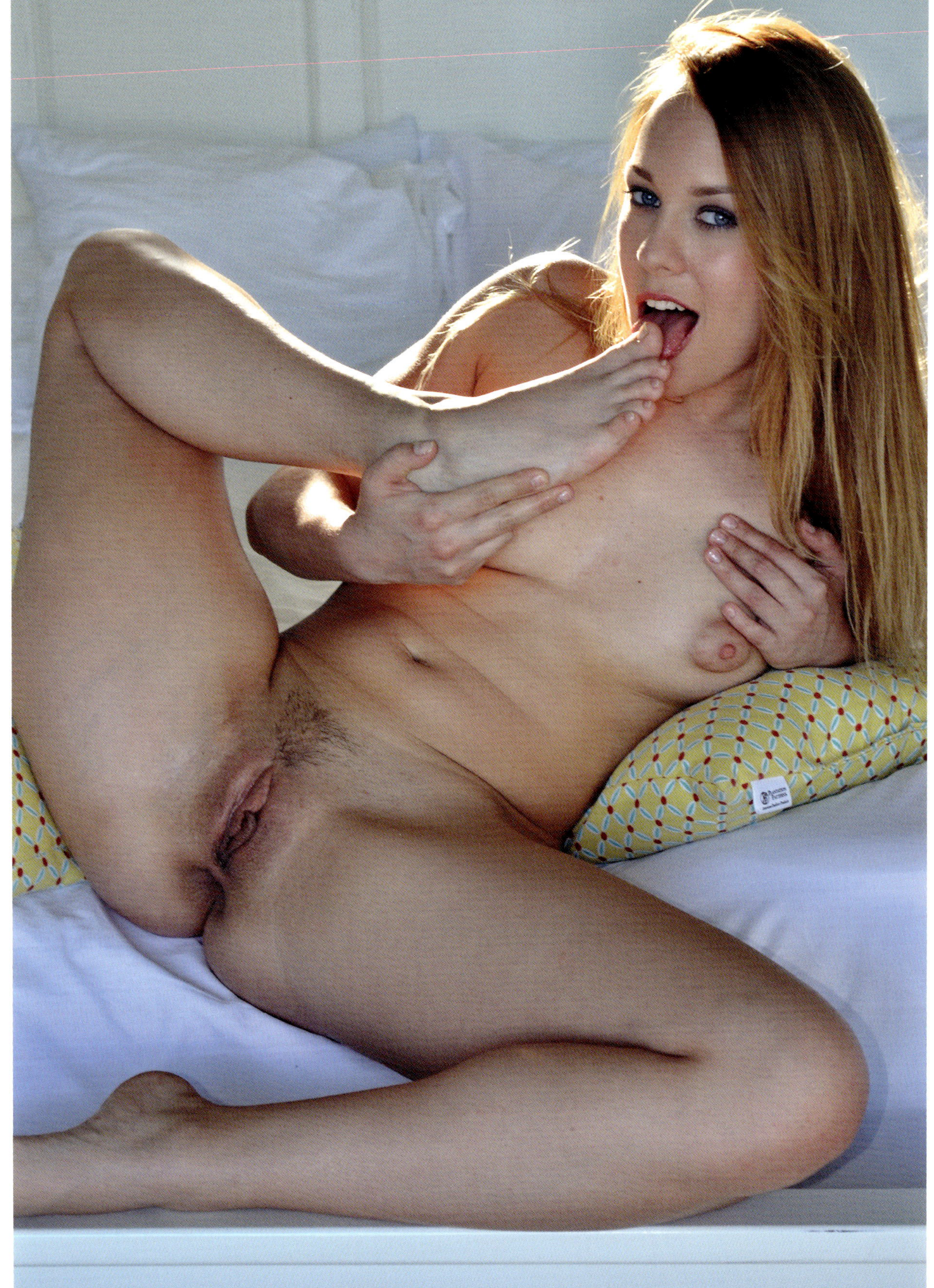

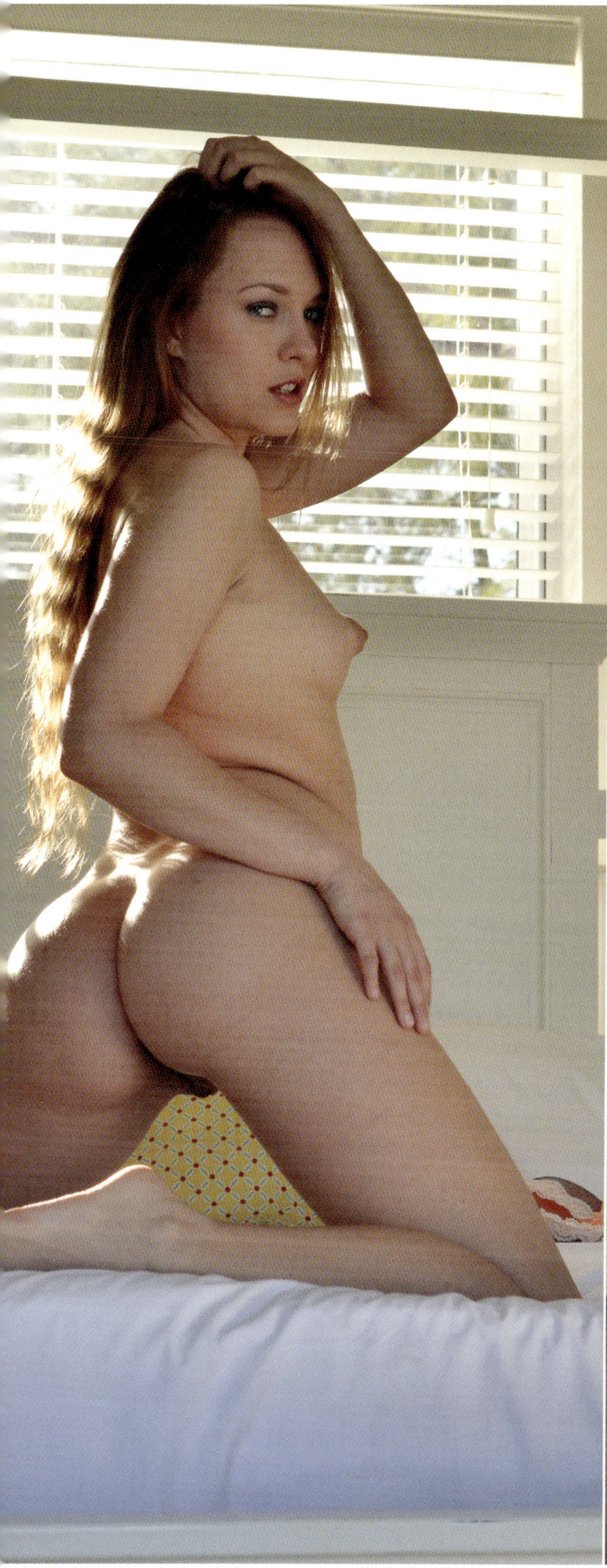

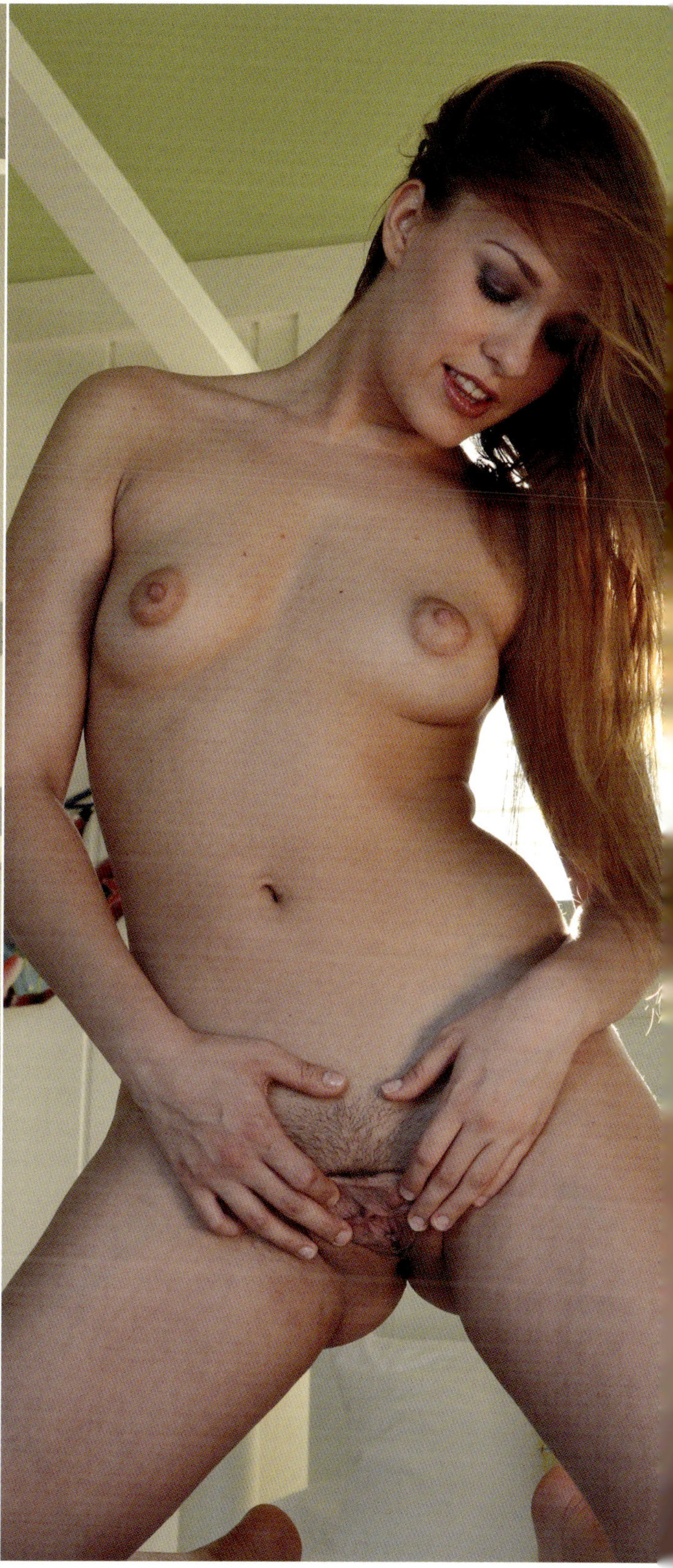

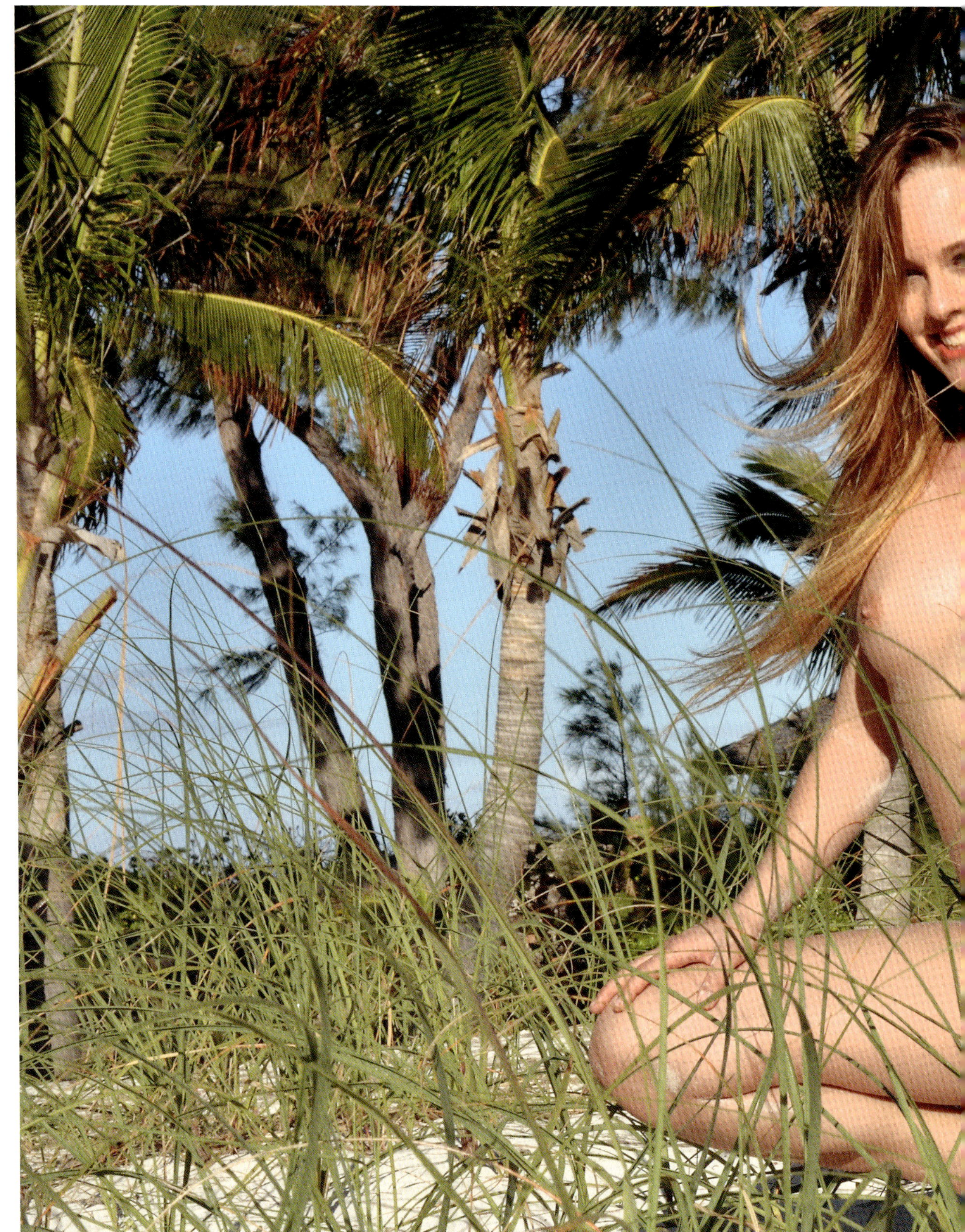



Vivien

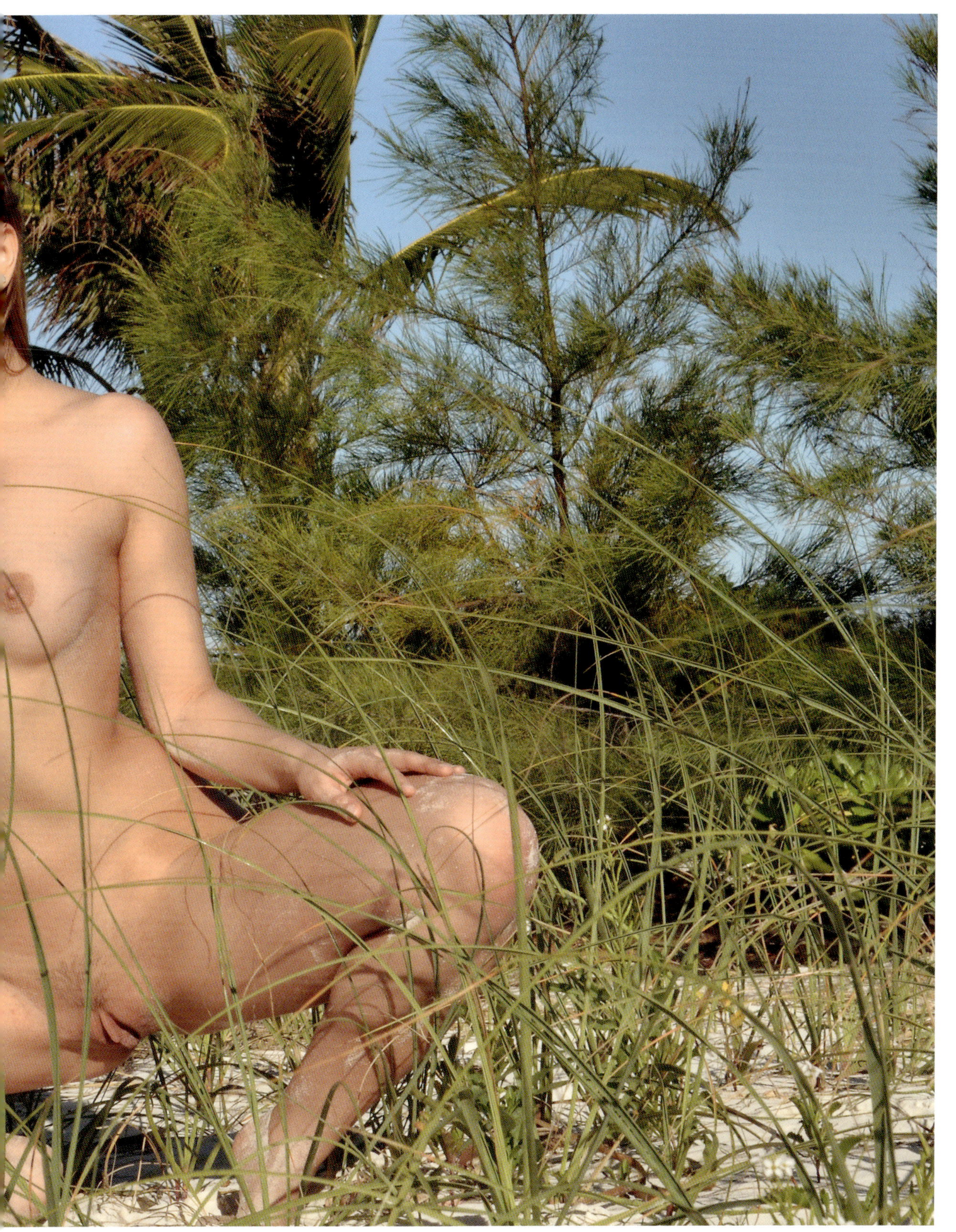

Vivien

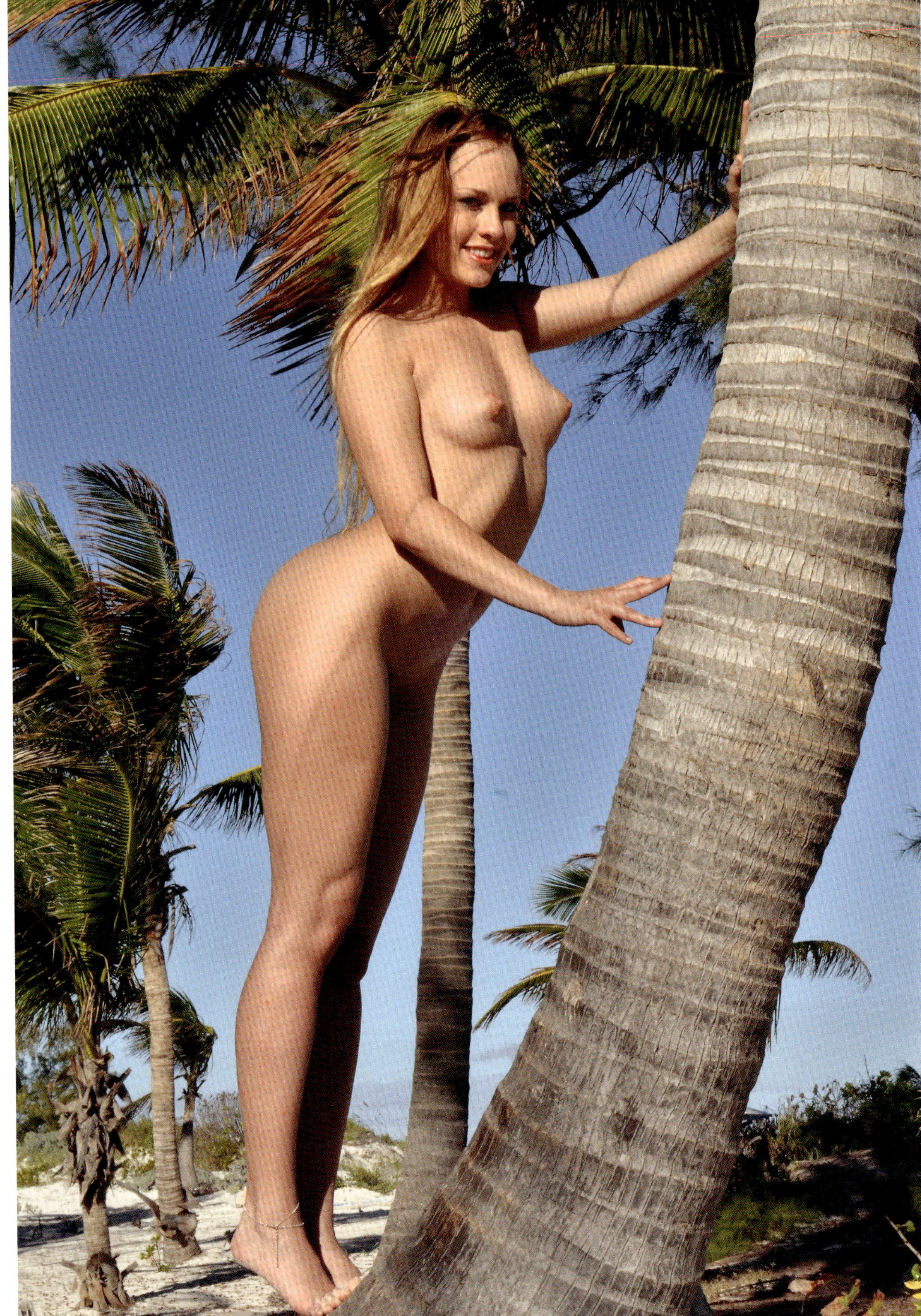

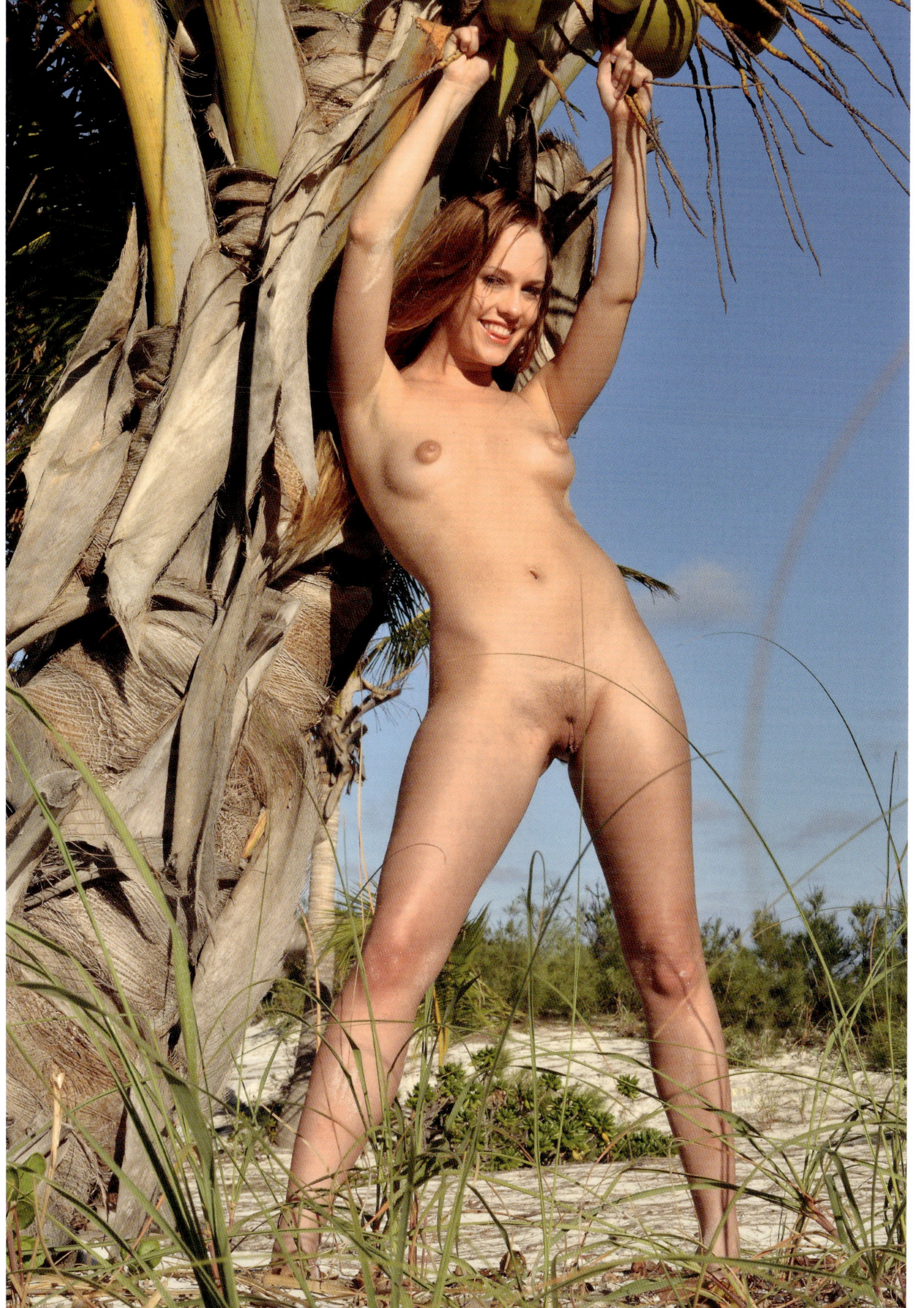

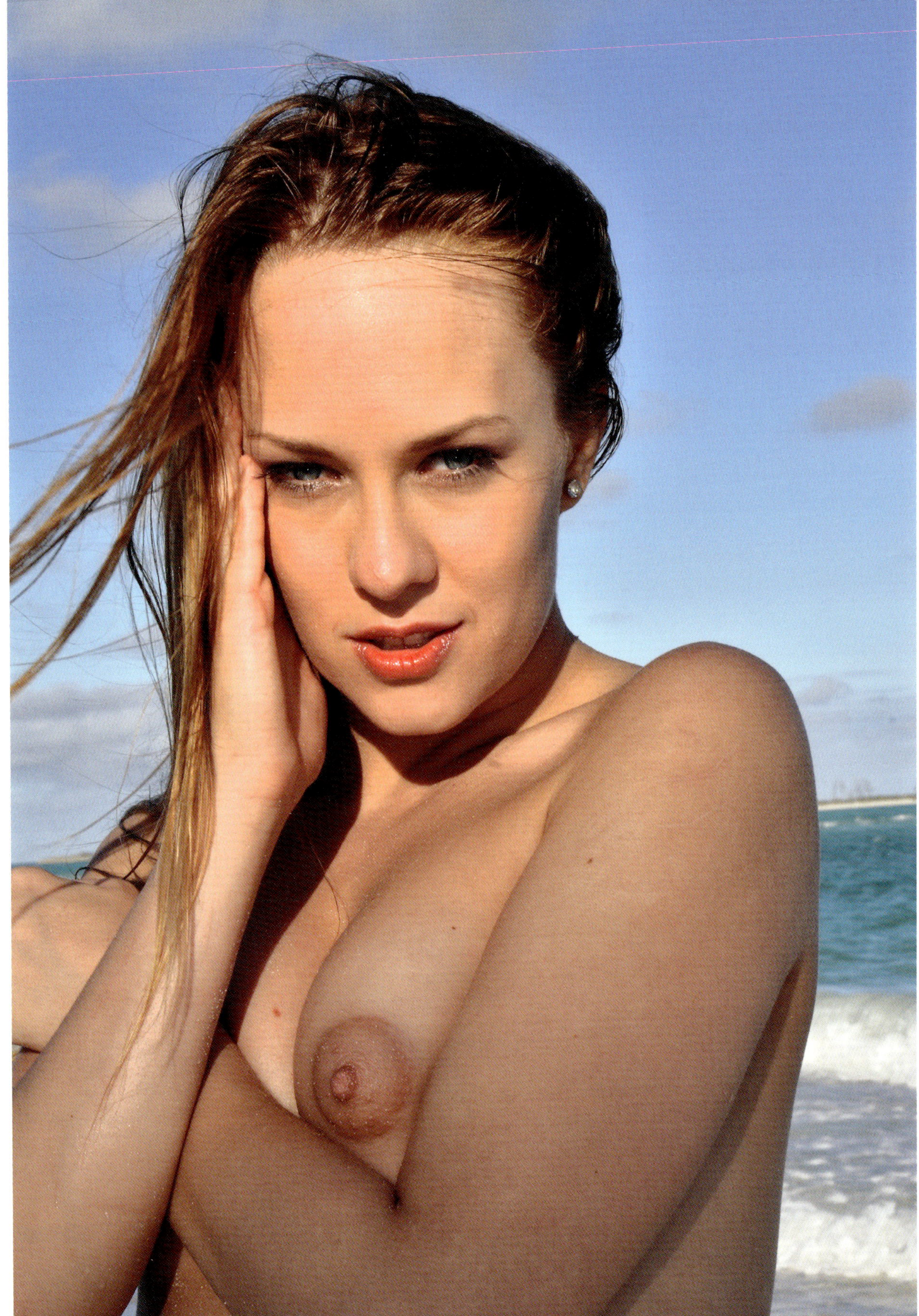

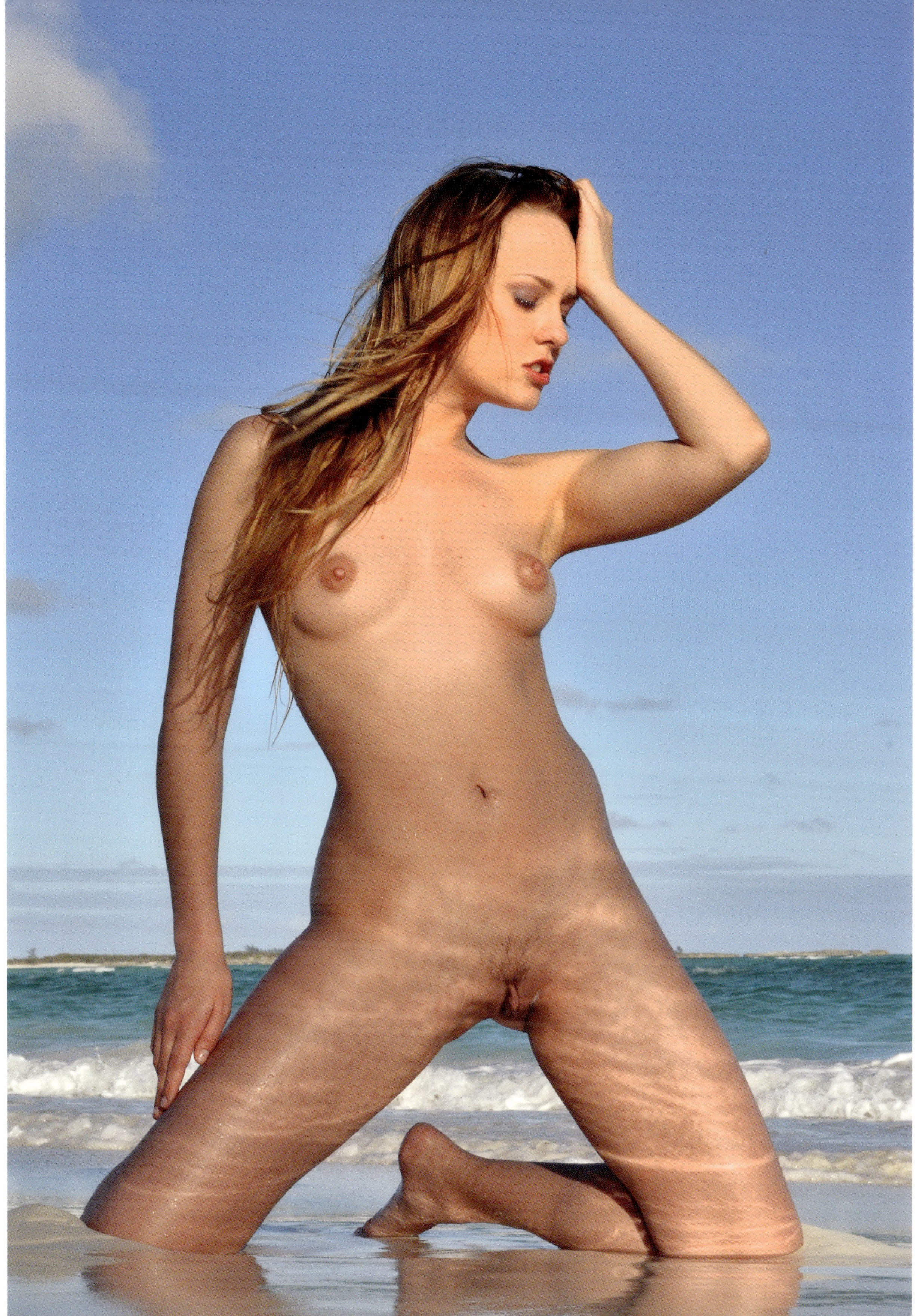

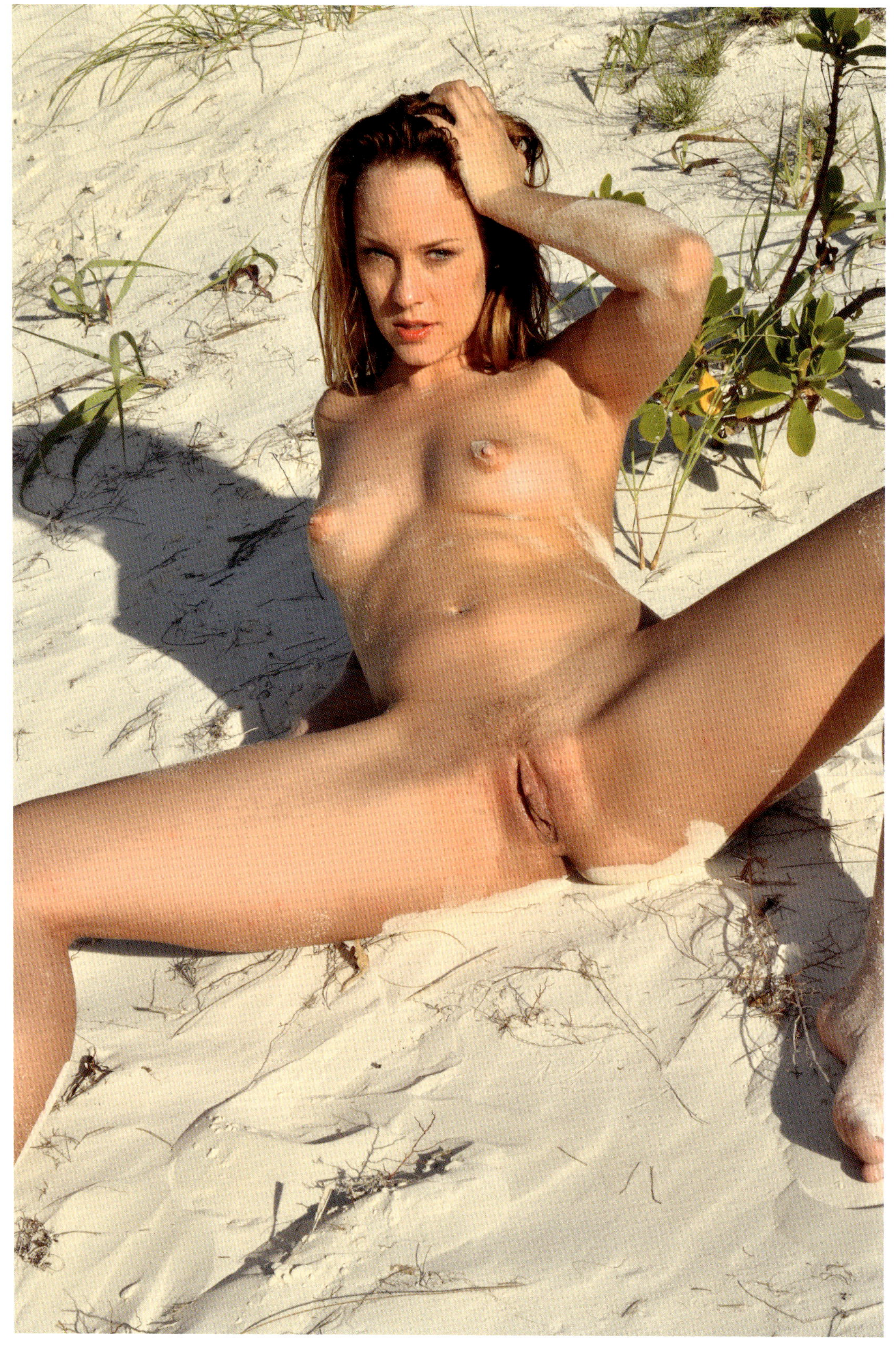

Vivien

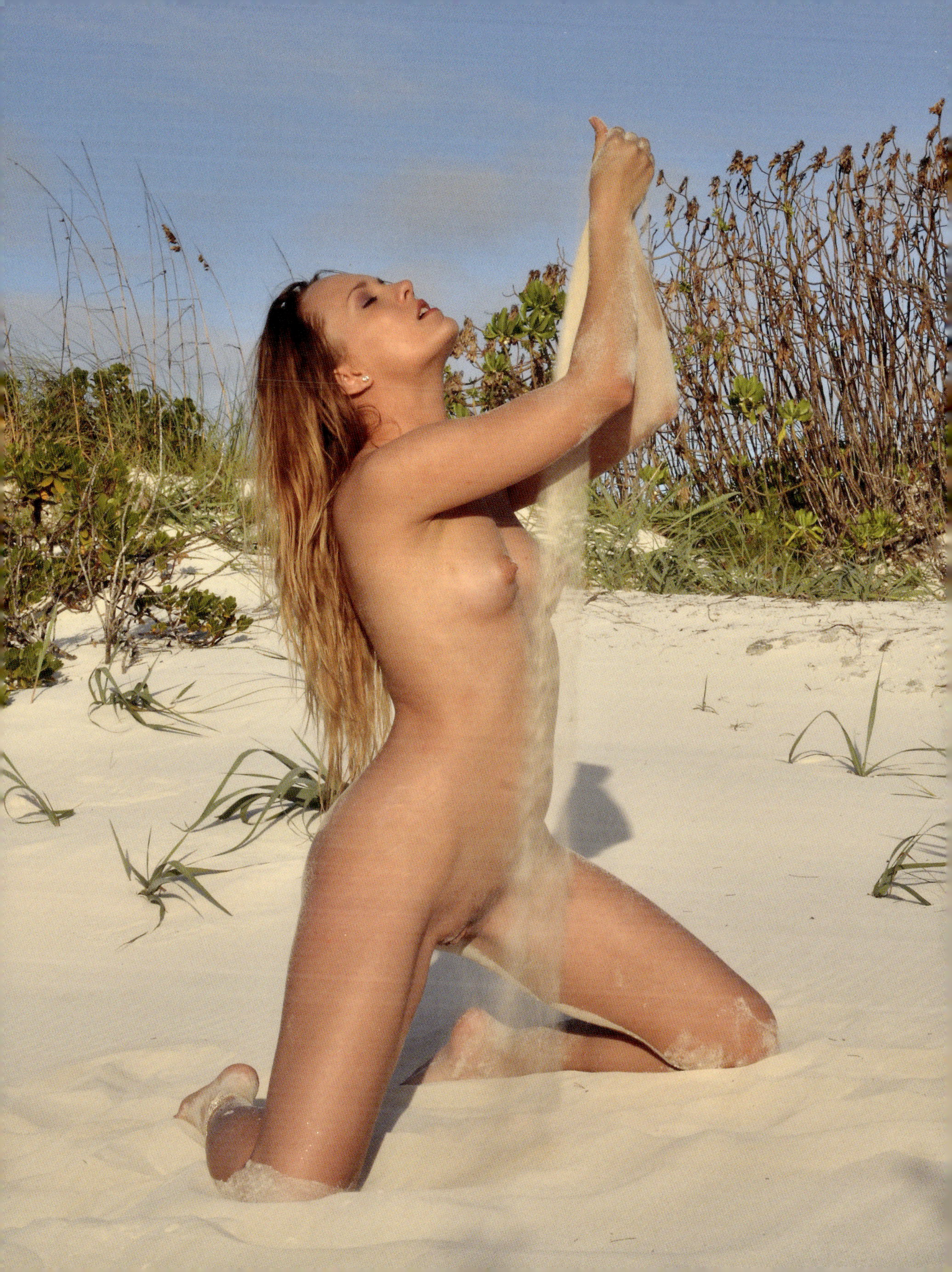

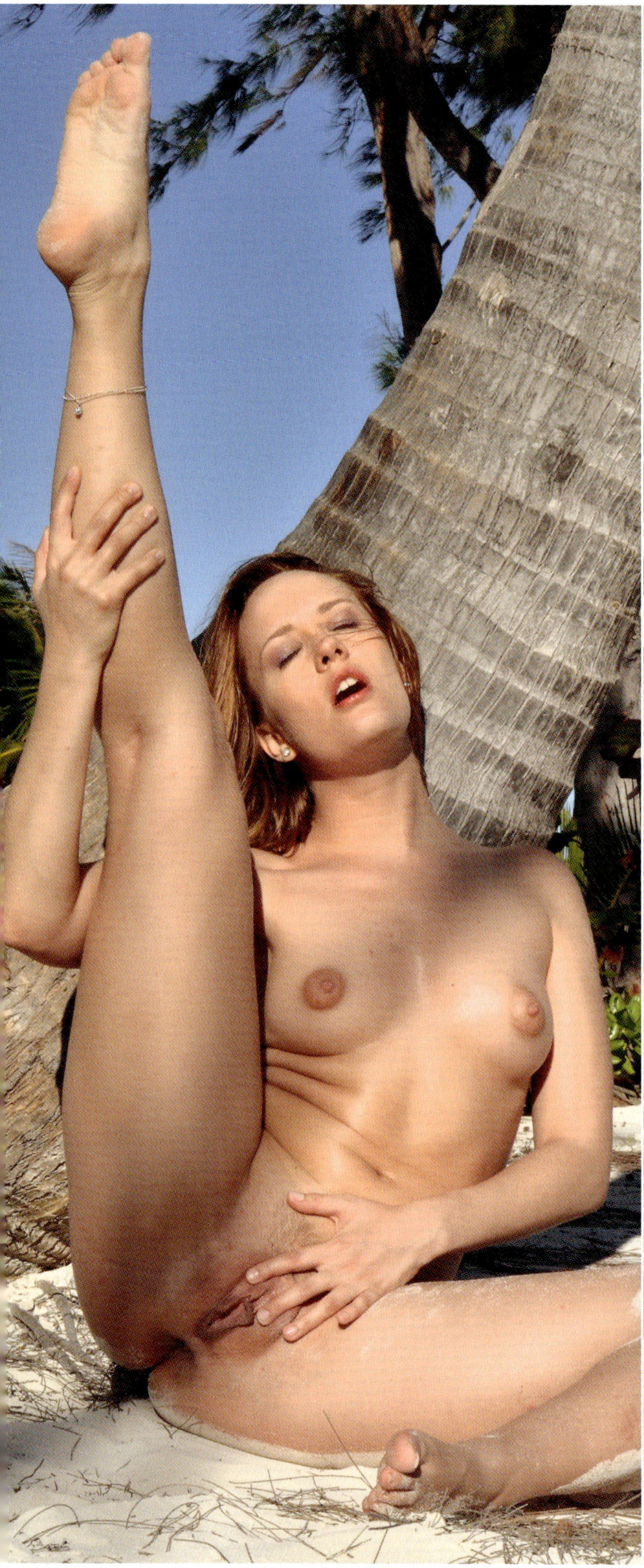

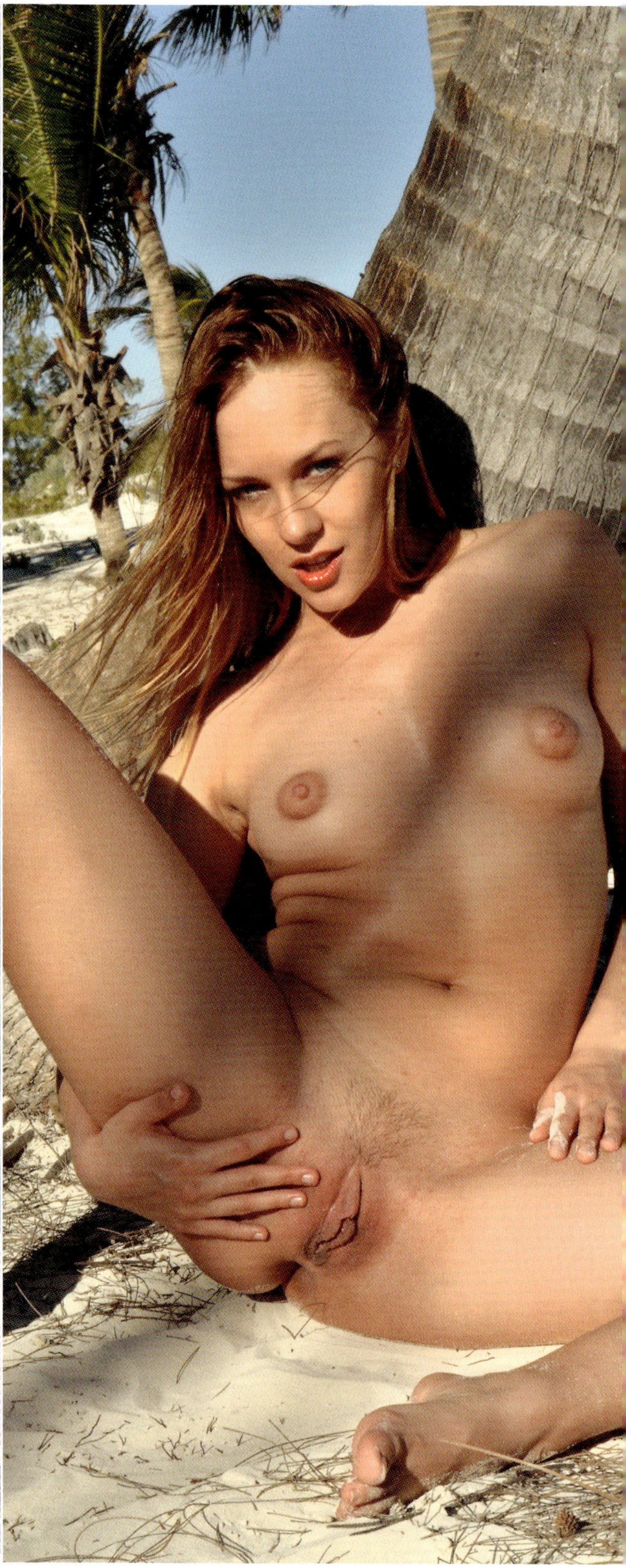

Vivien

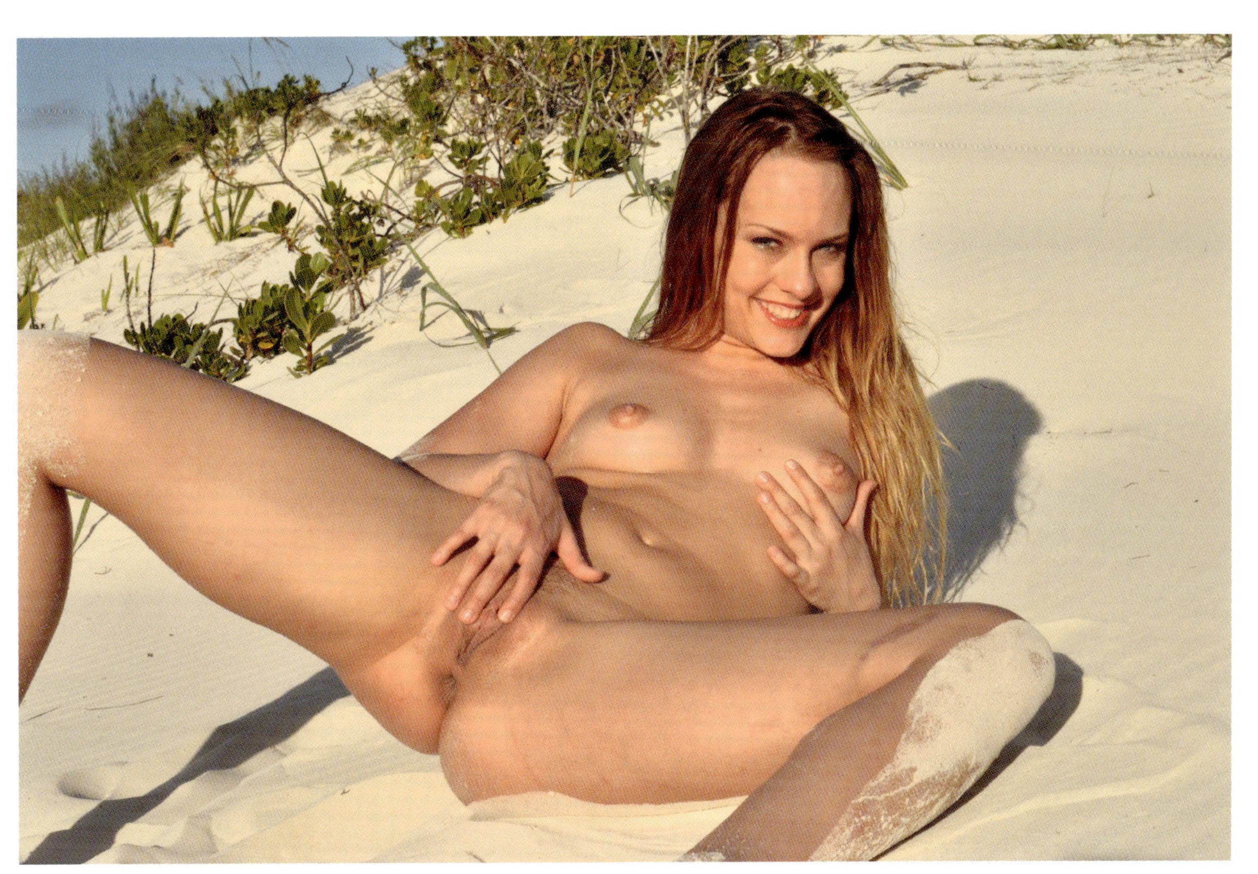

Vivien

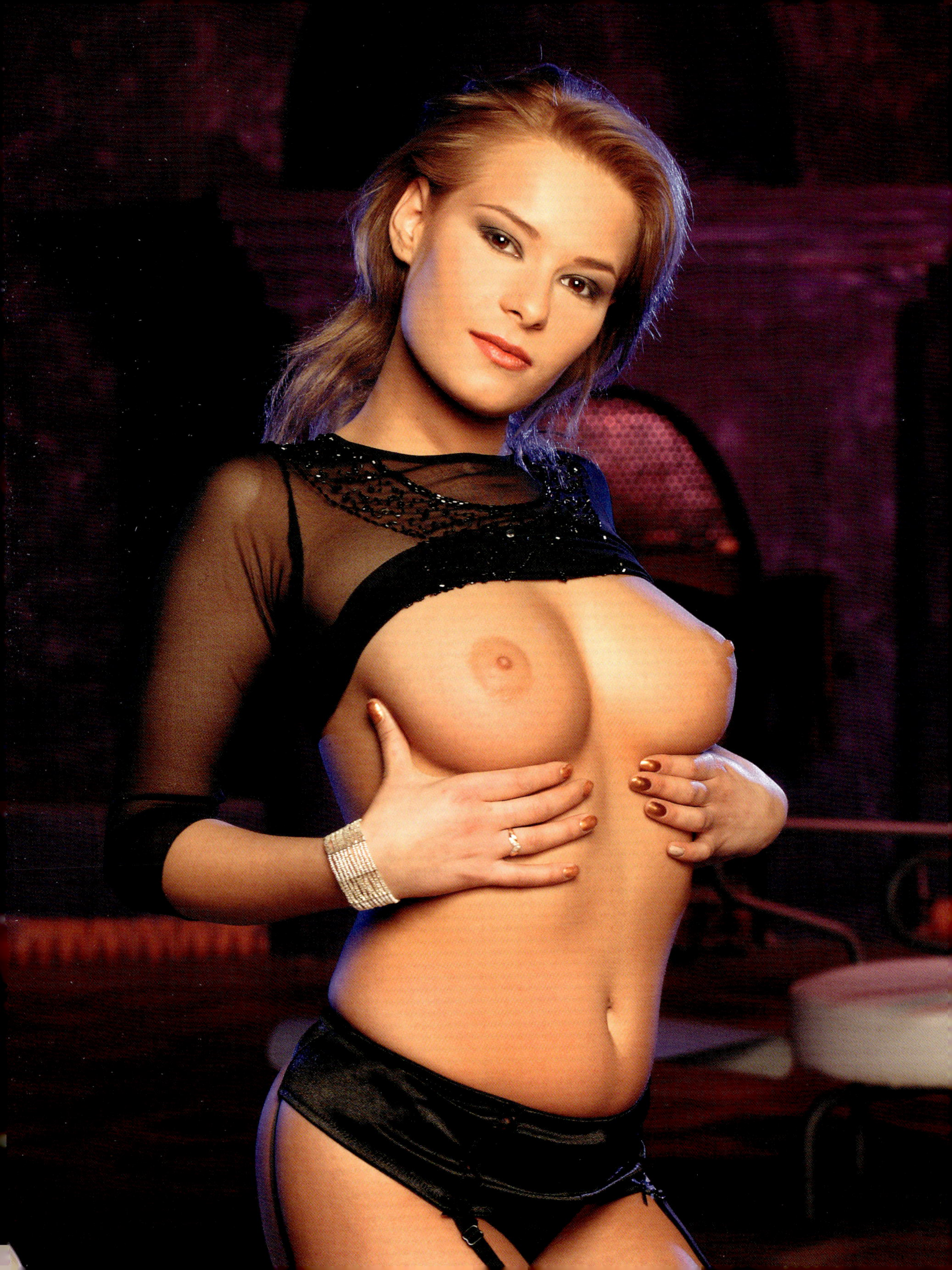

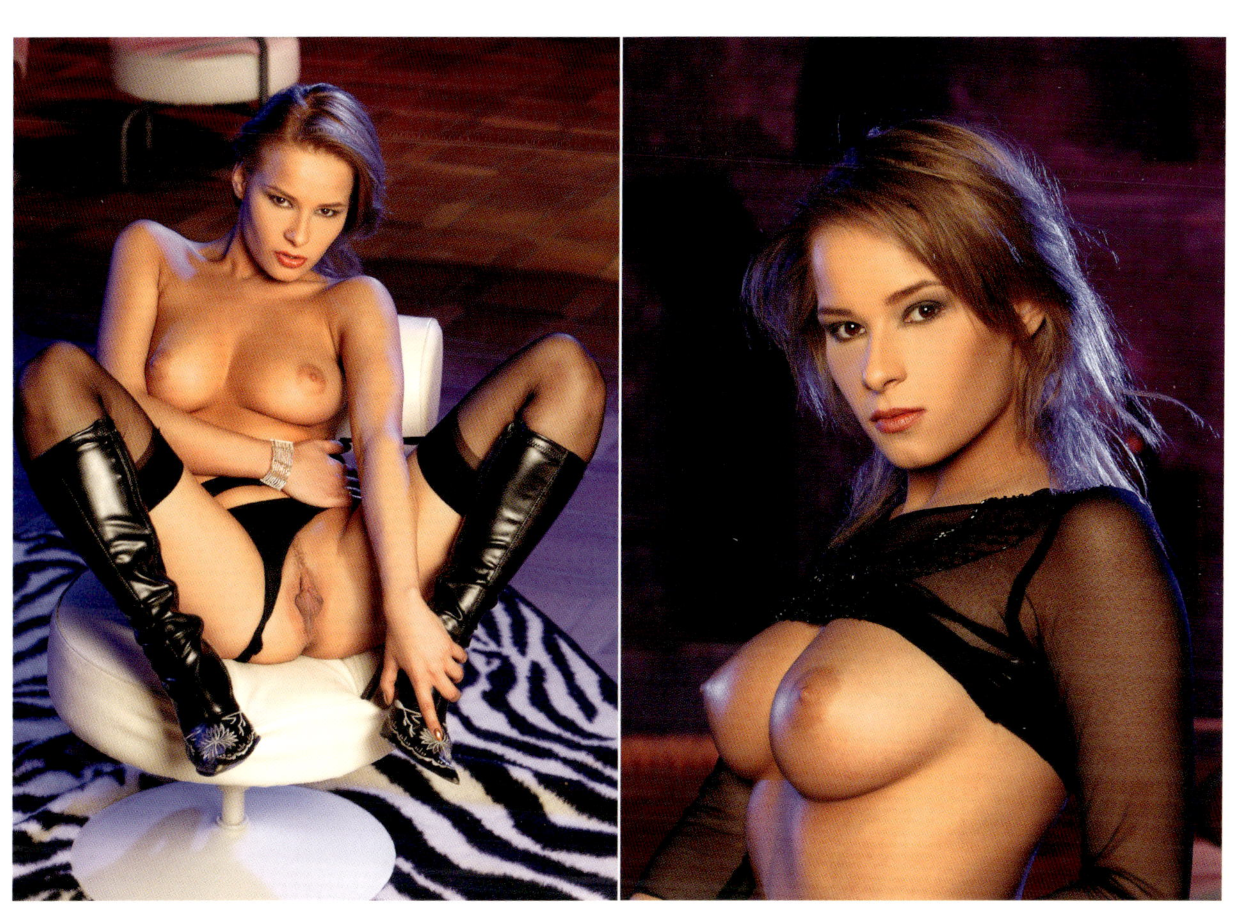

Jenia

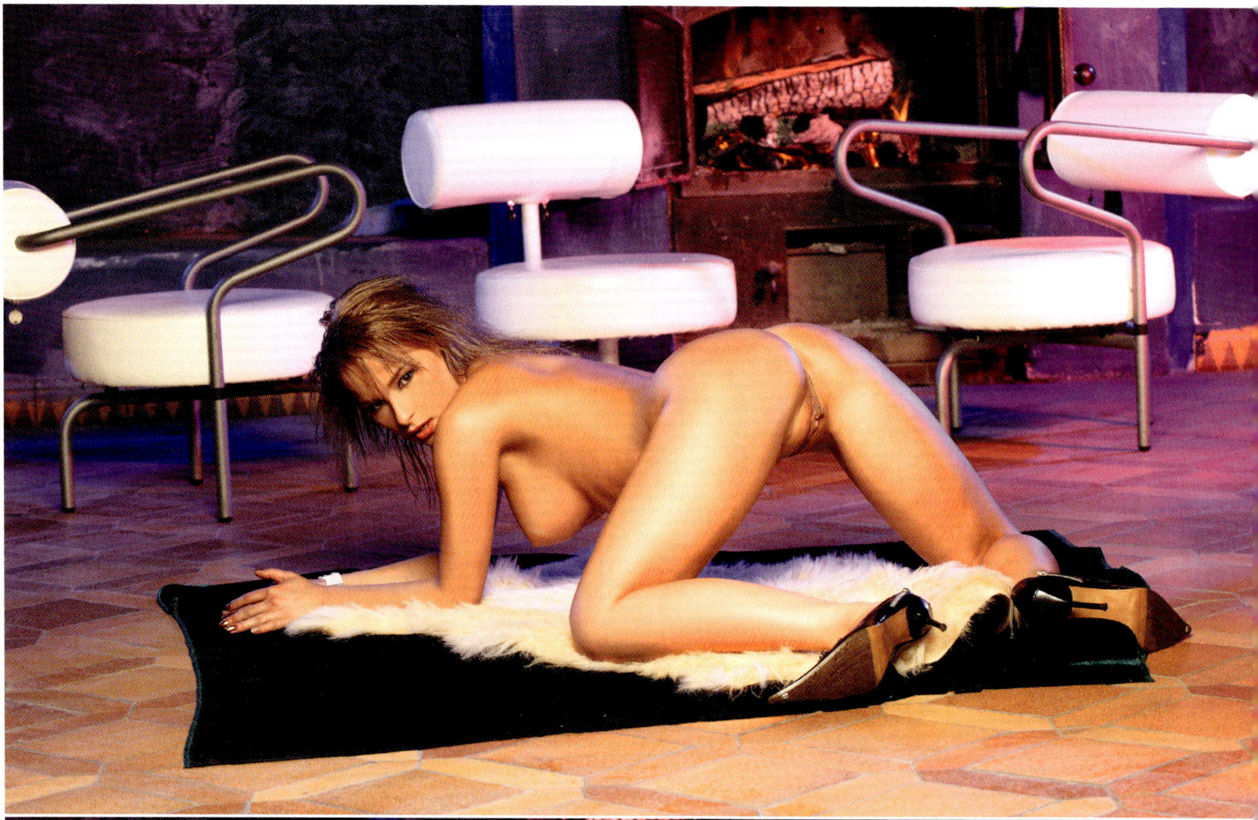

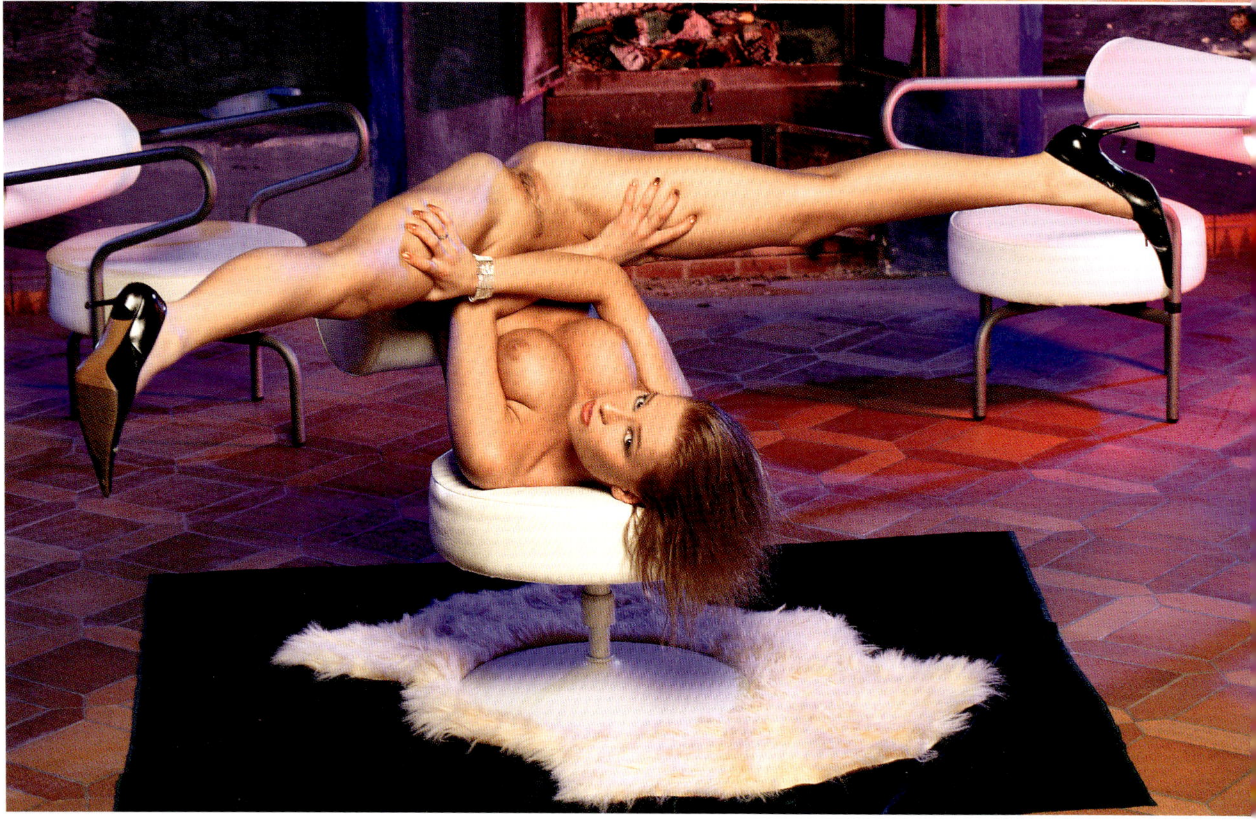

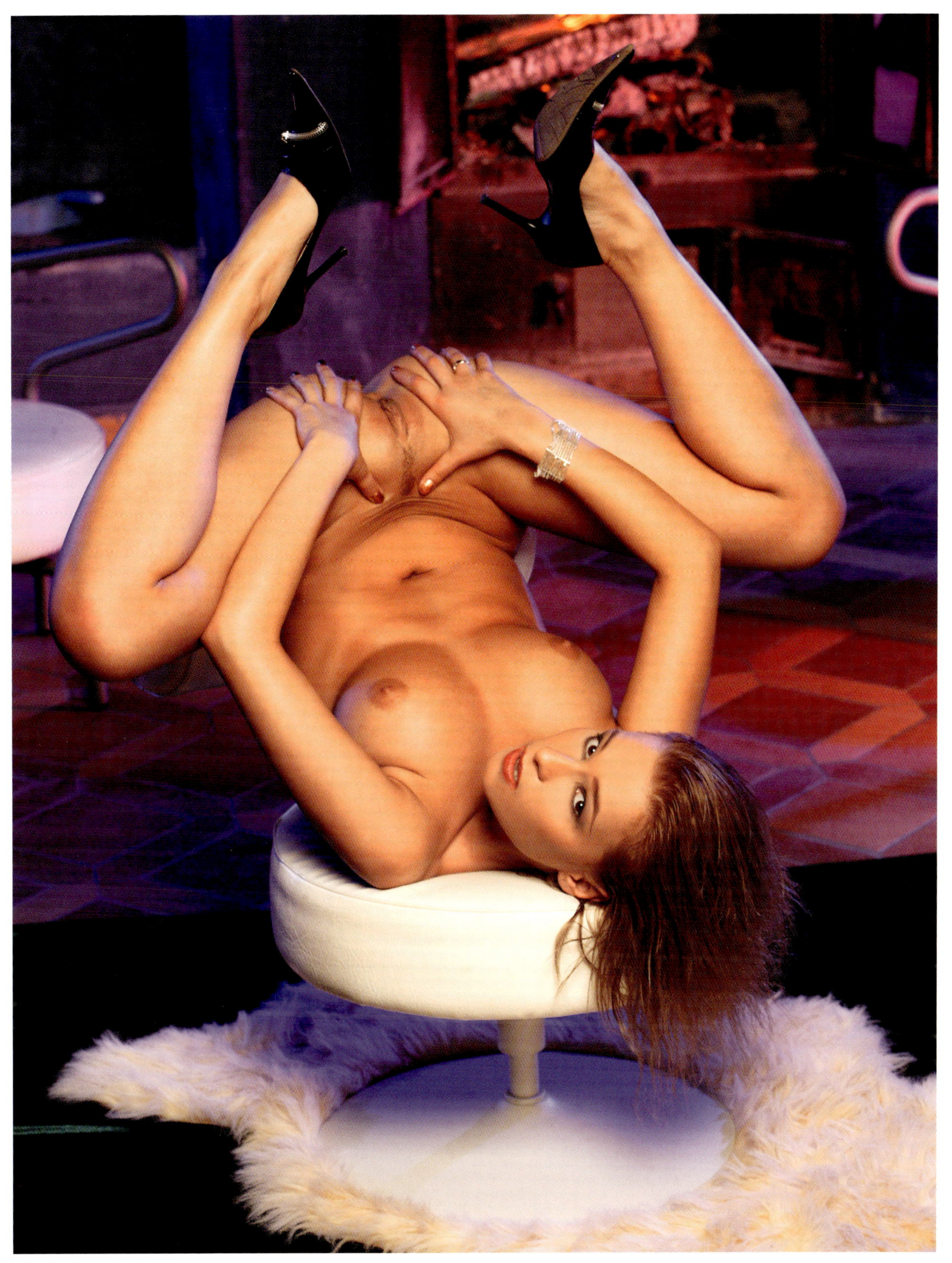

Jenia

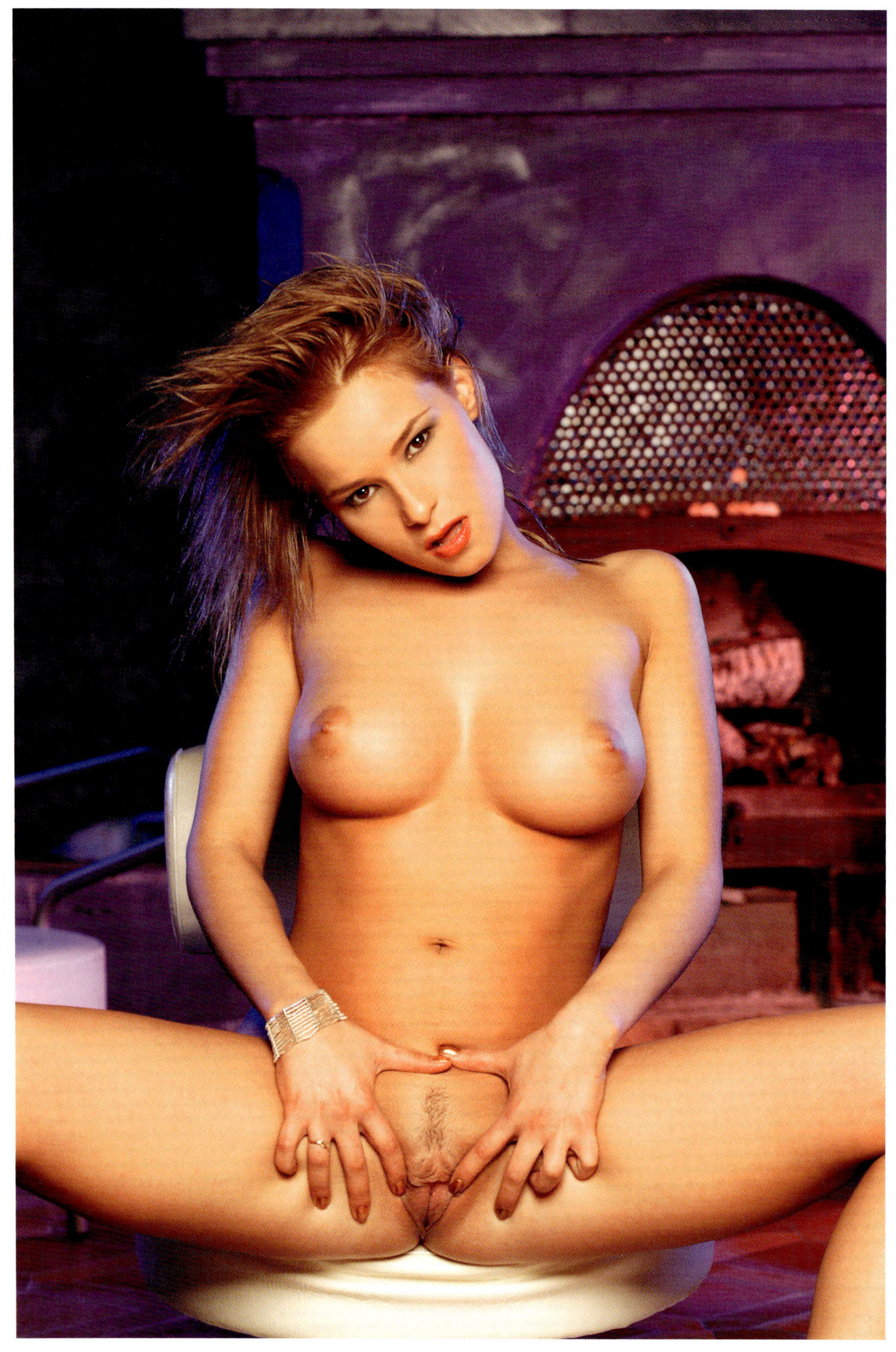

Jenia

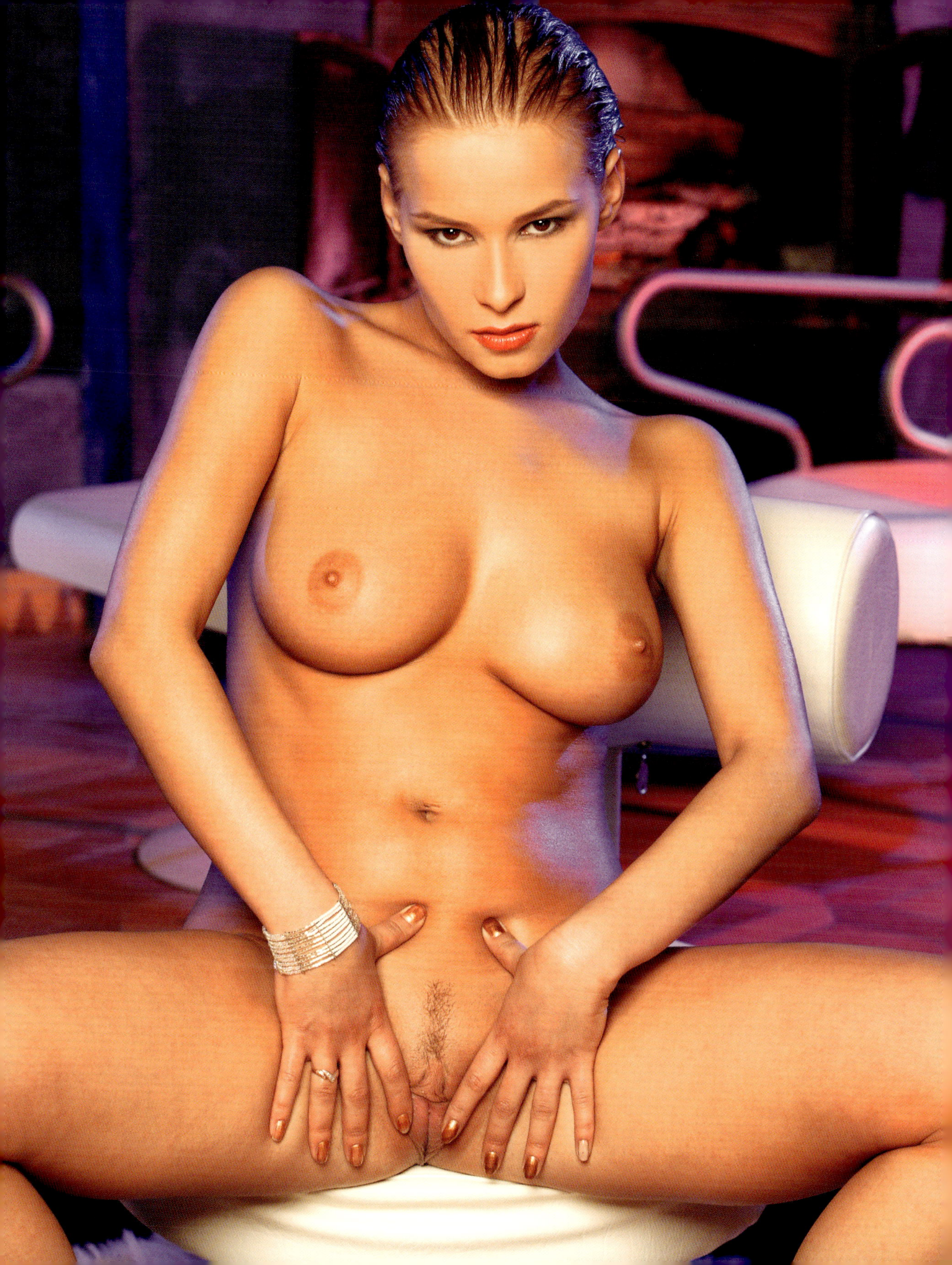

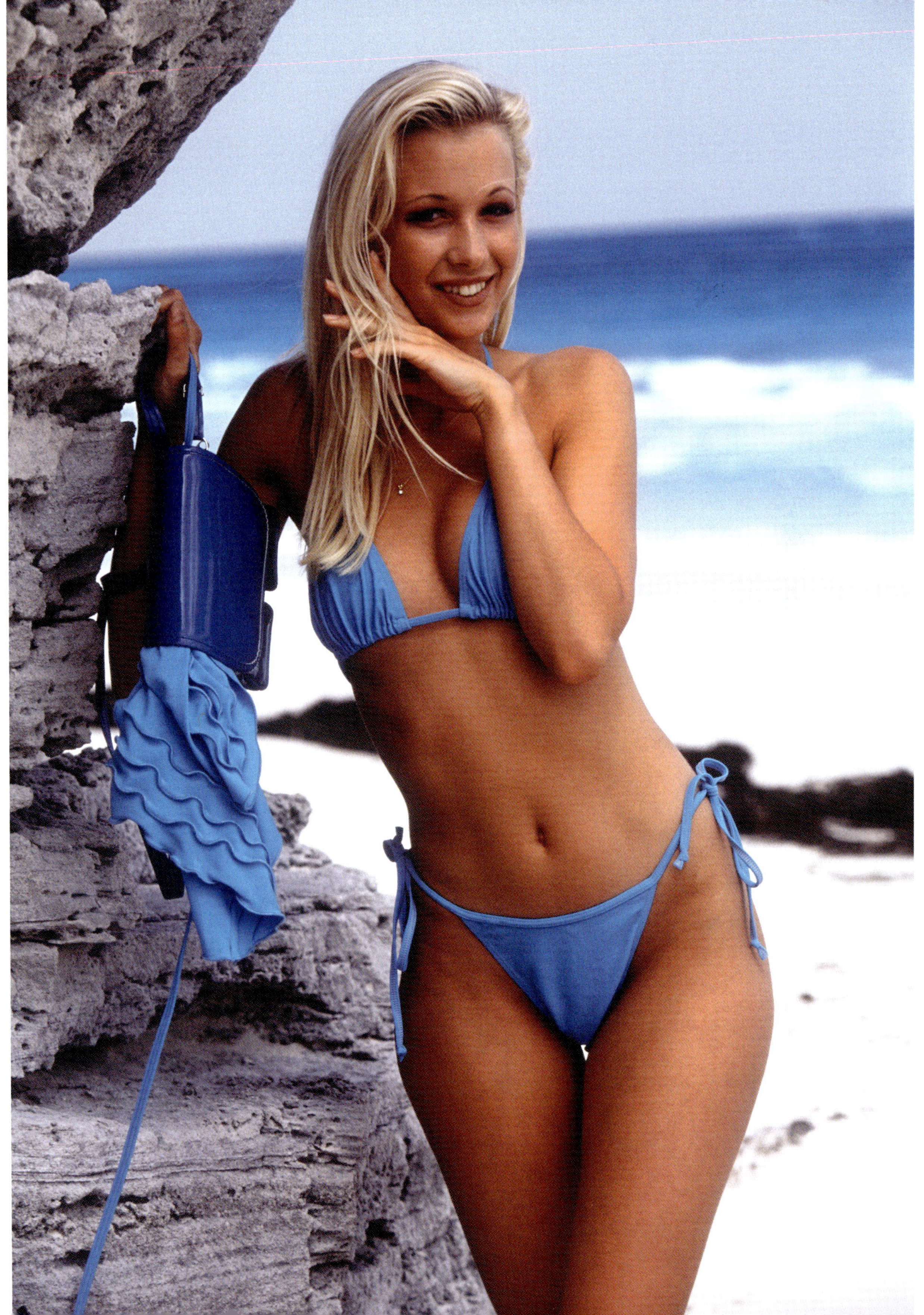

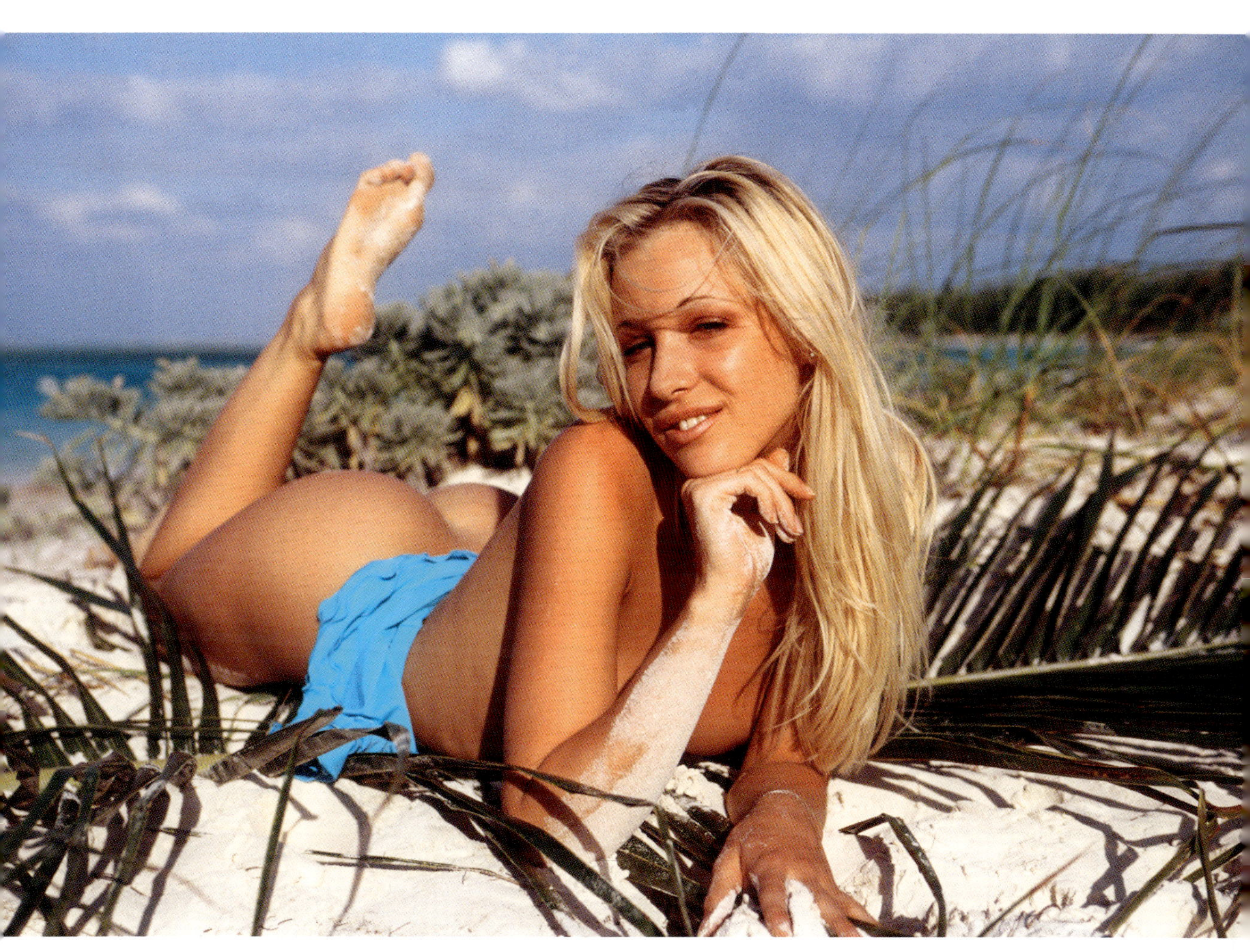

Jana

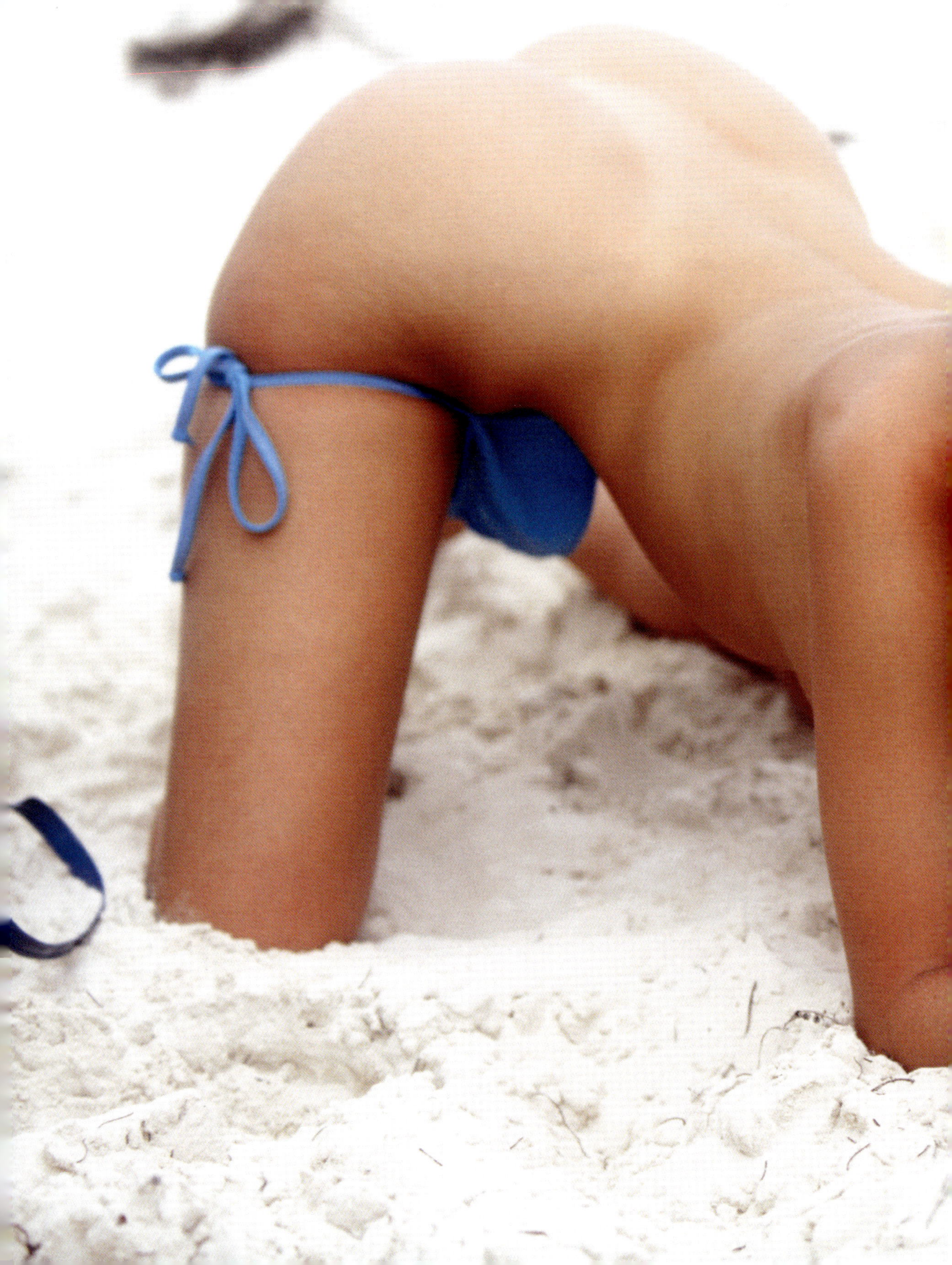

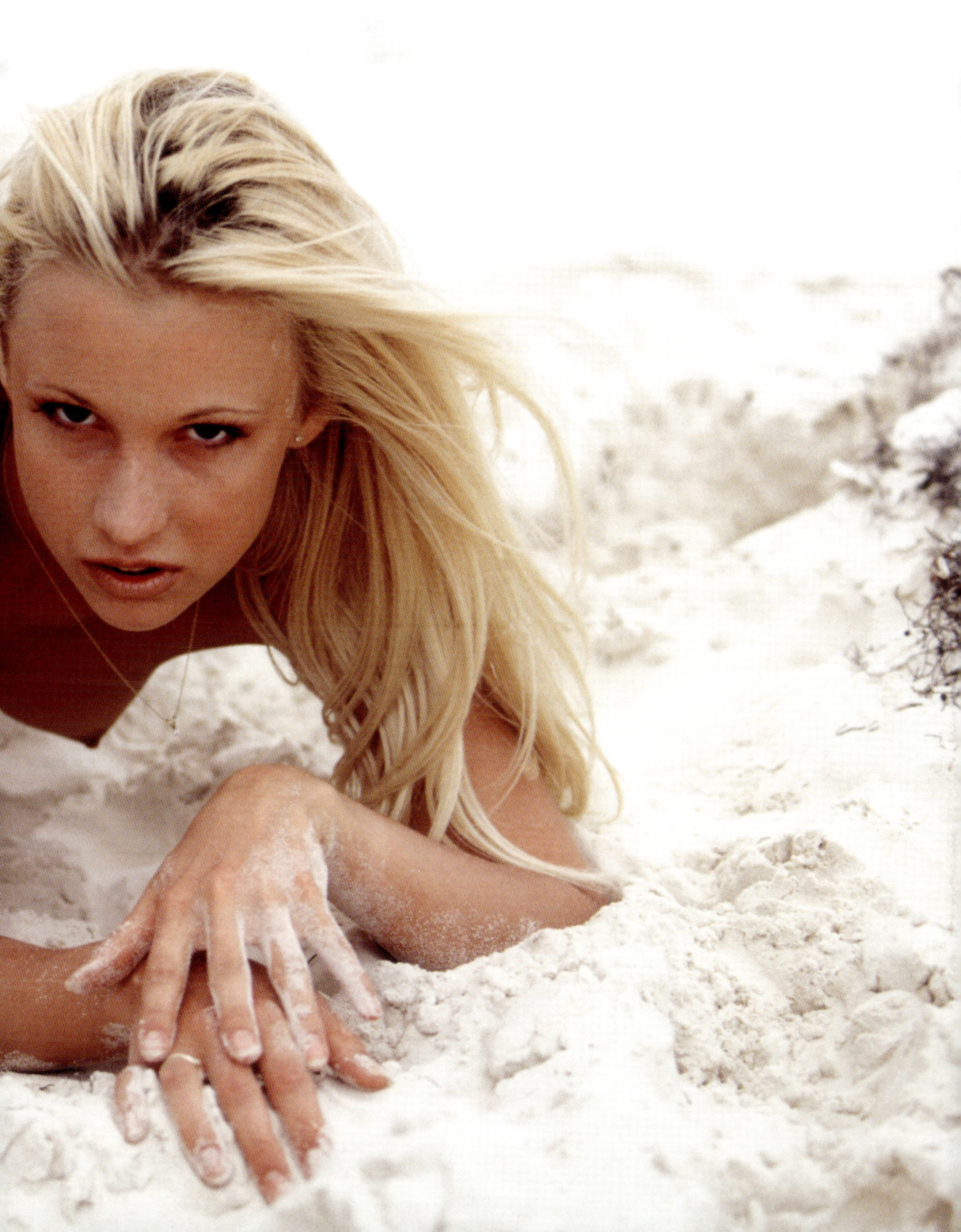

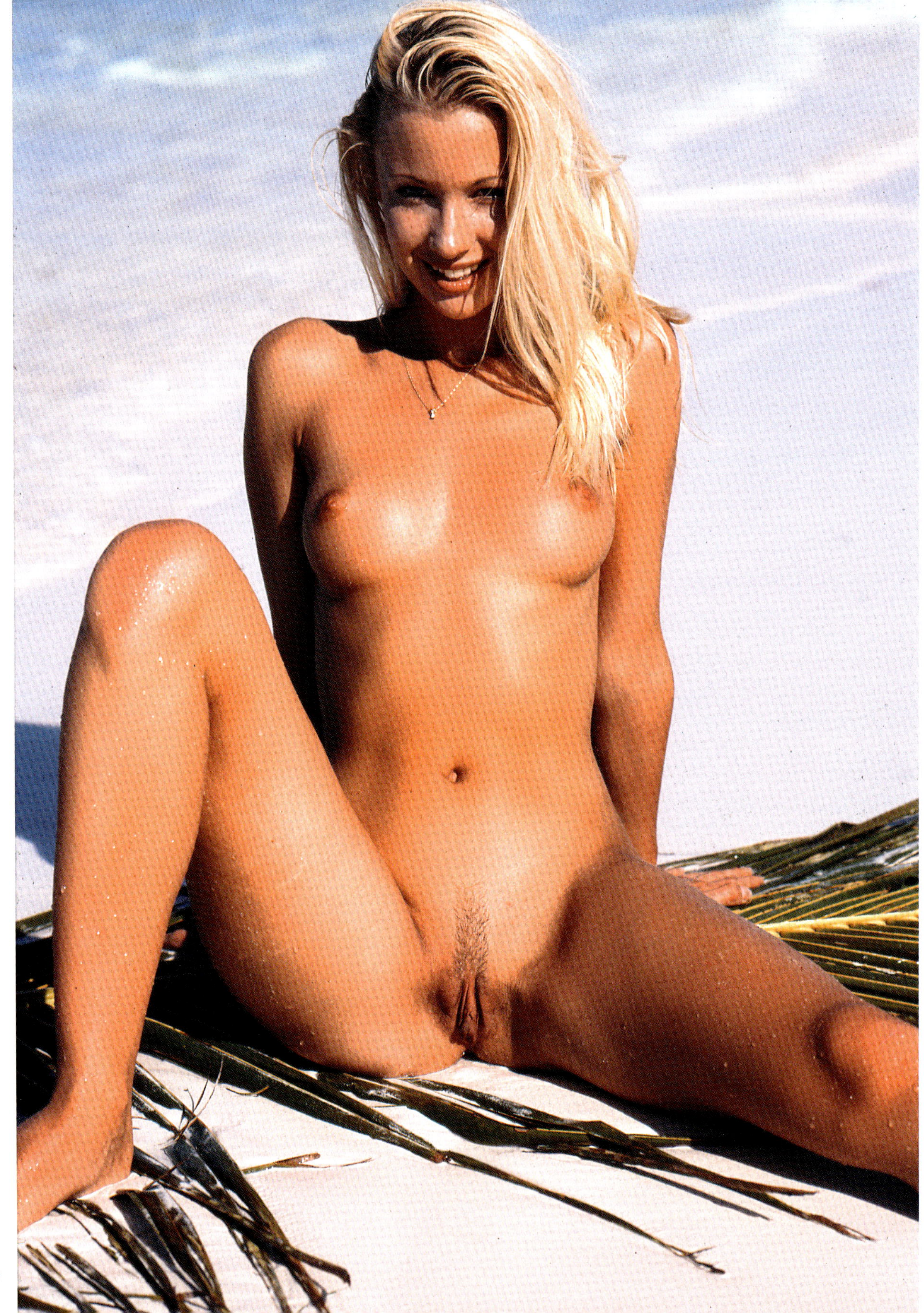

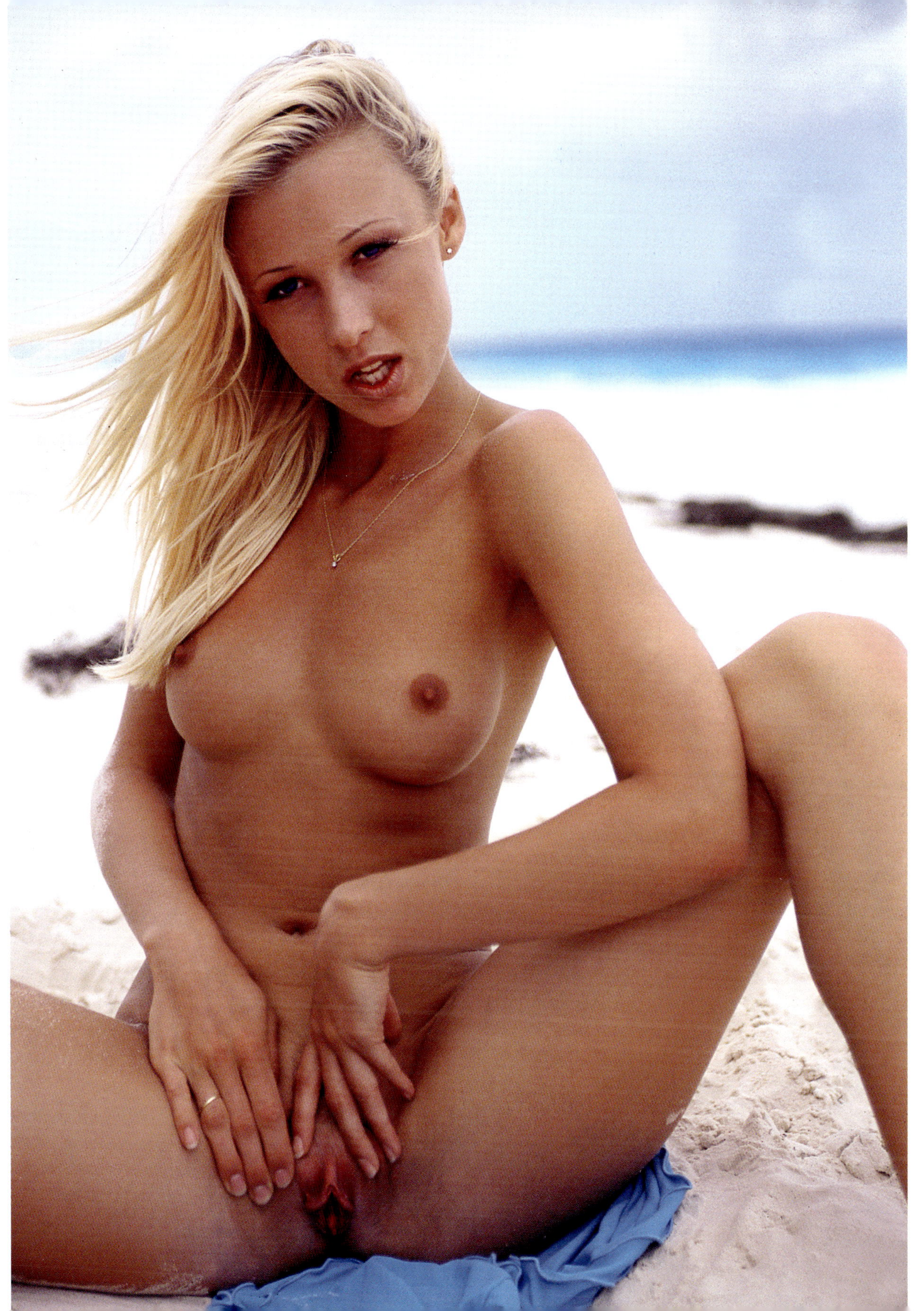

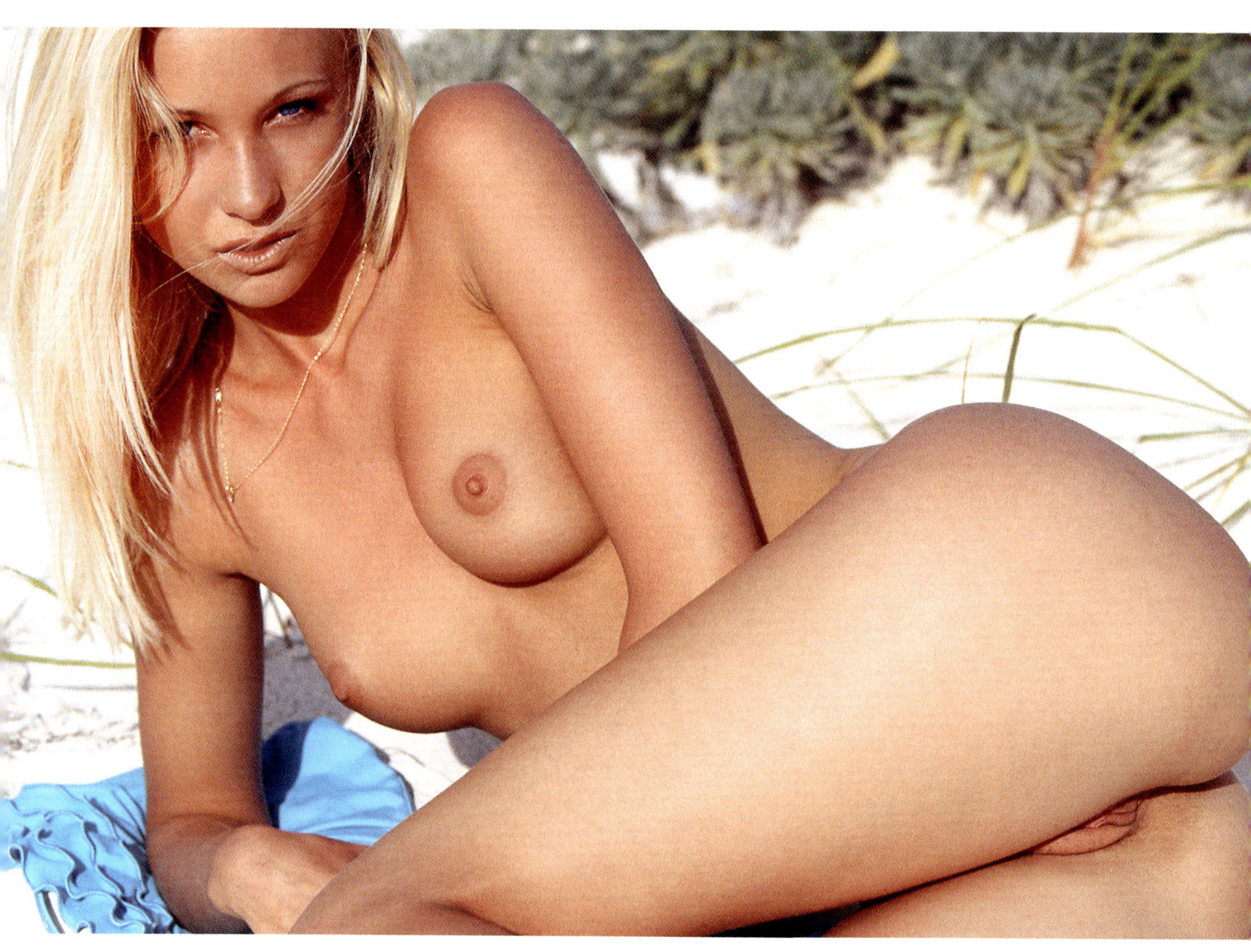

Jana

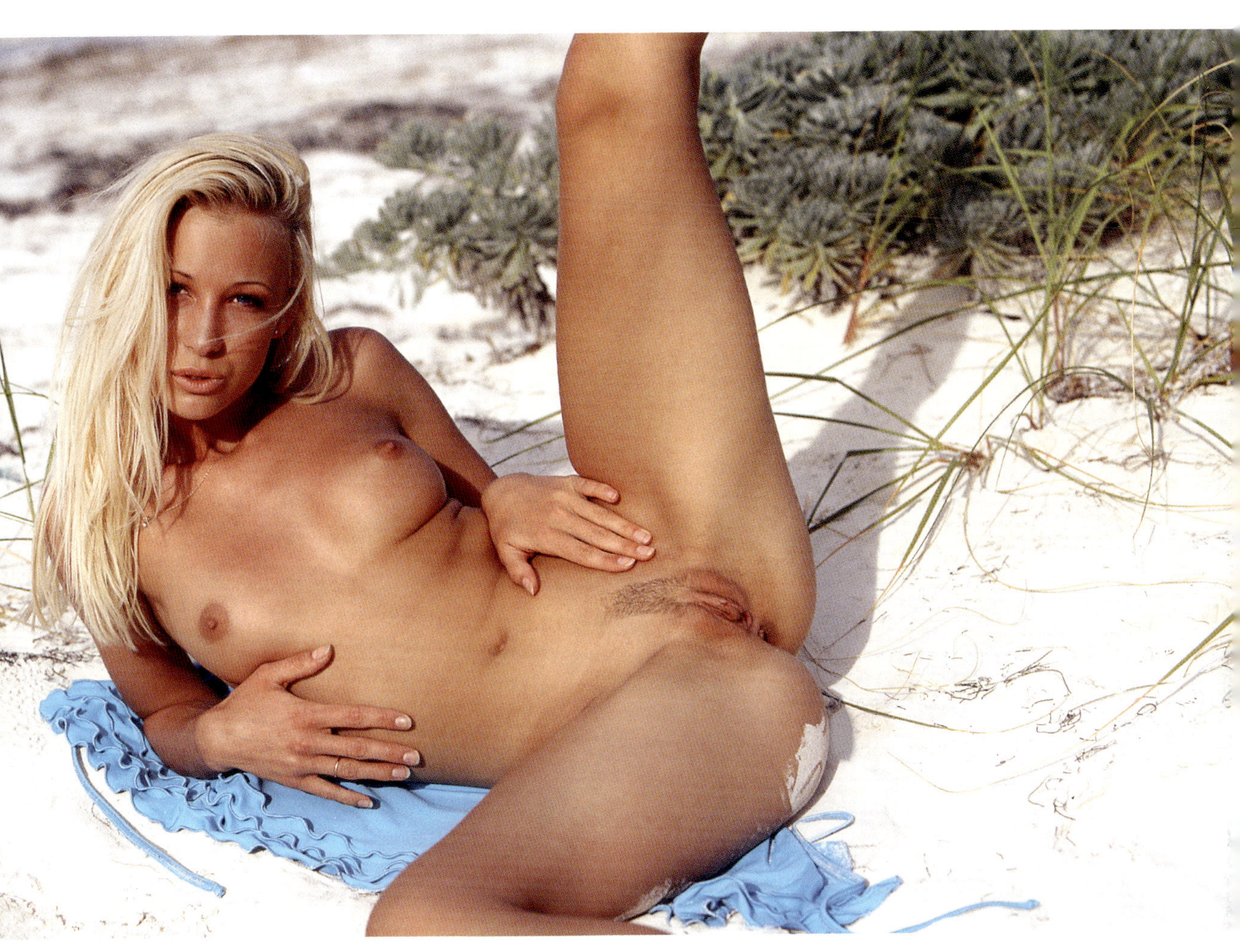

Jana

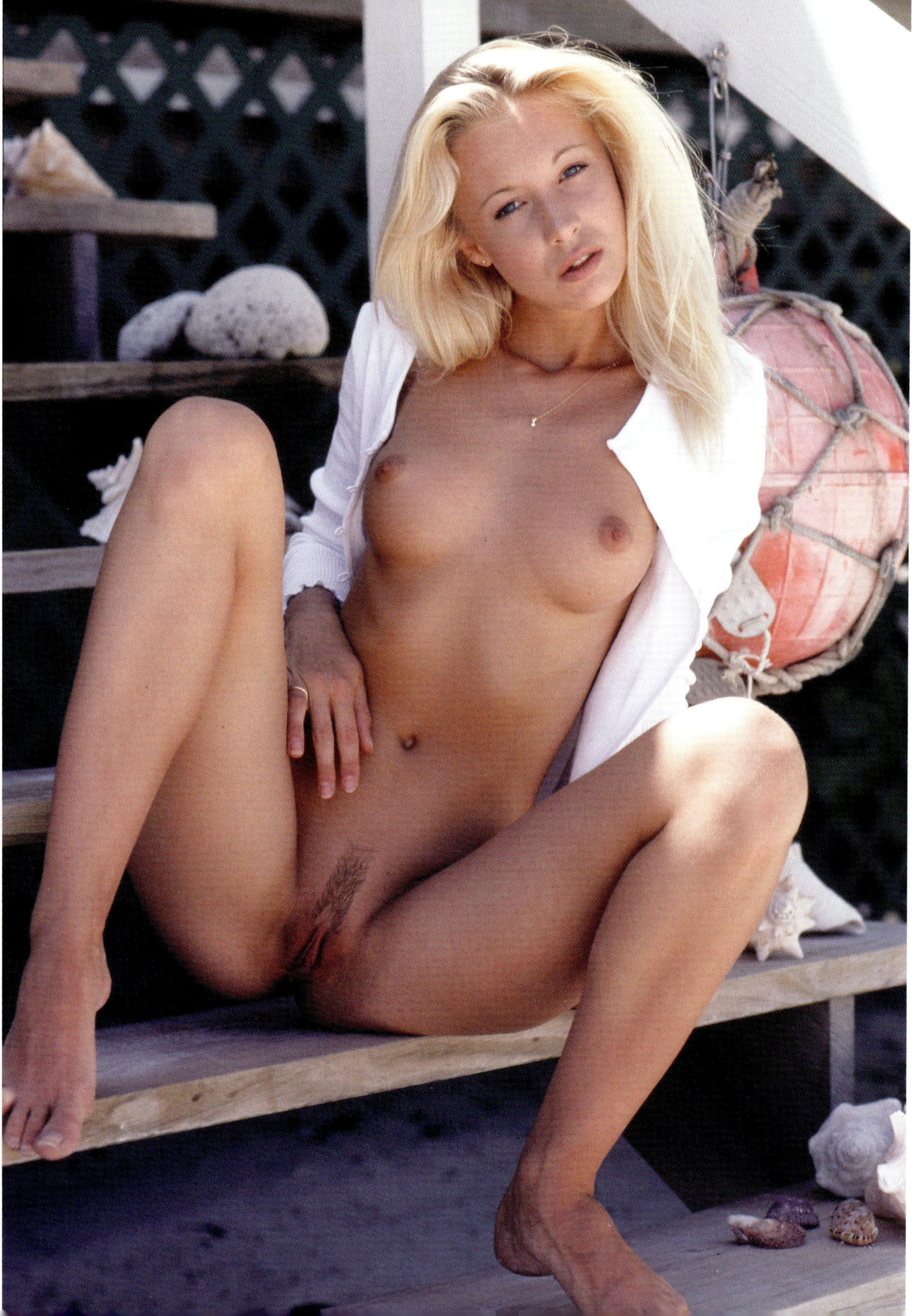

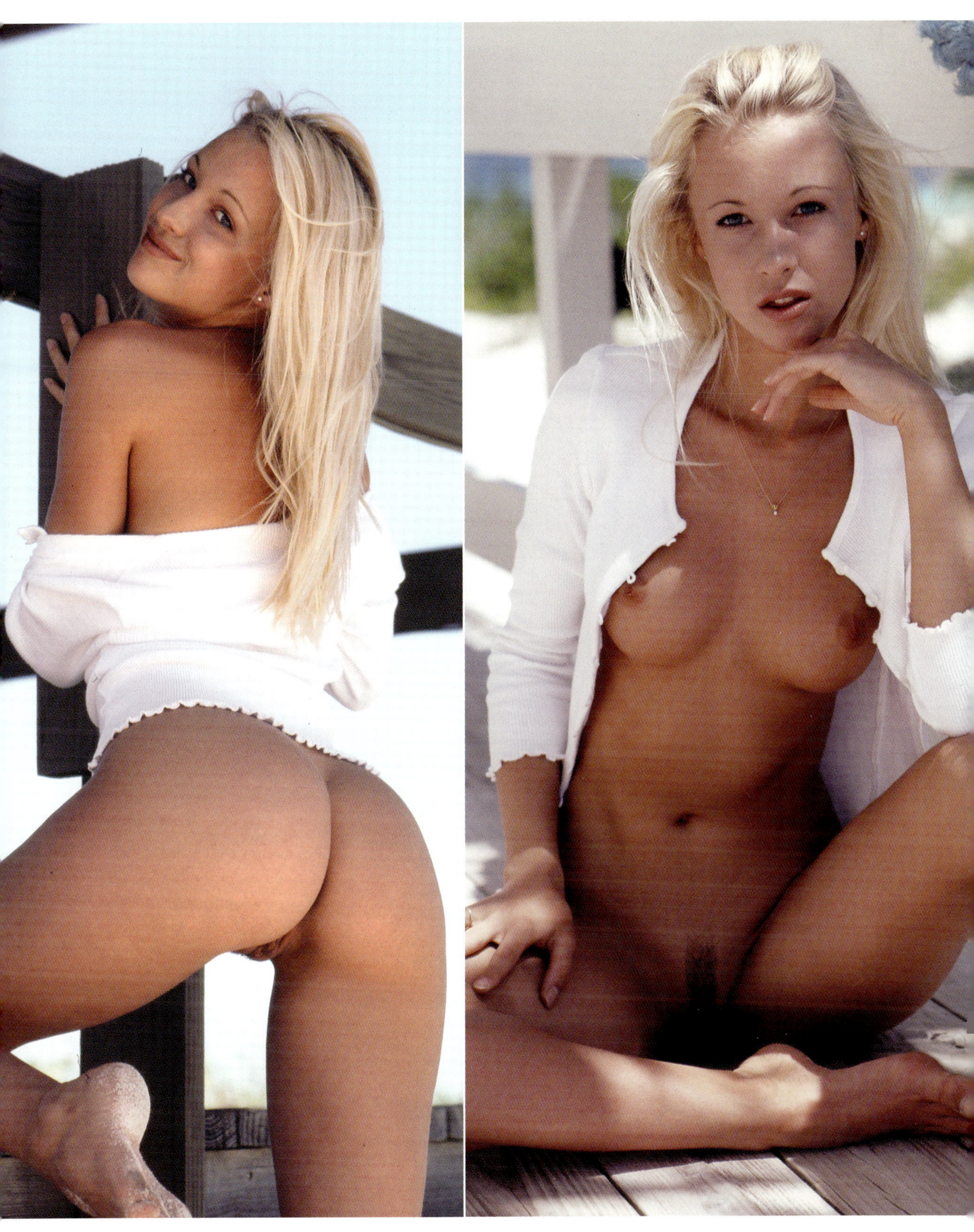

Jana

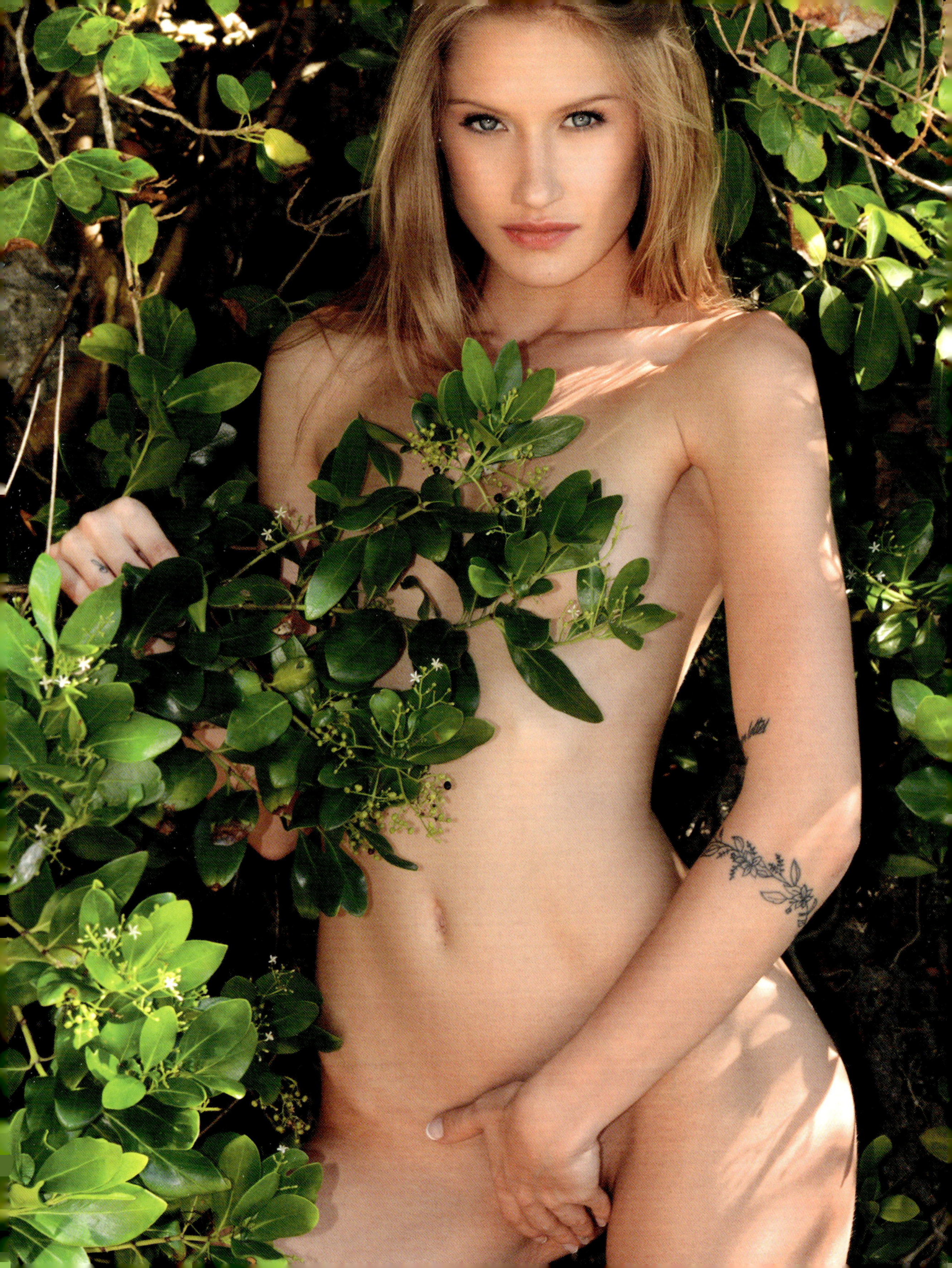

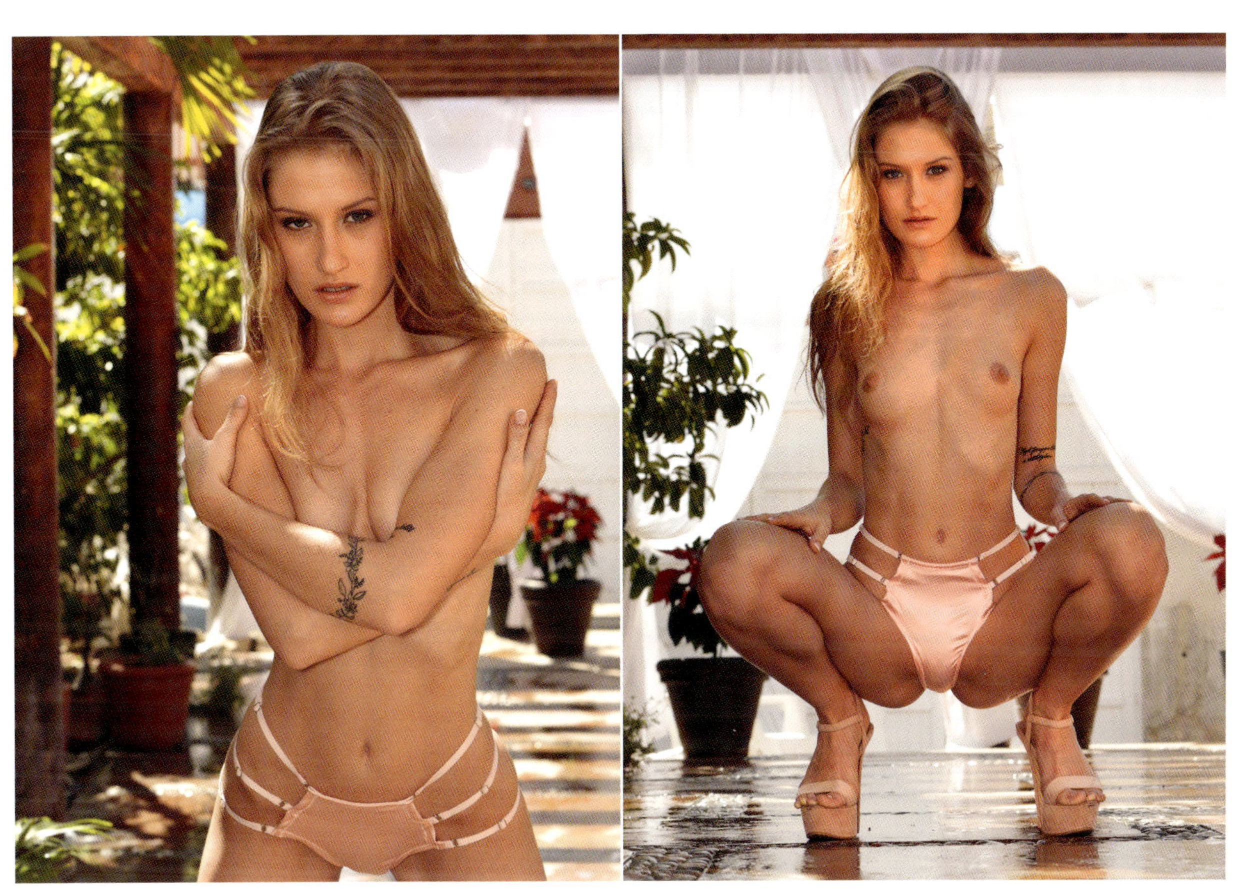

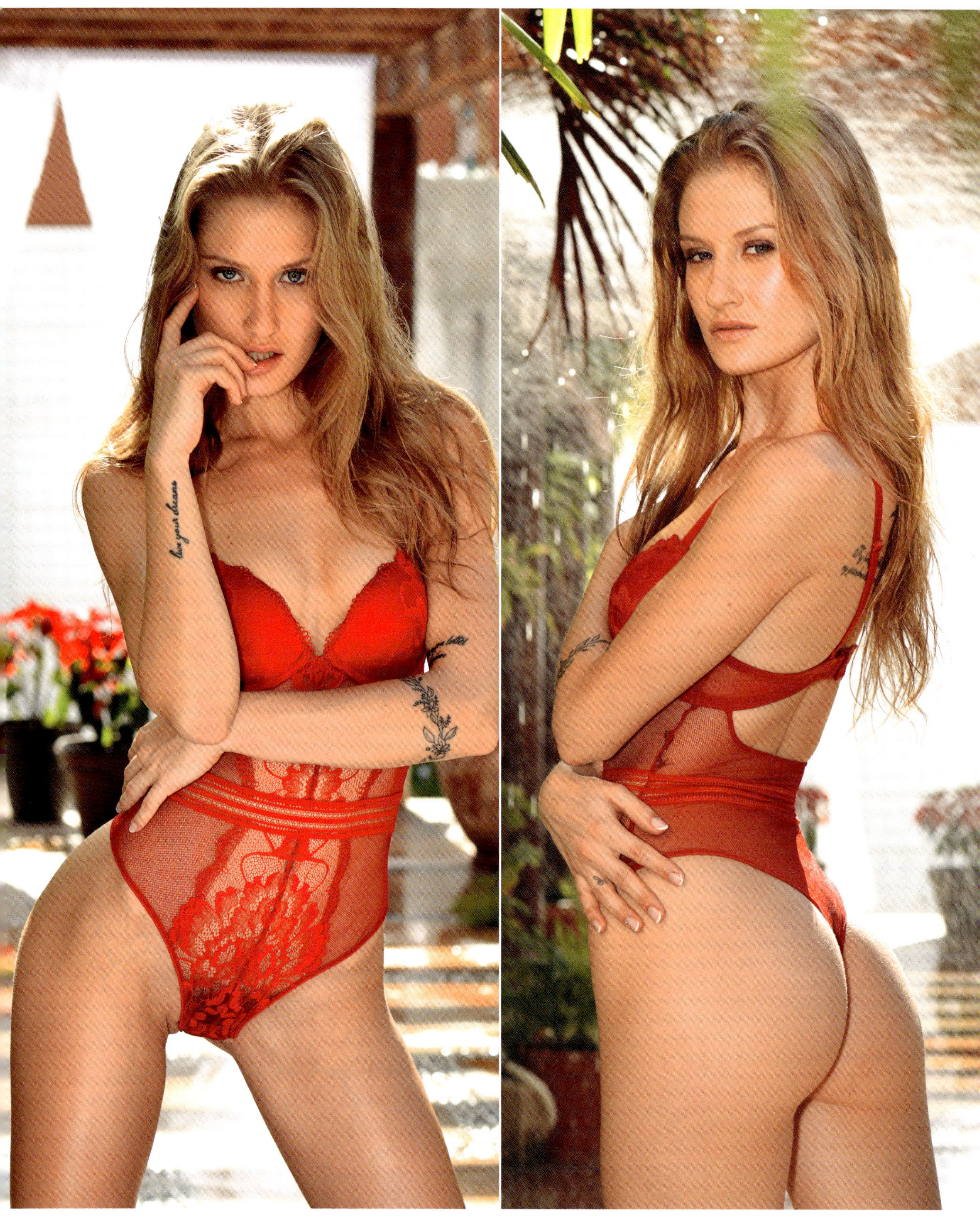



Tiffany

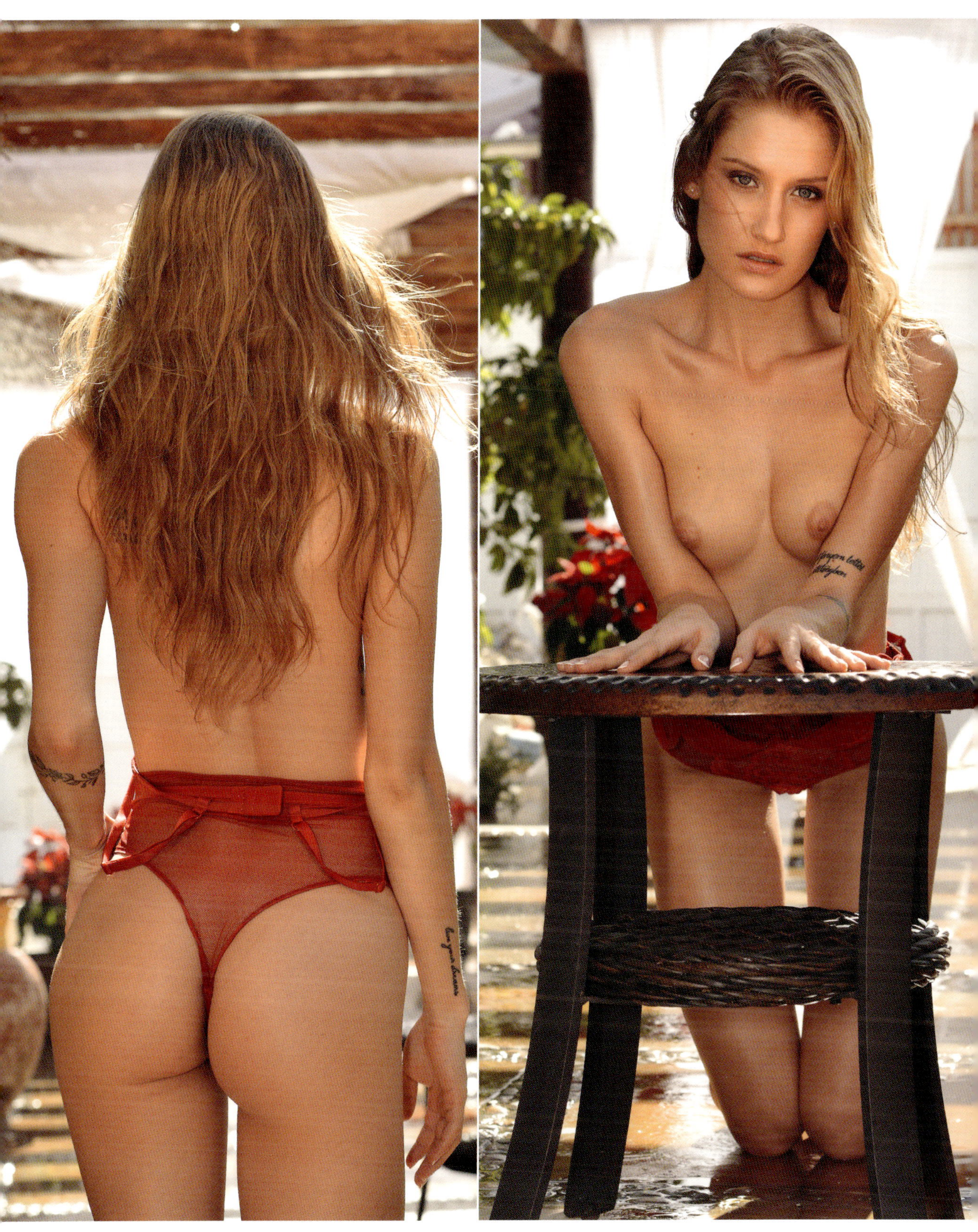

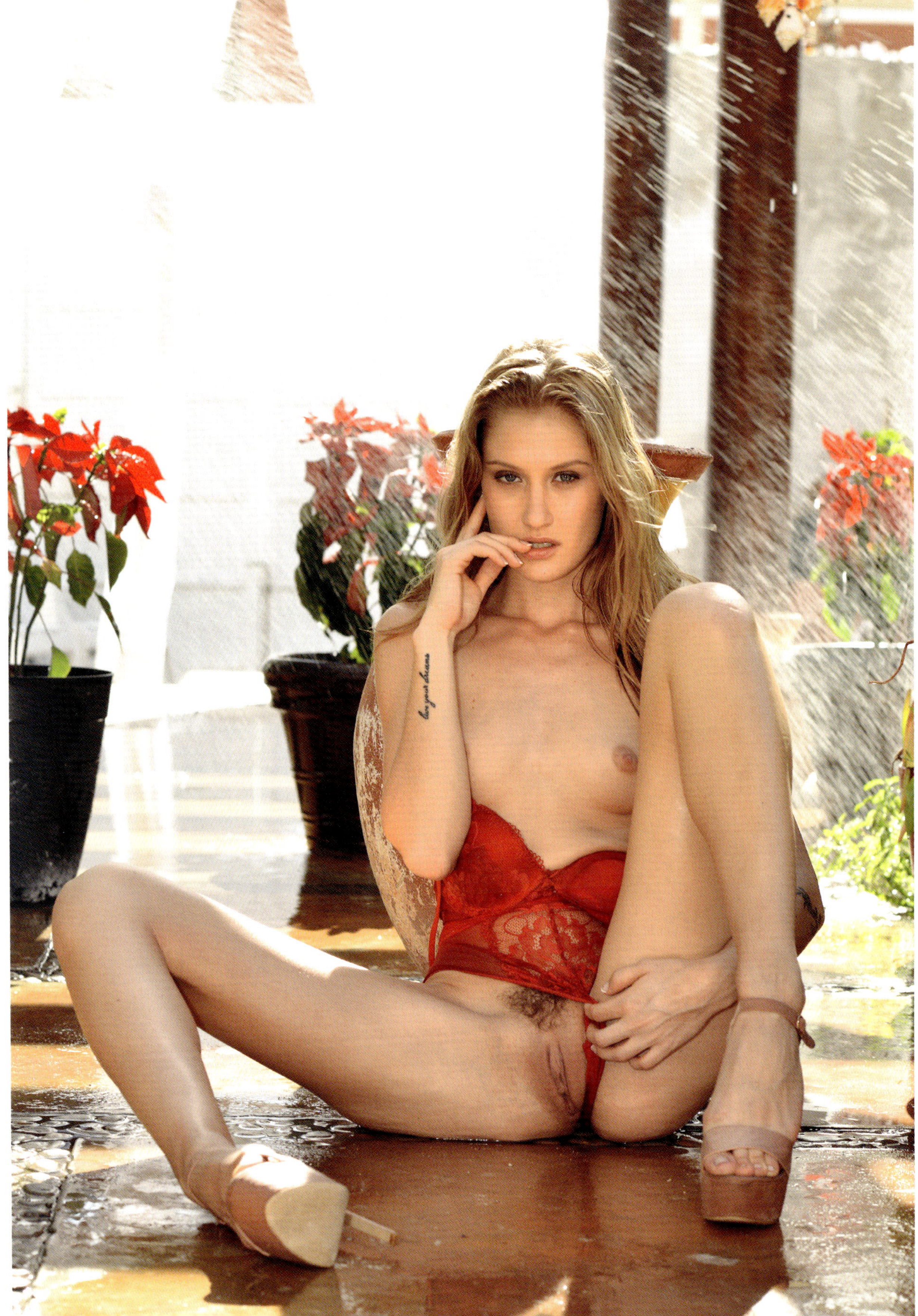

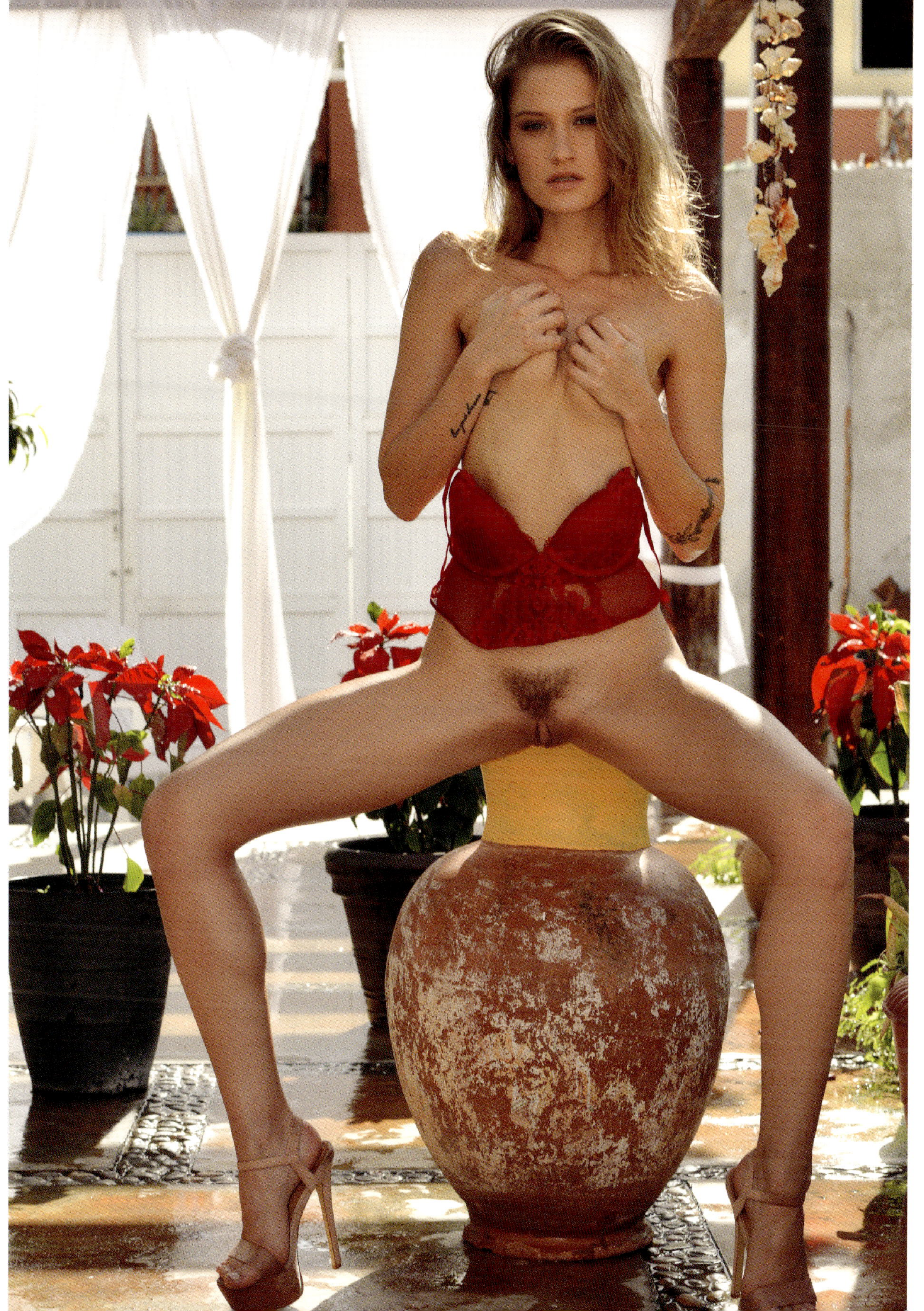

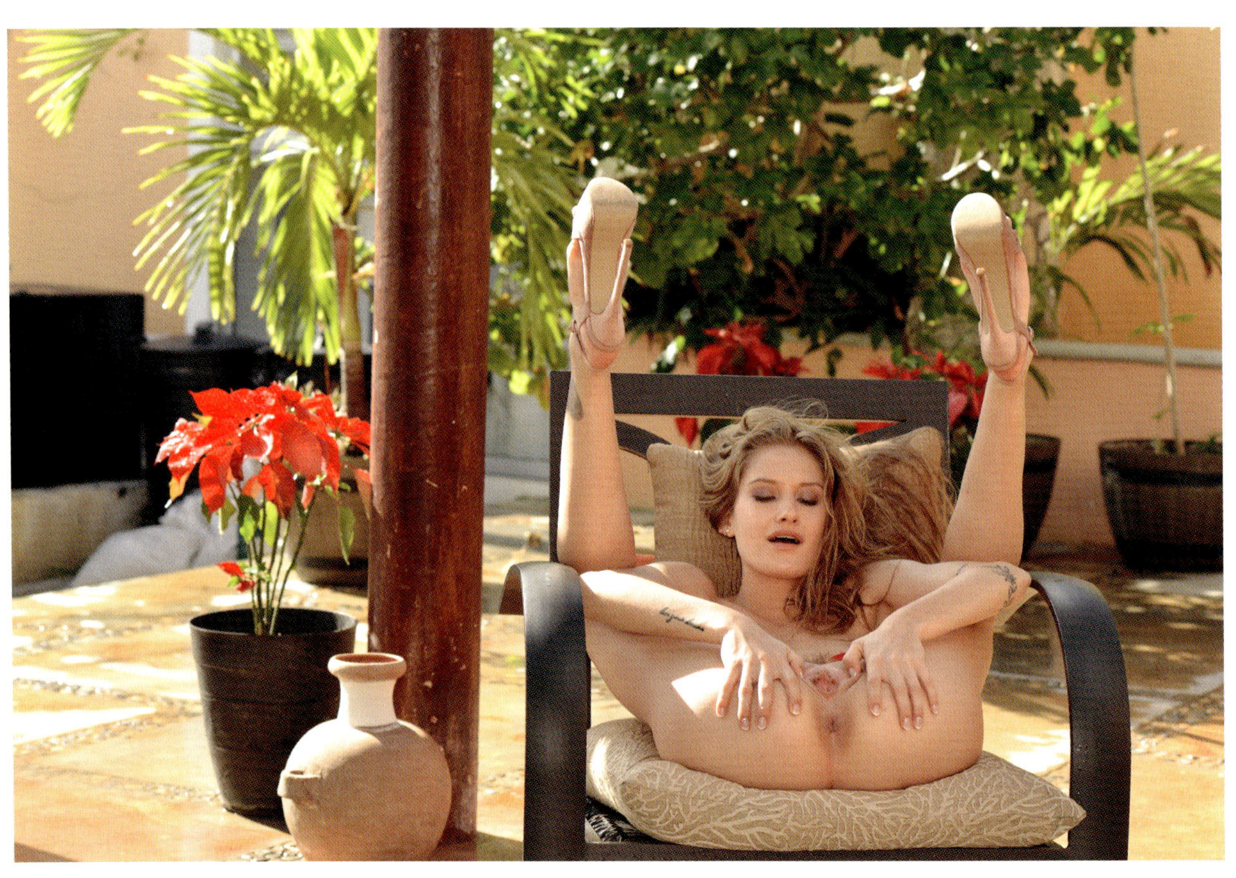



Tiffany

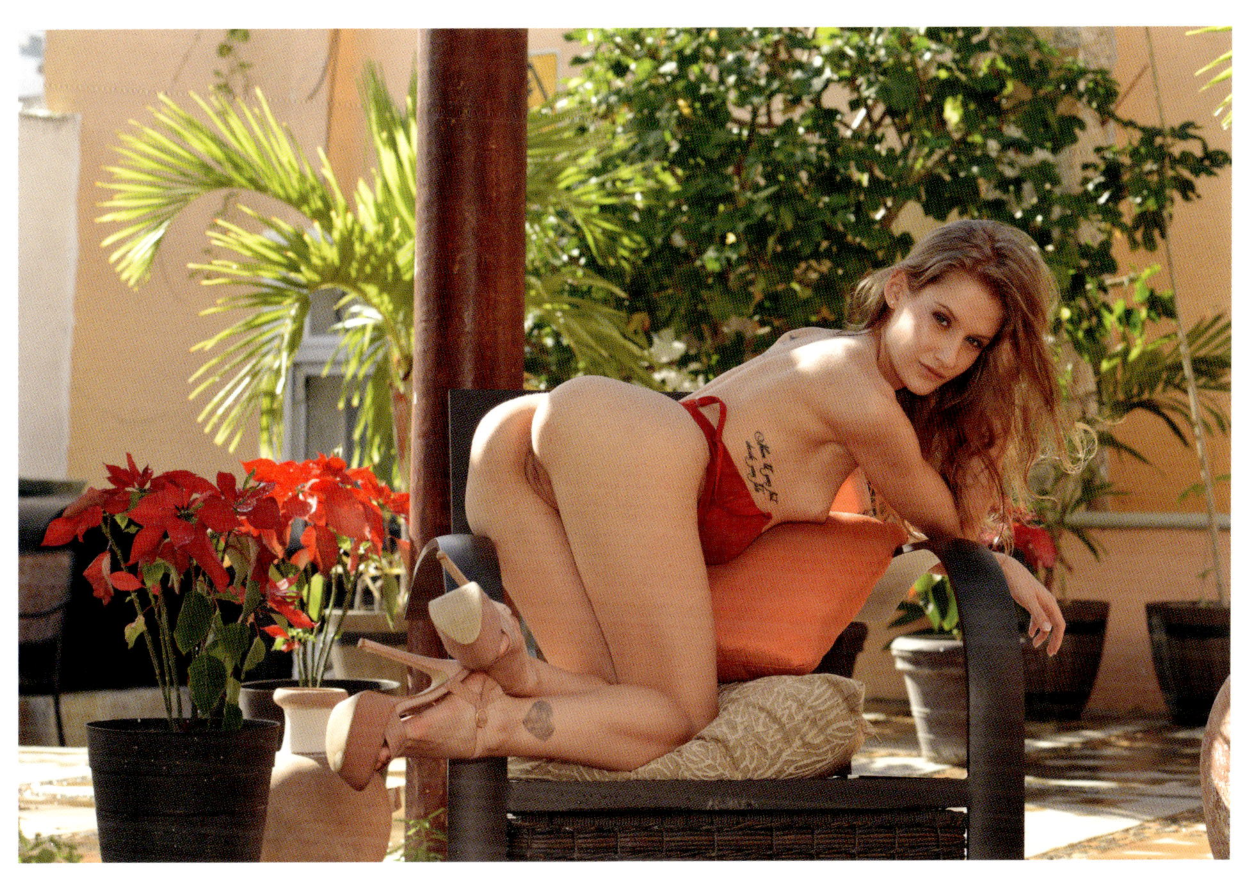

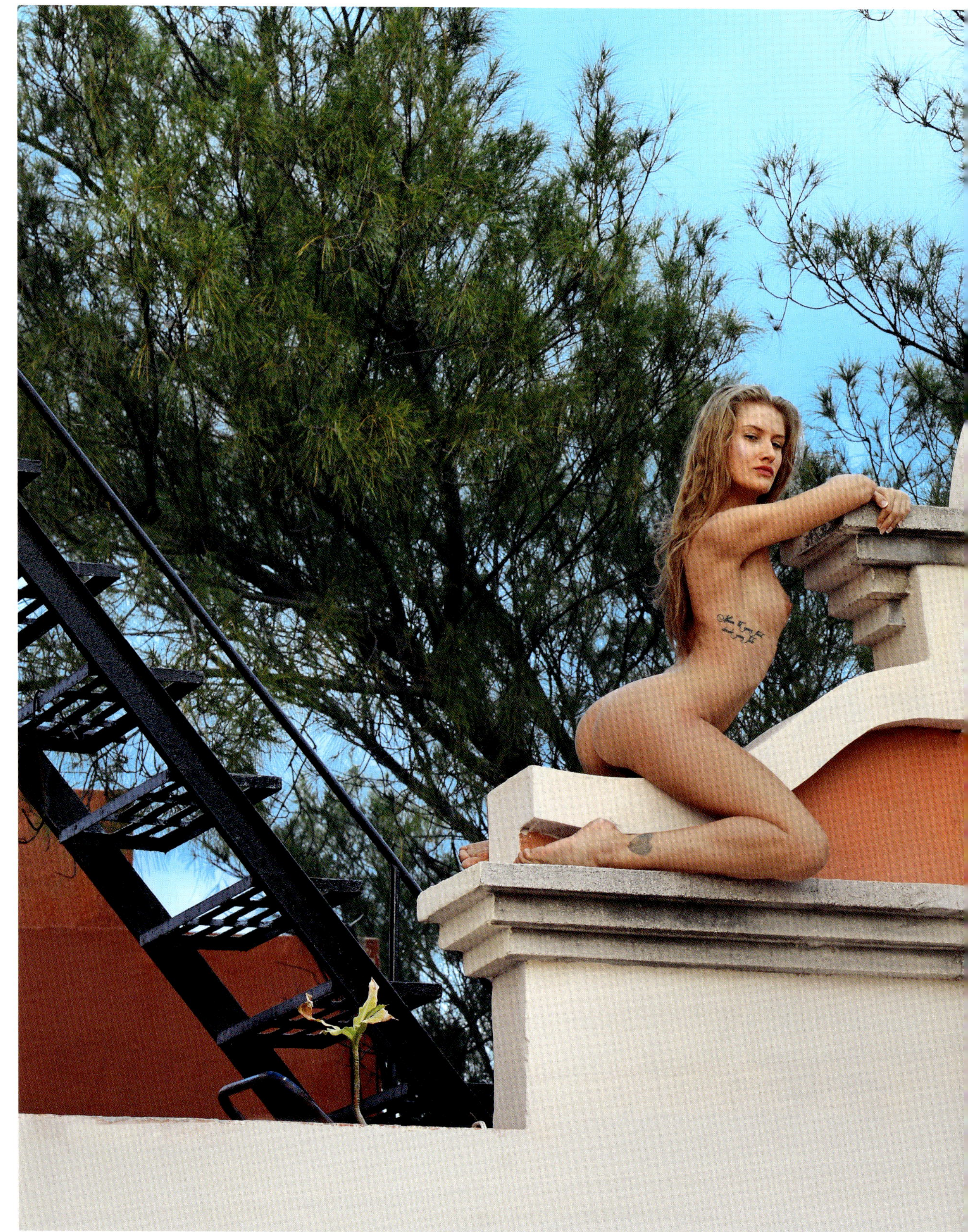

Tiffany

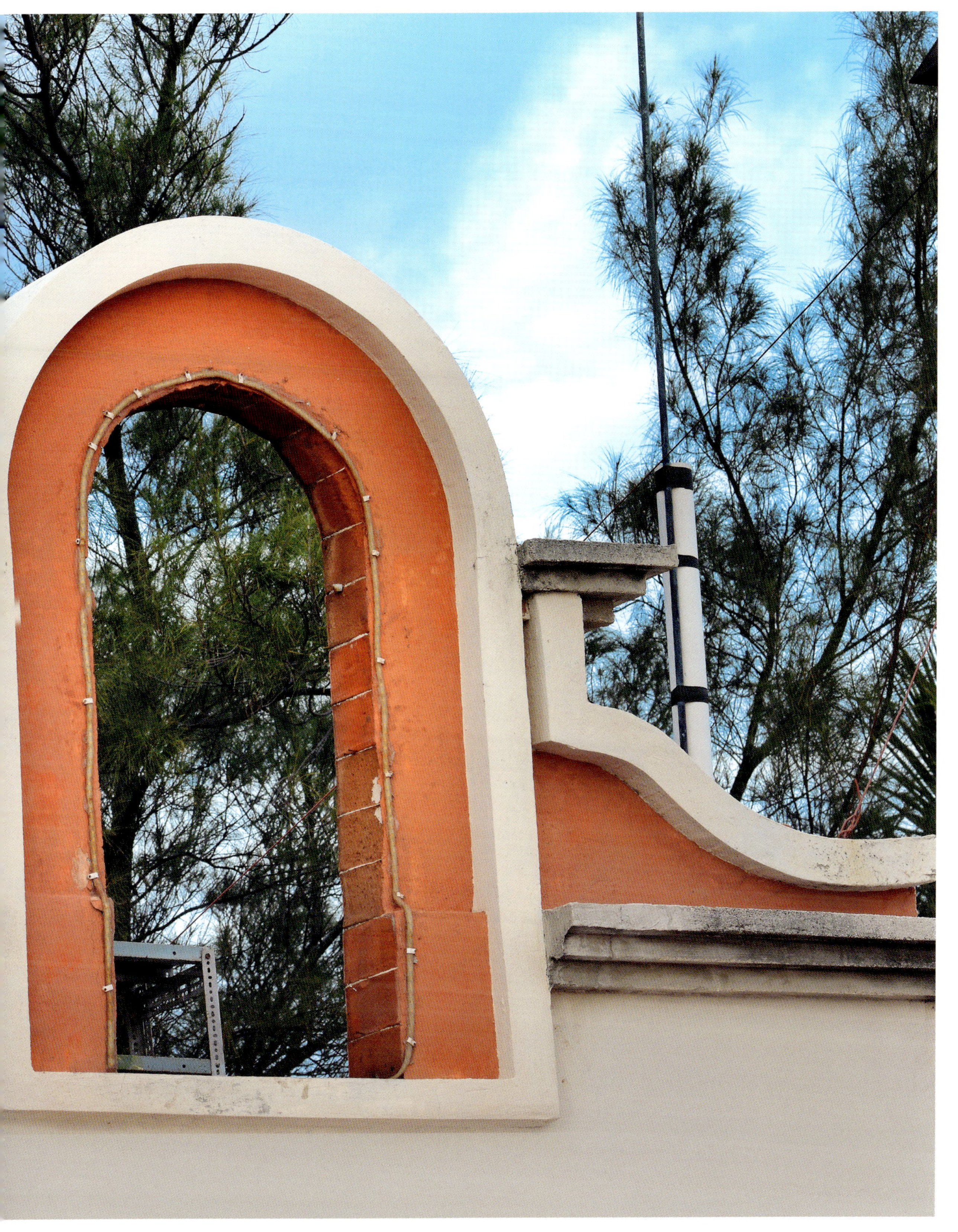

Tiffany

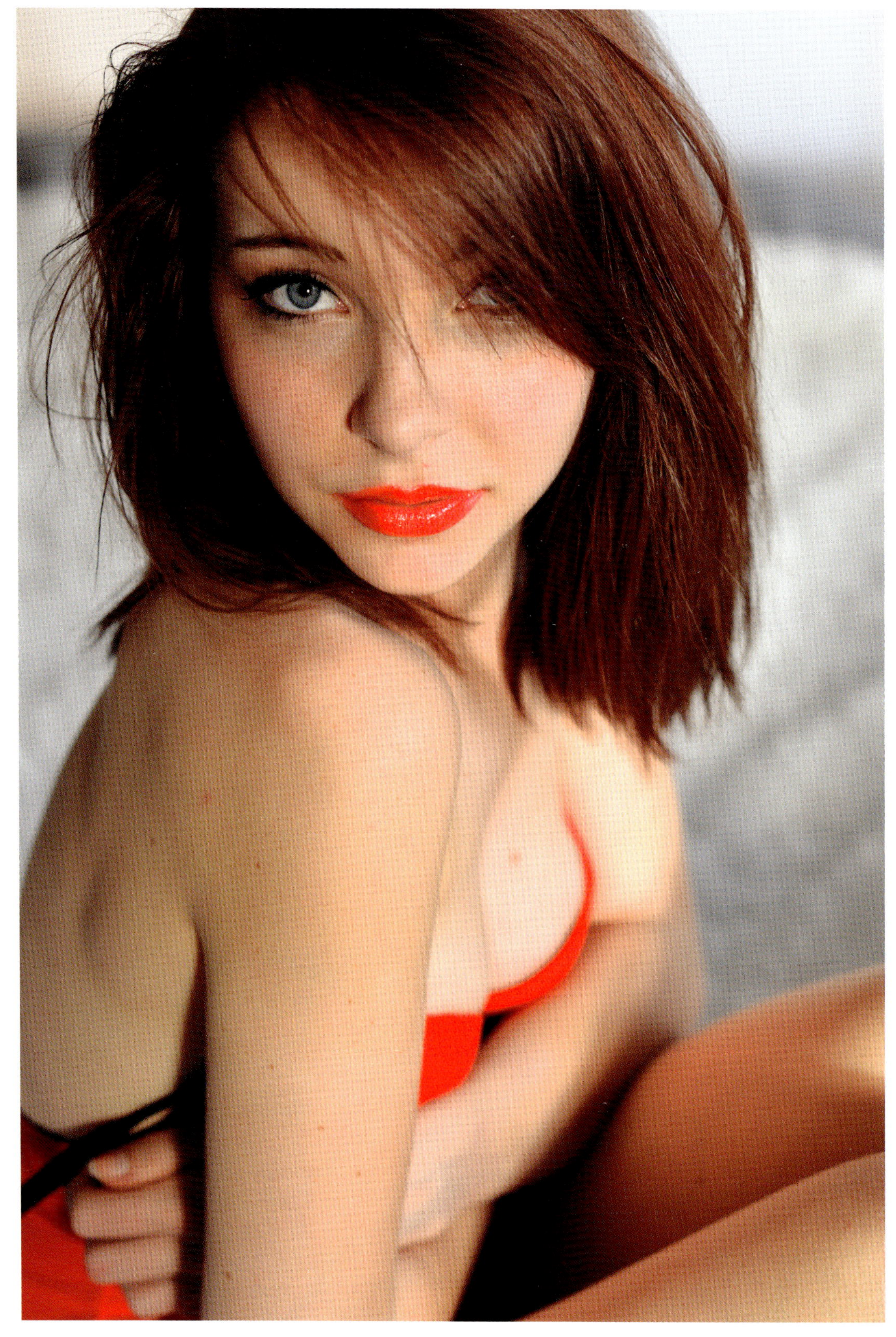

Emilie

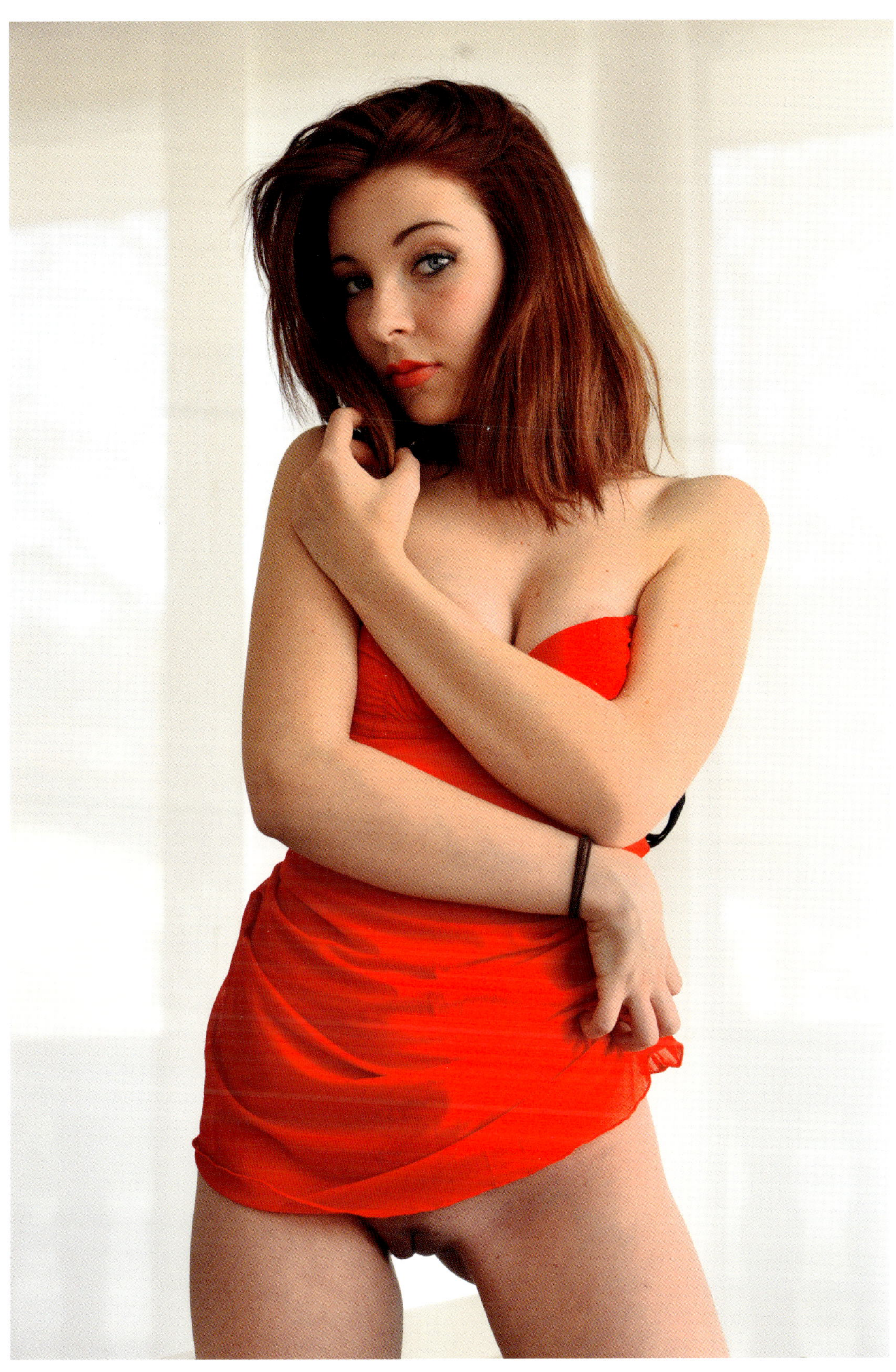

Emilie

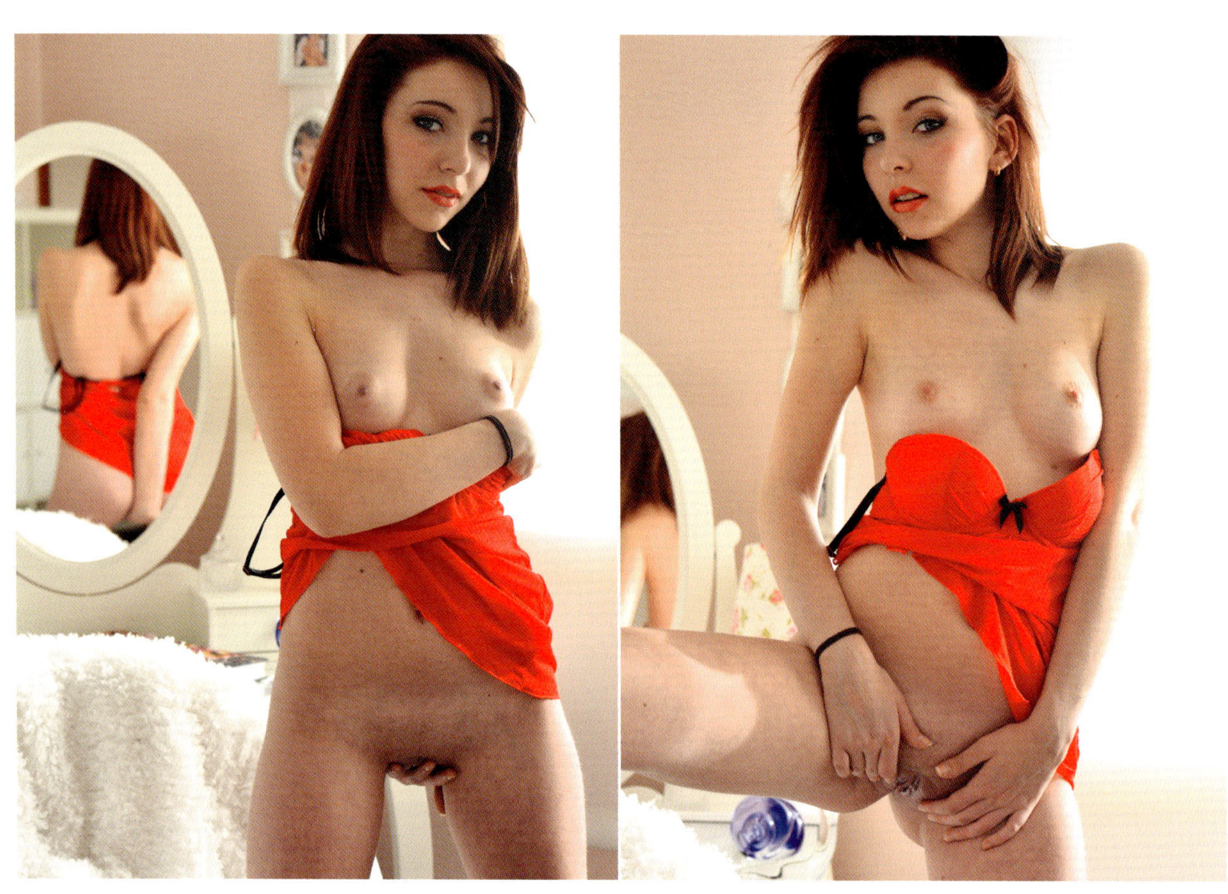



Emilie

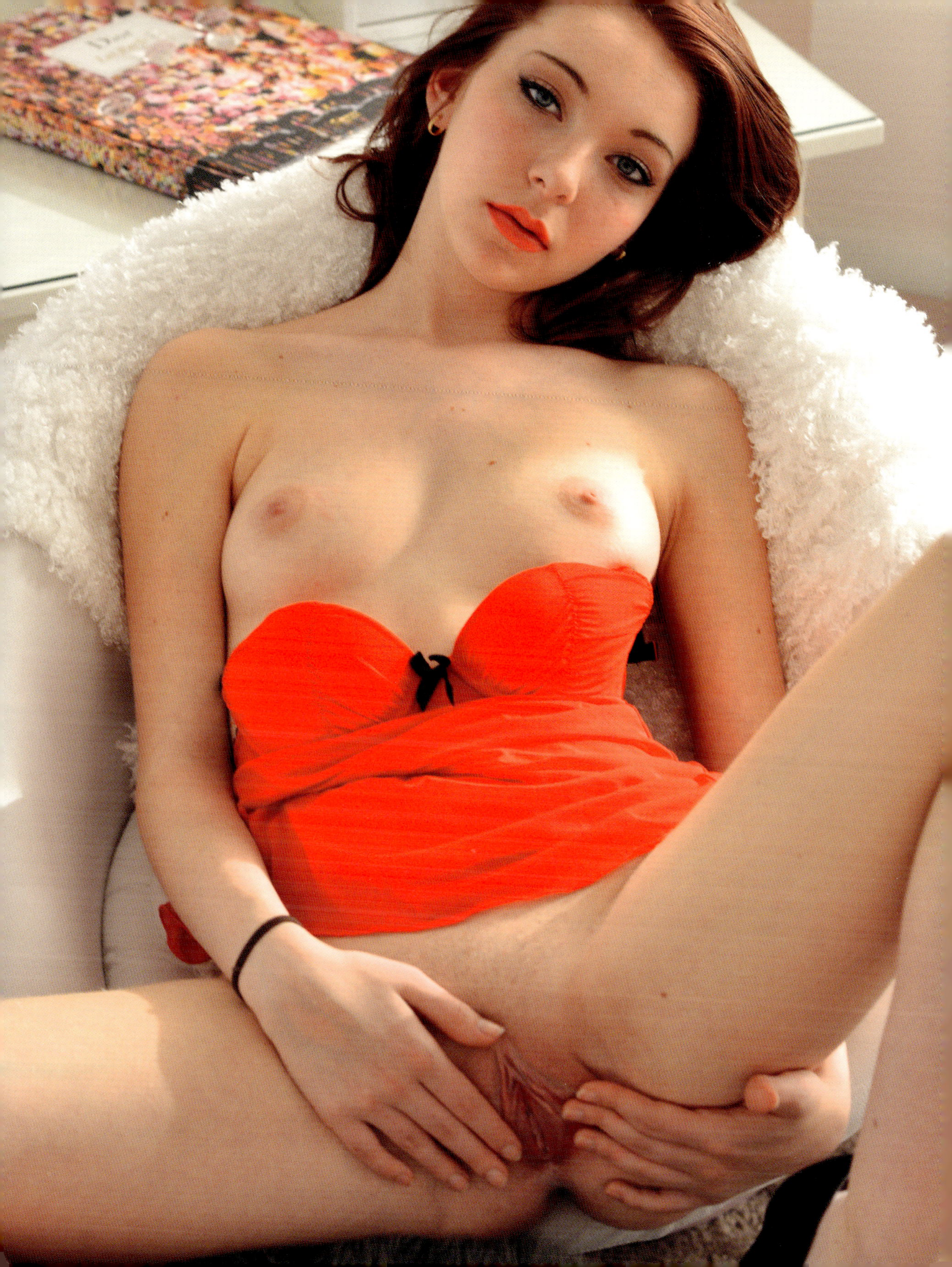

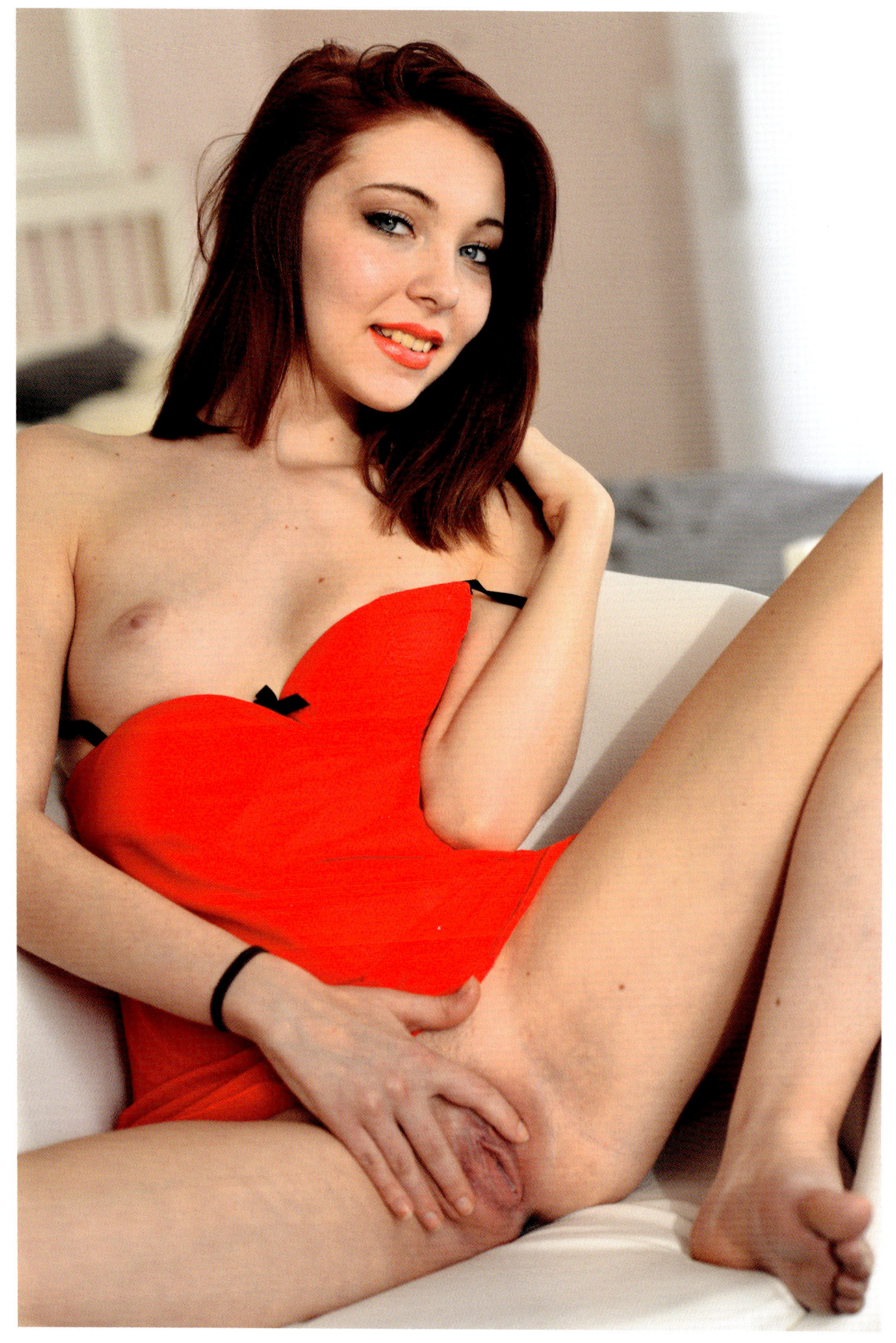

Emilie

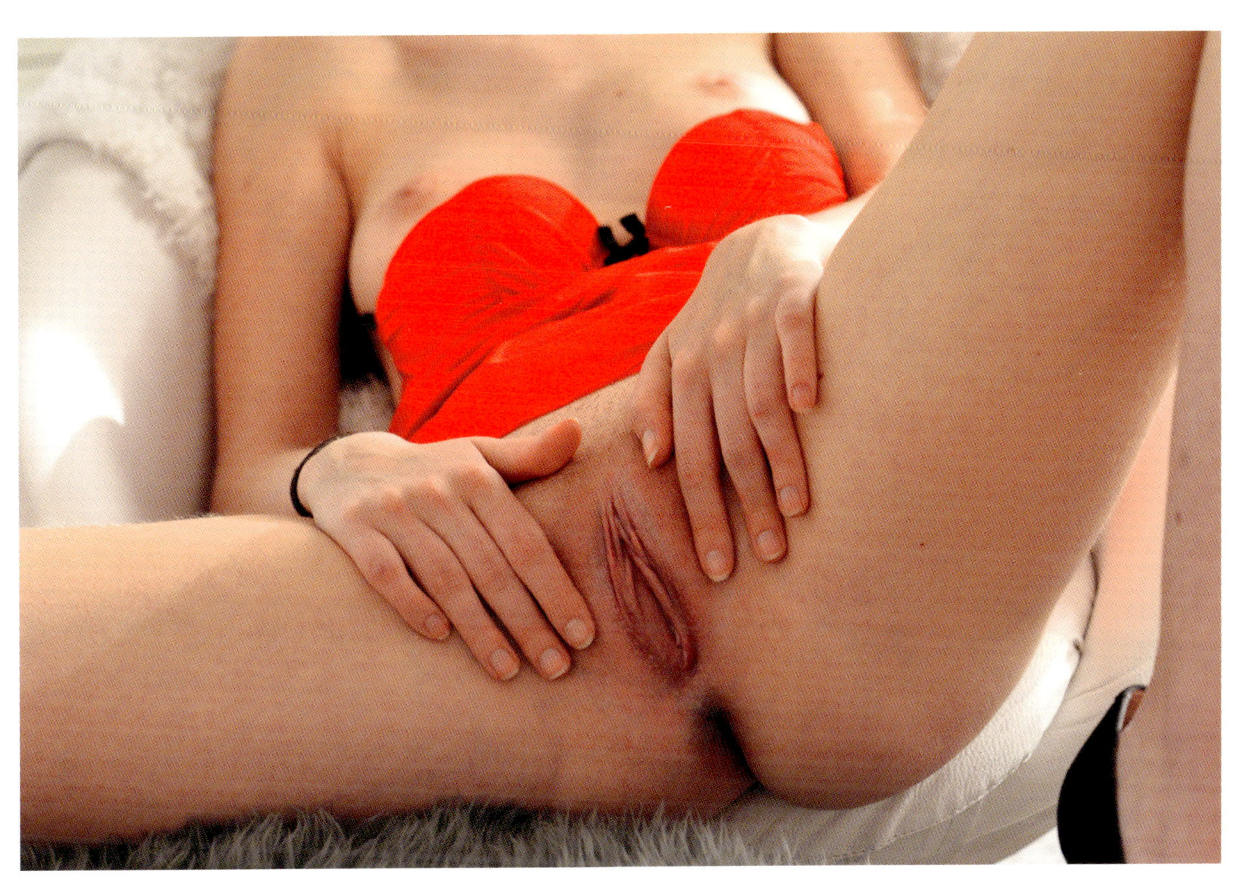

Emilie

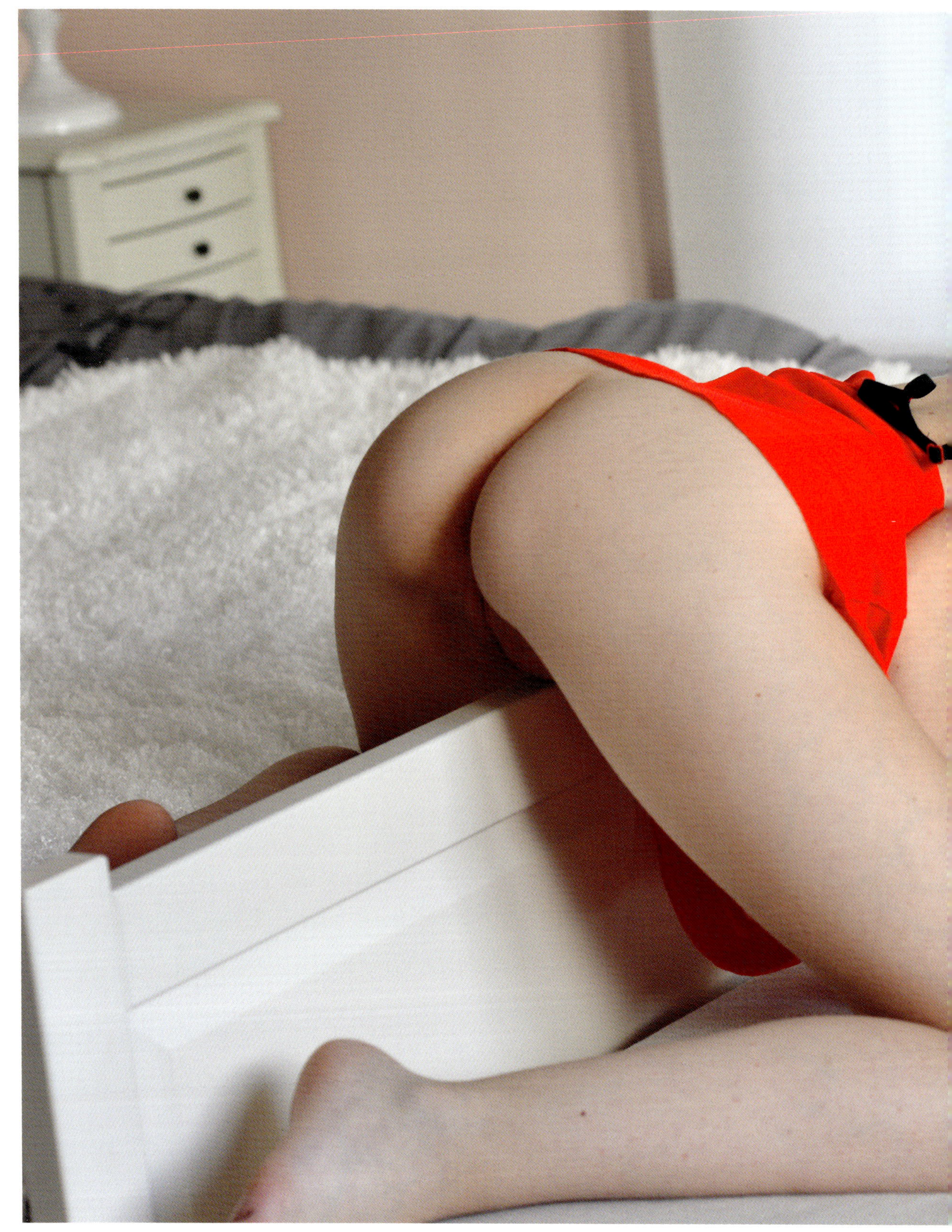



Emilie

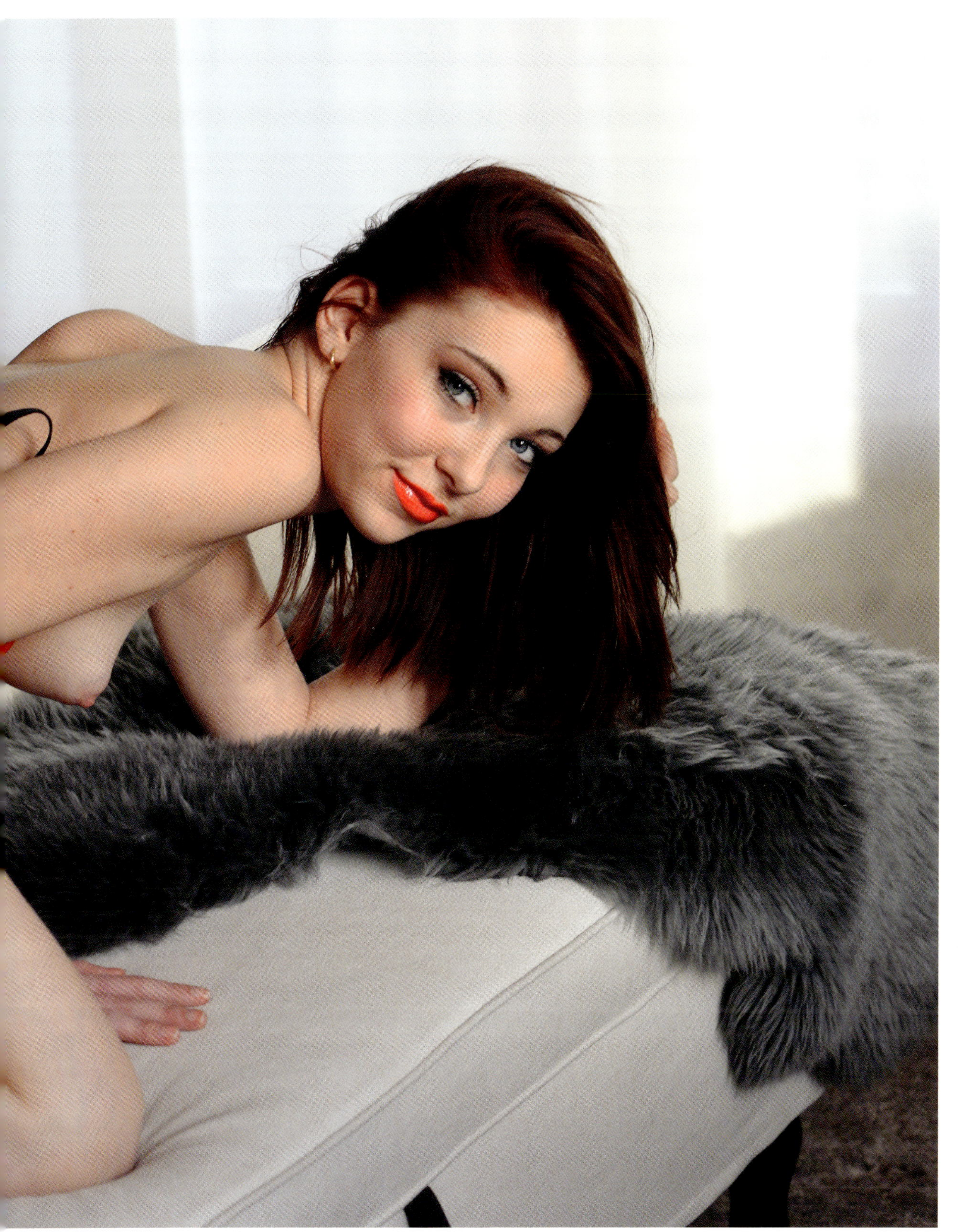

Emilie

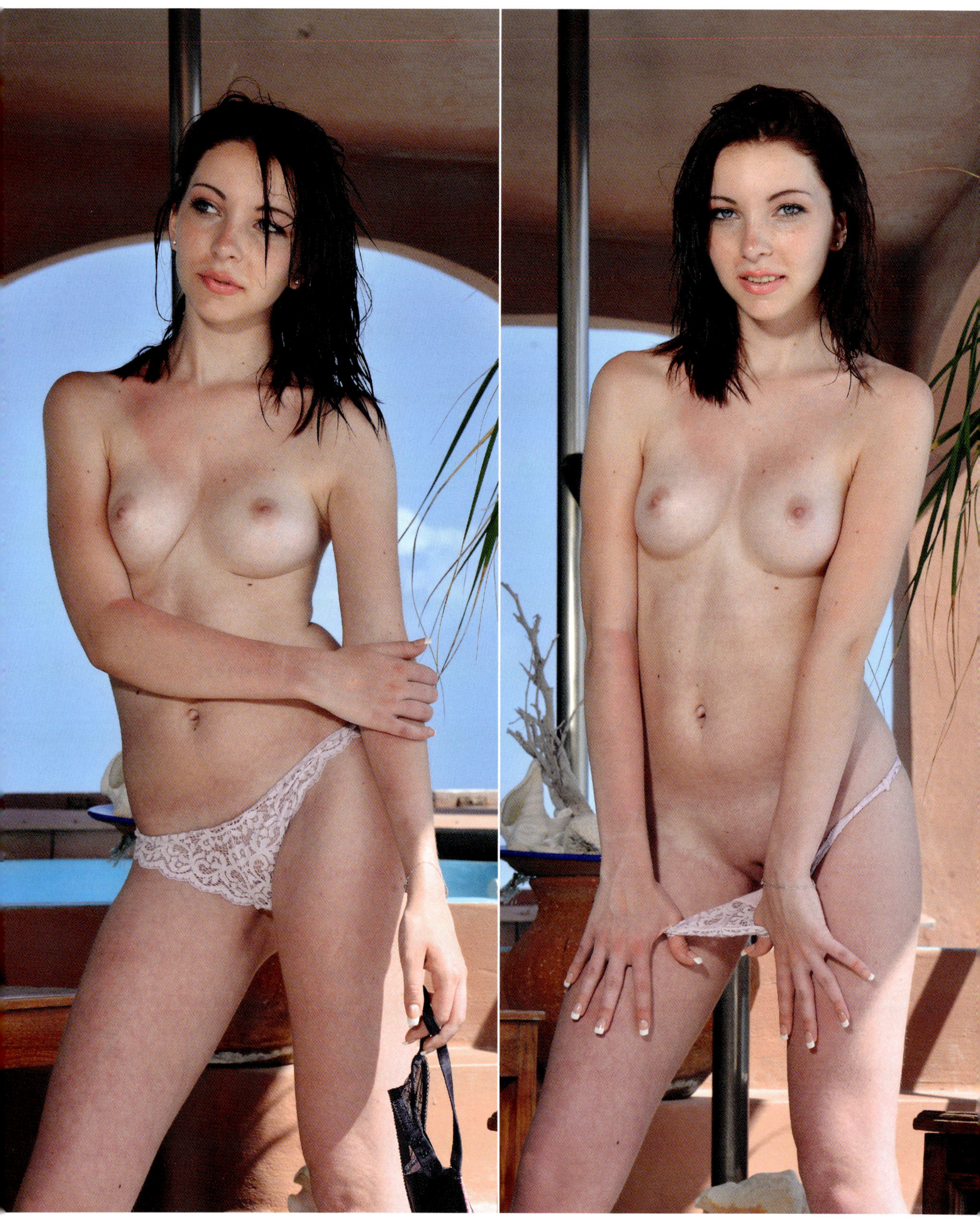

Emilie

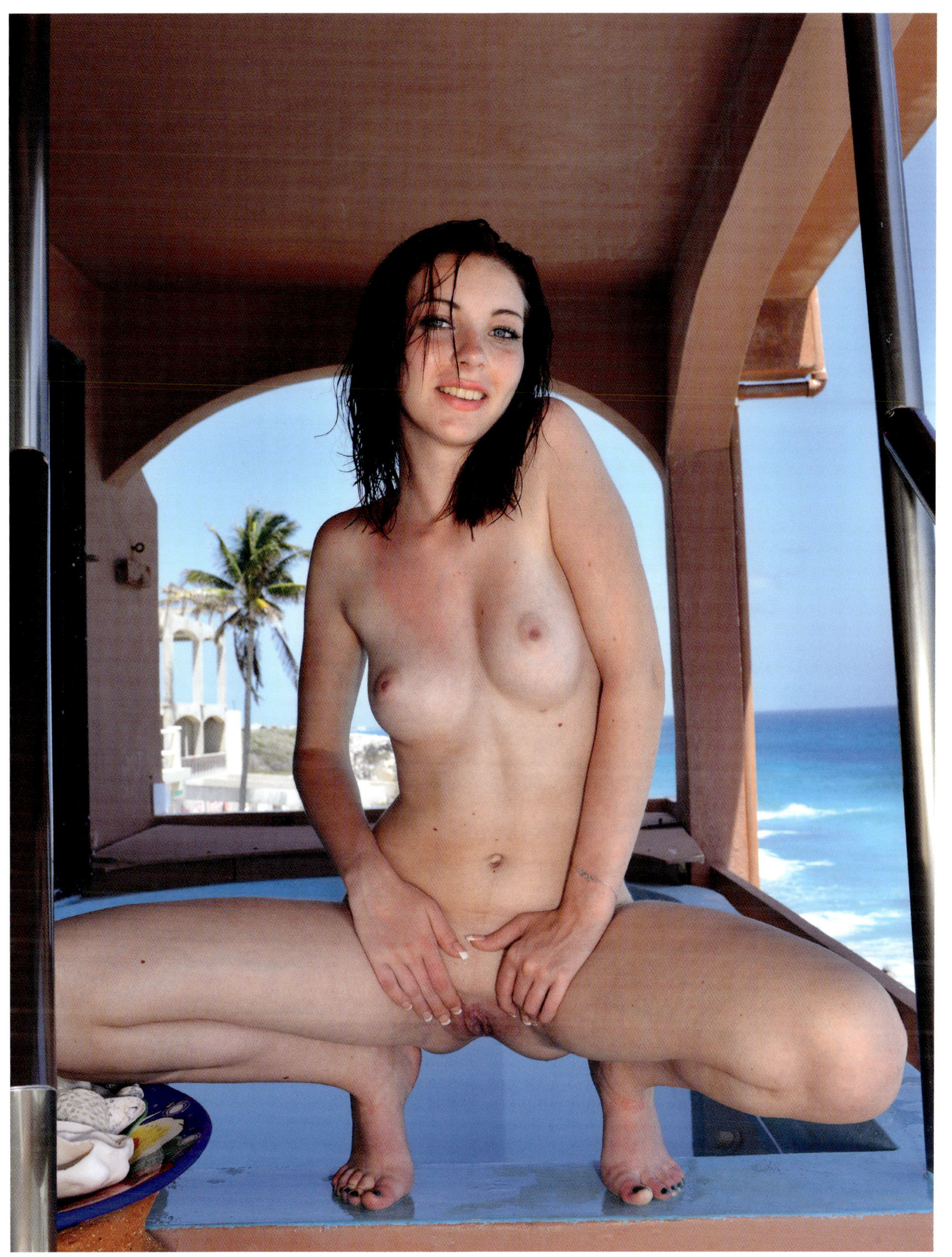

Emilie

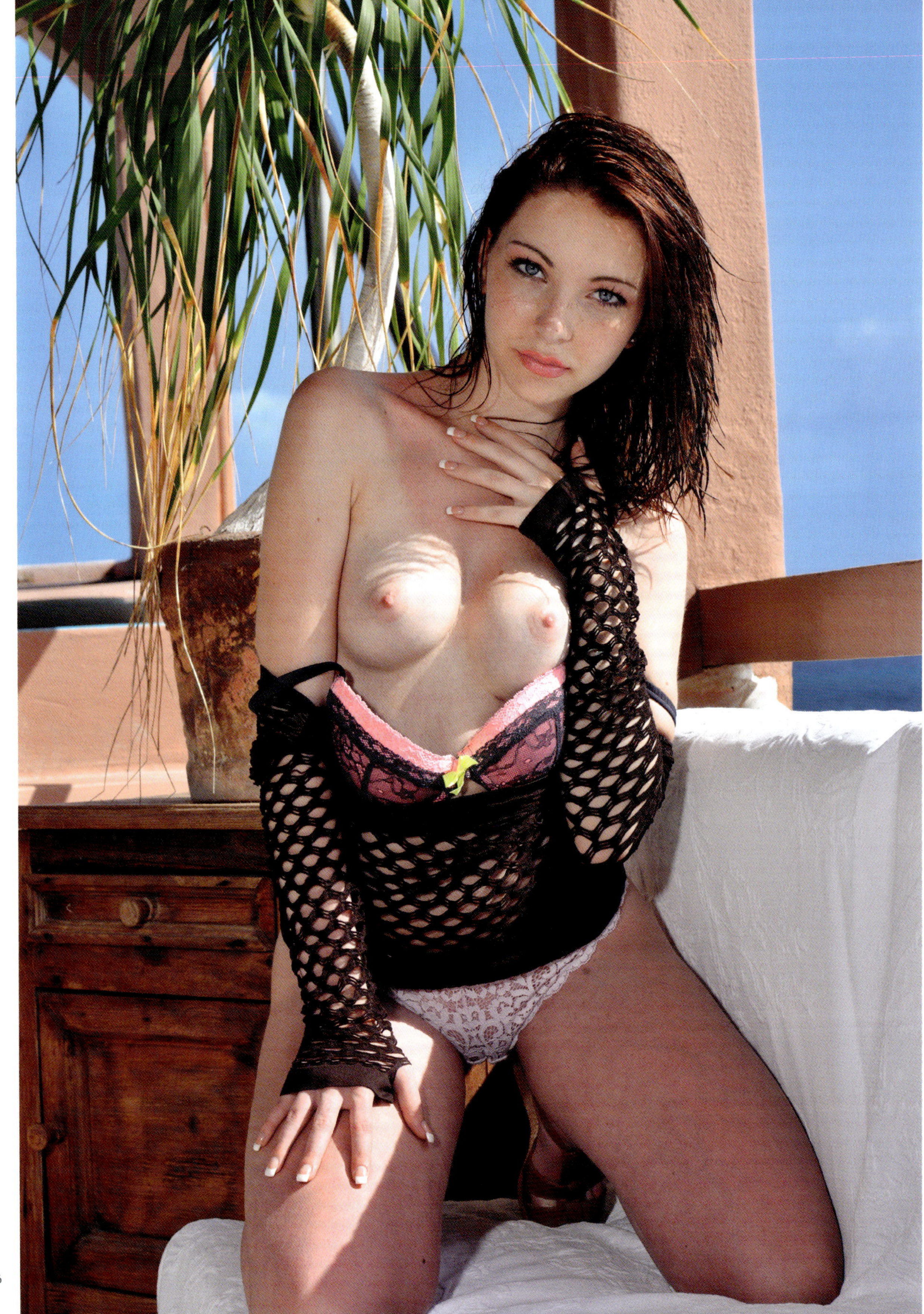

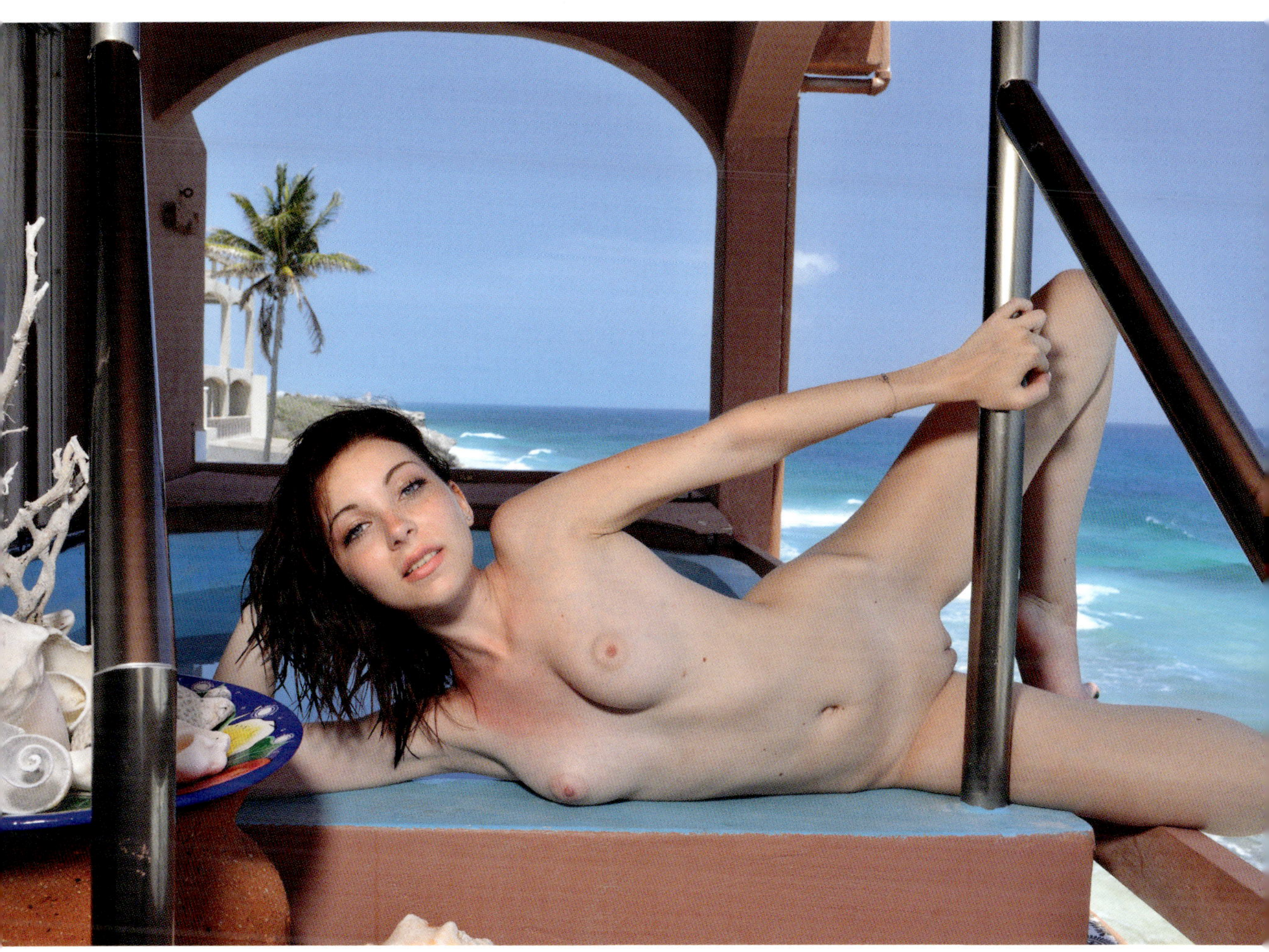

Emilie

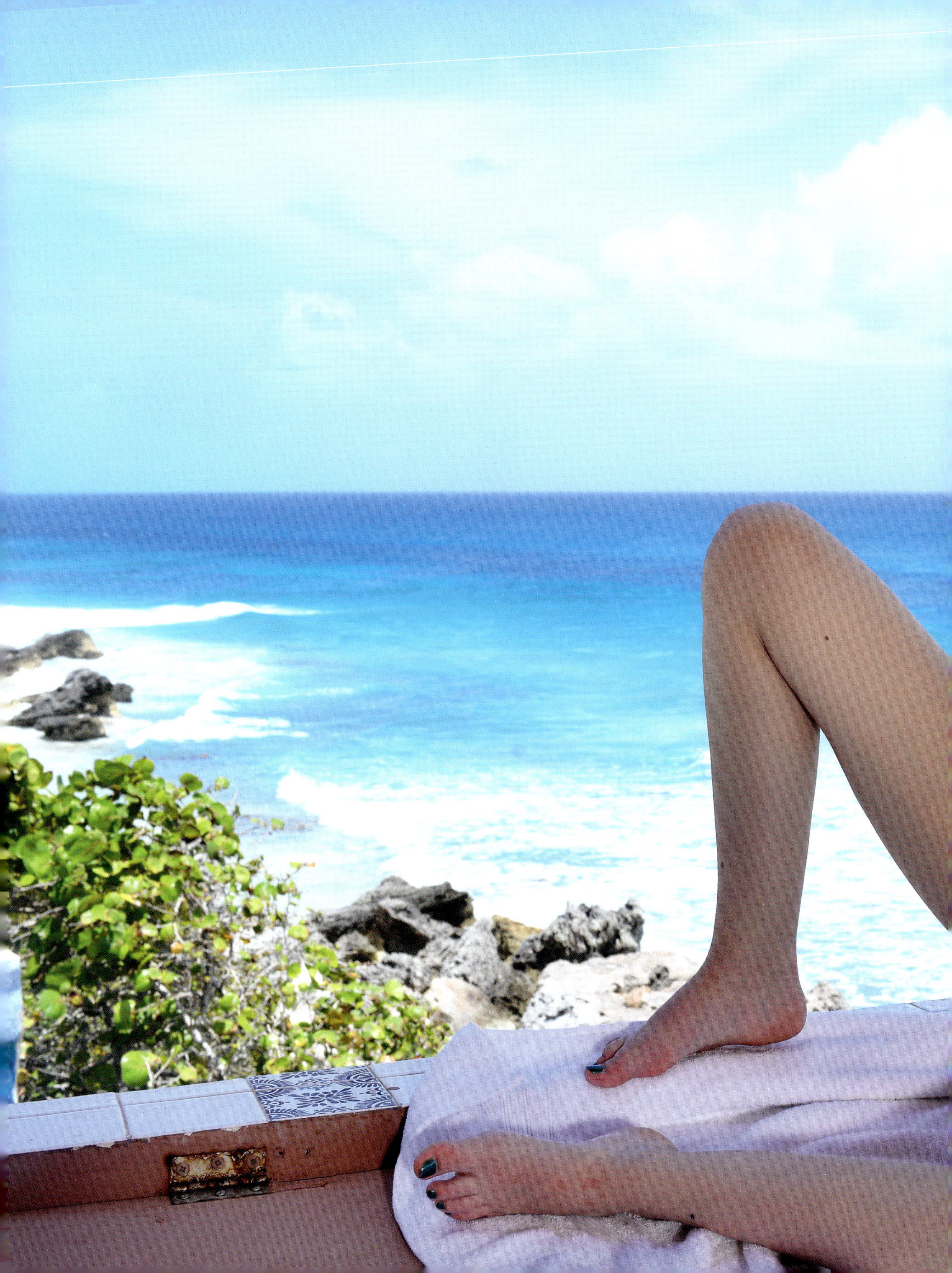

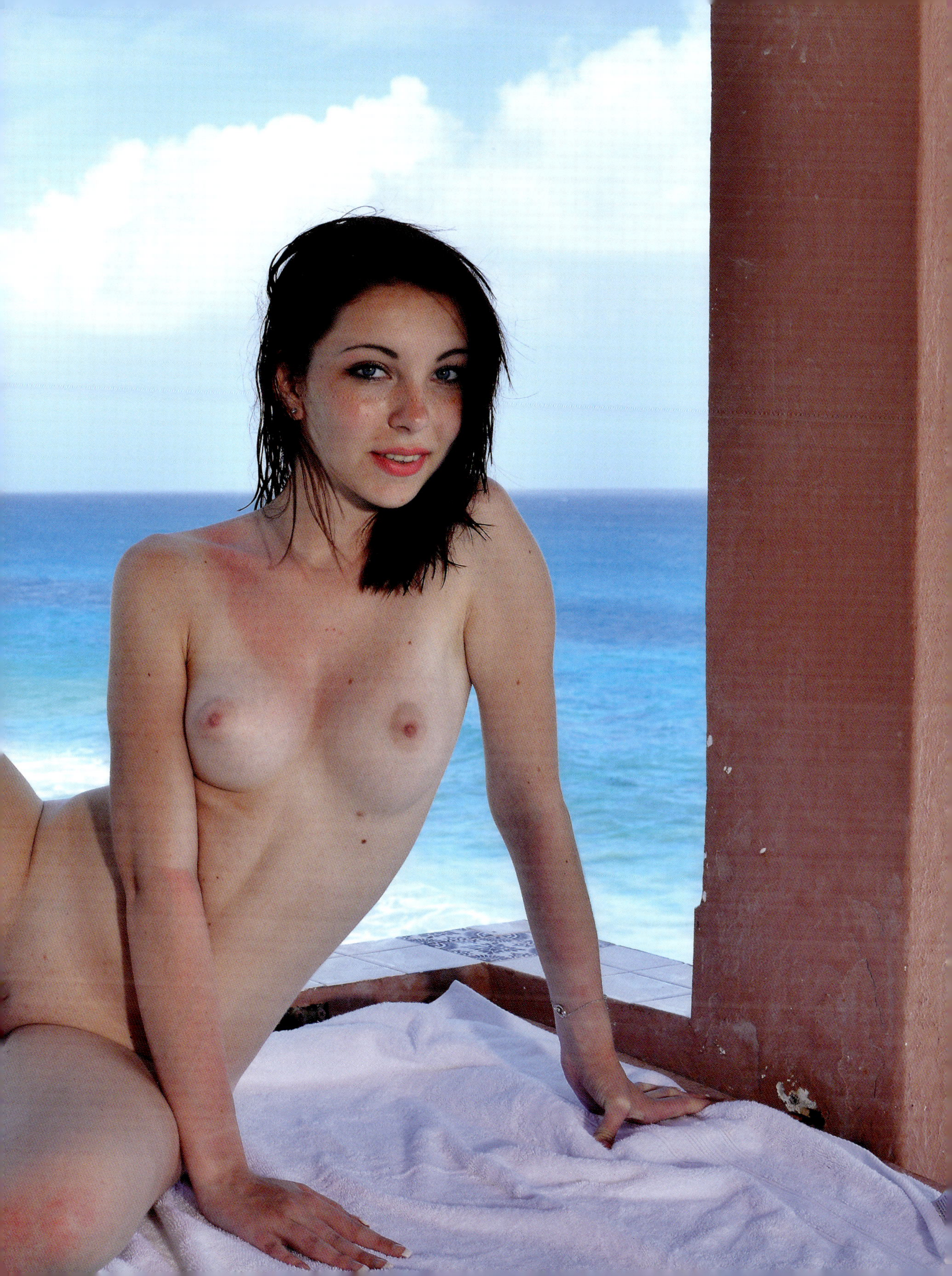

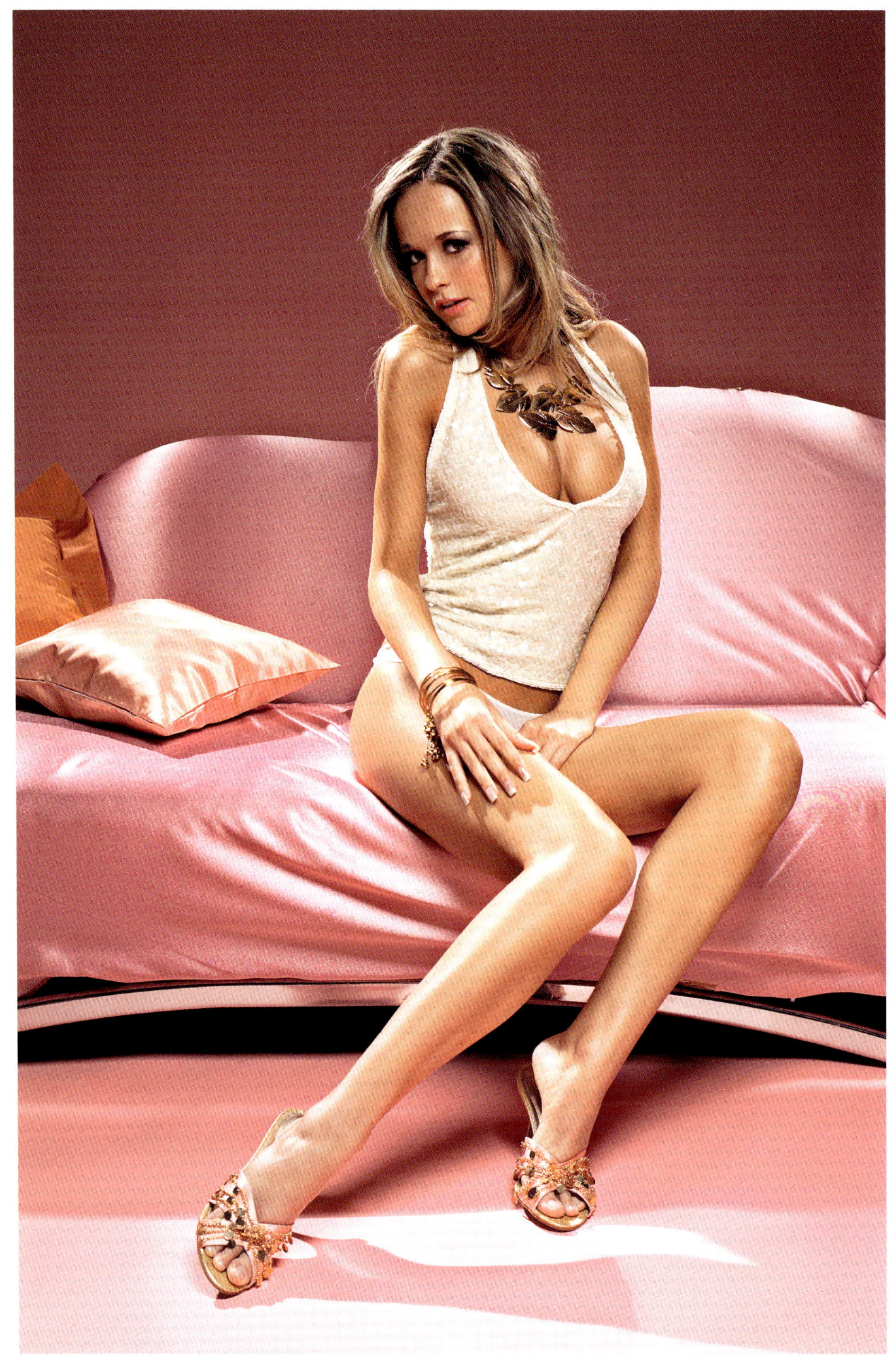

Klaudia

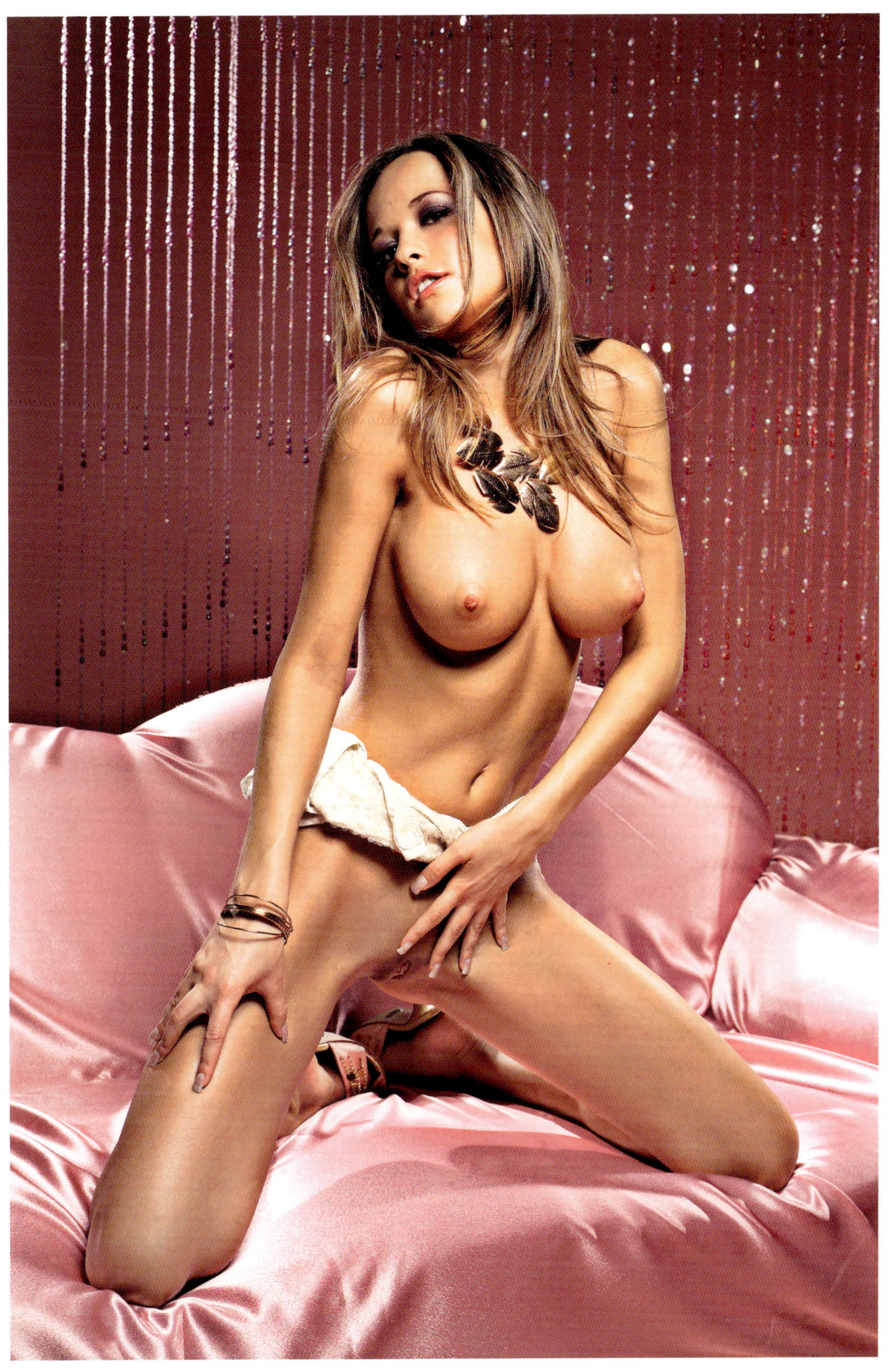

Klaudia

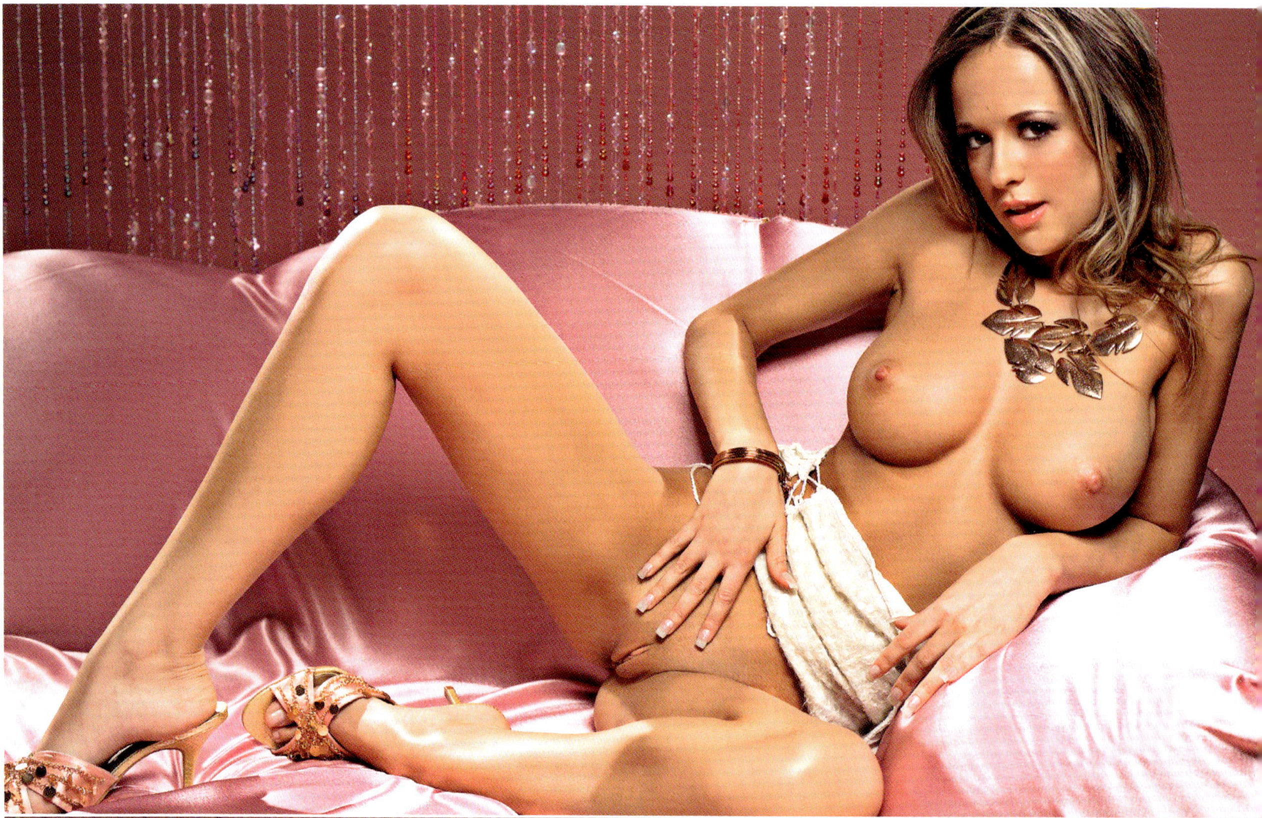

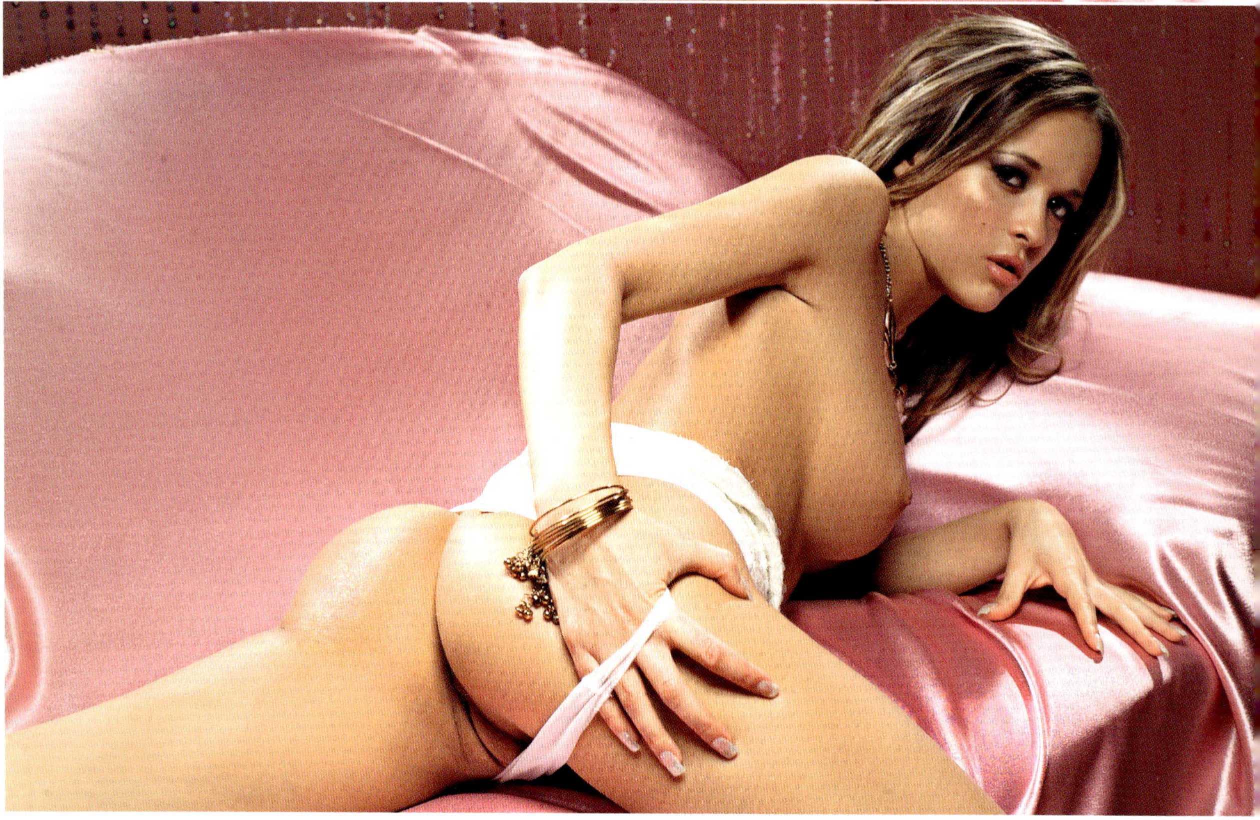

Klaudia

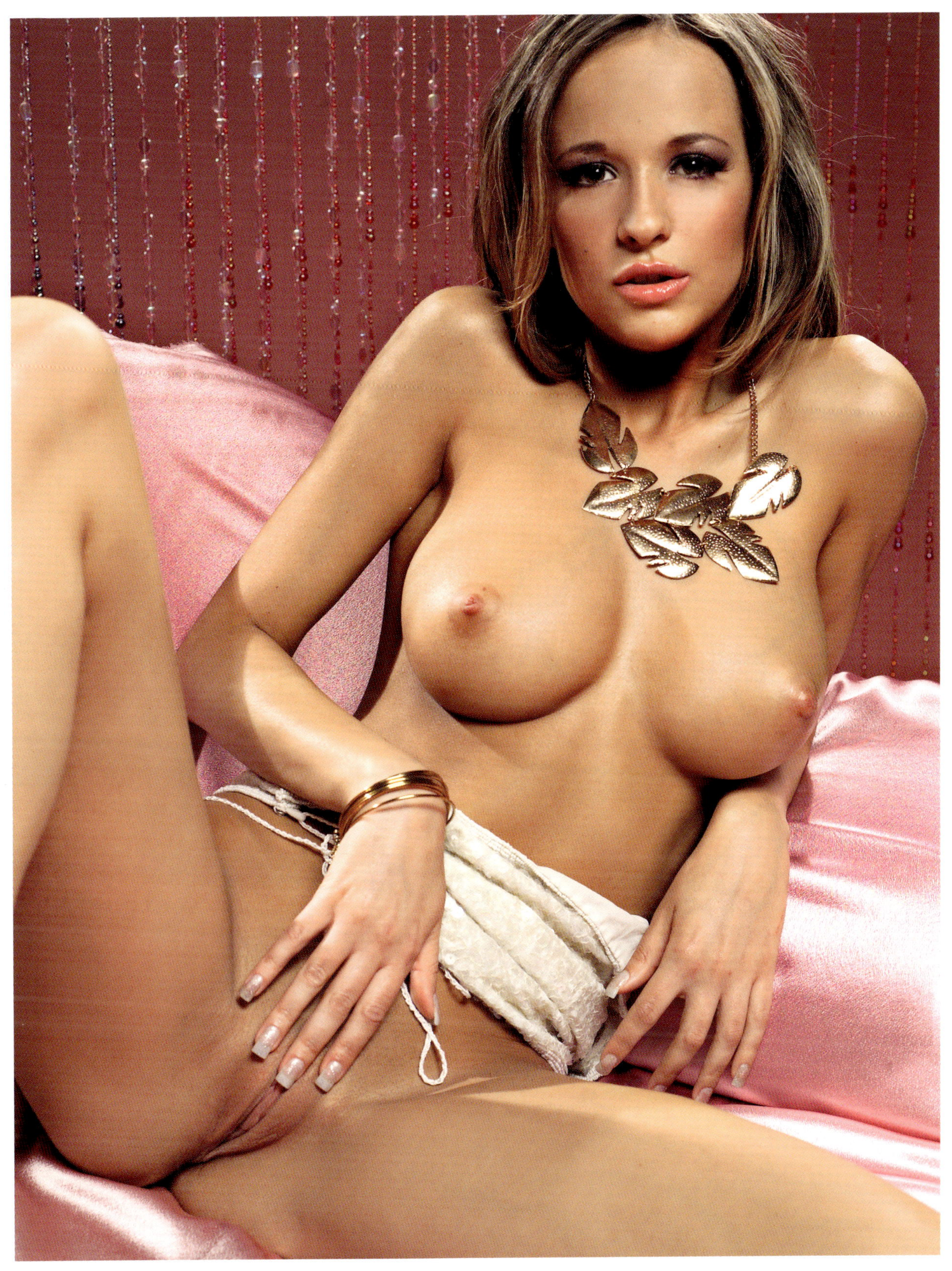

Klaudia

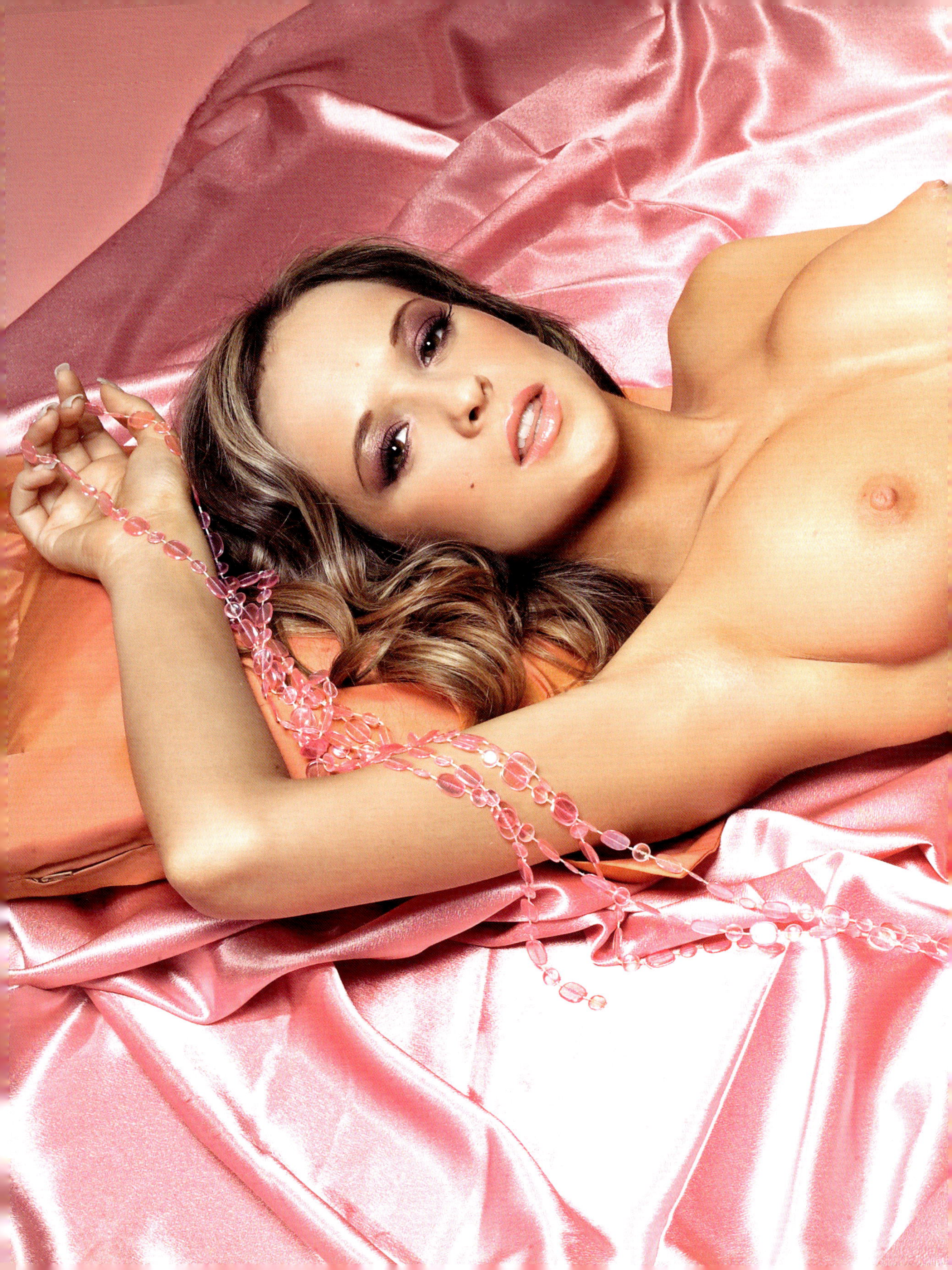

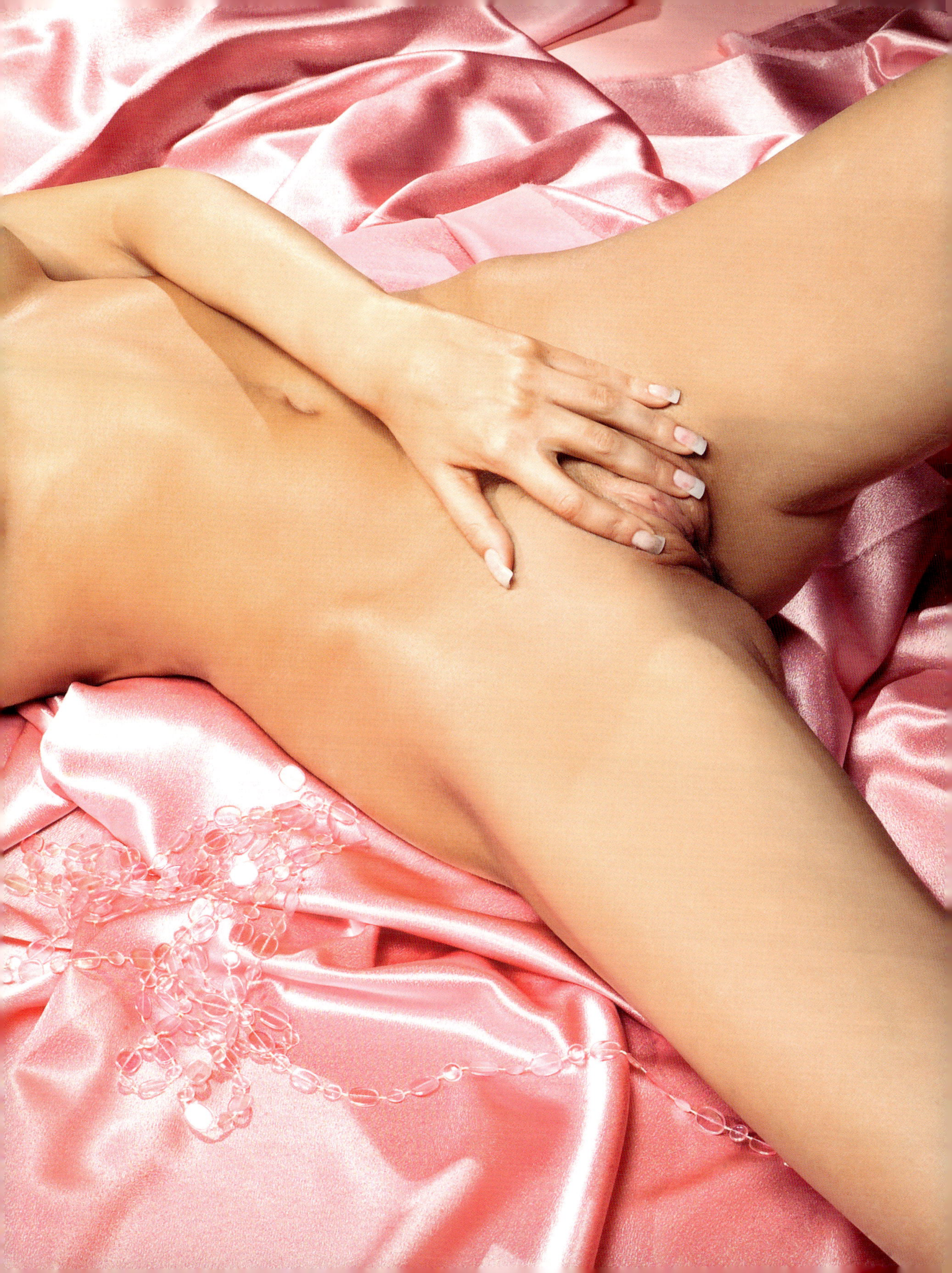

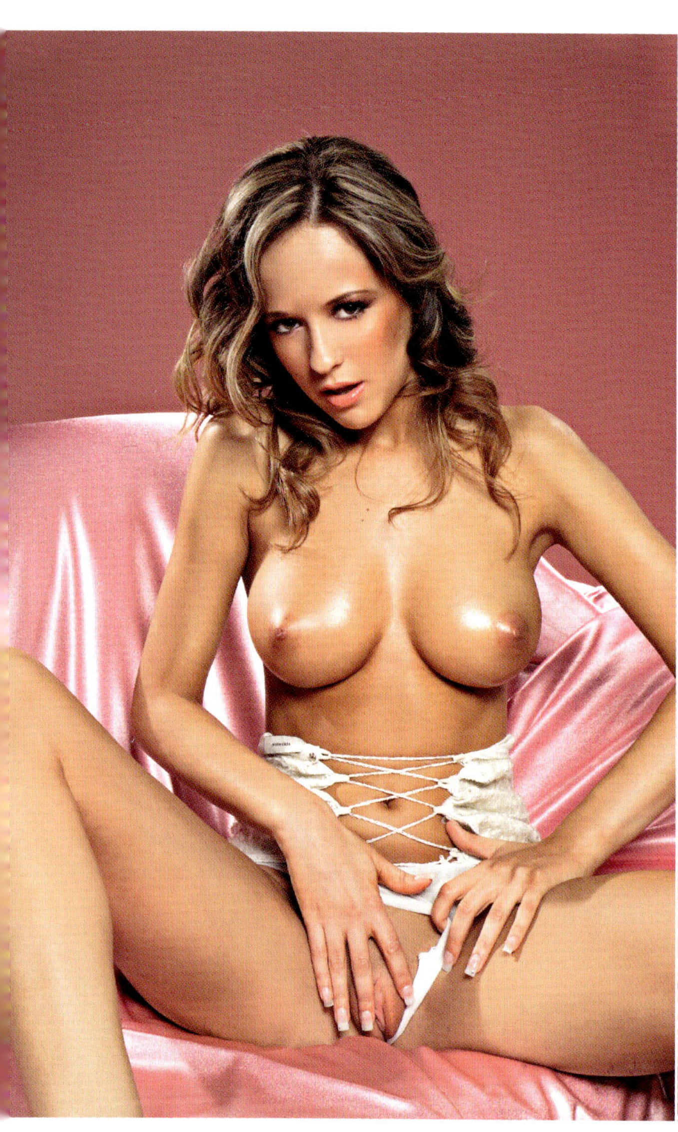

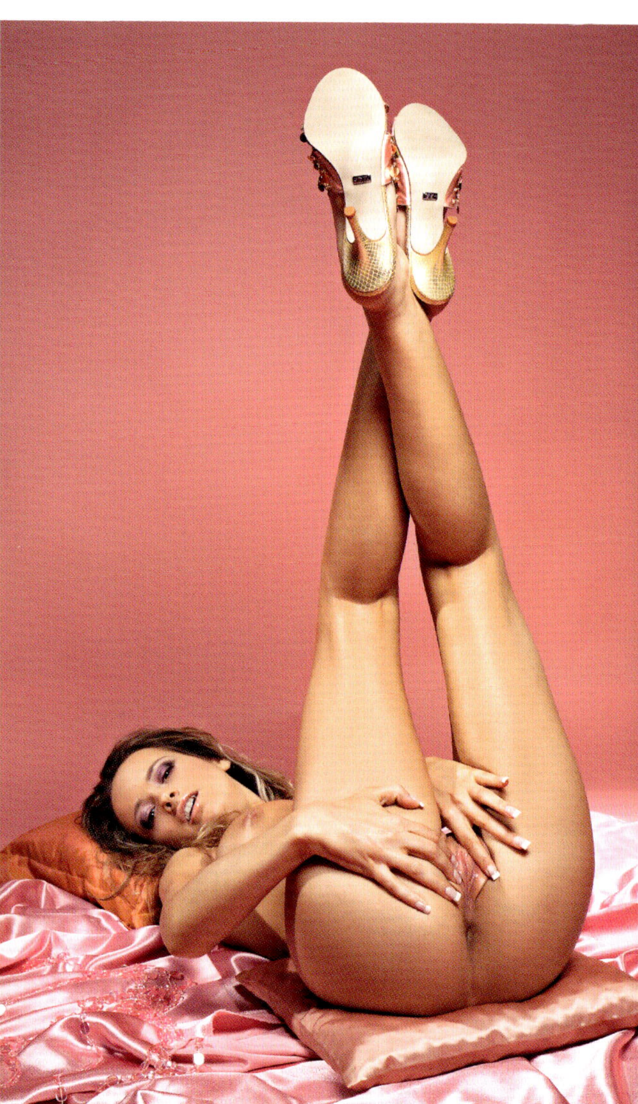



Klaudia

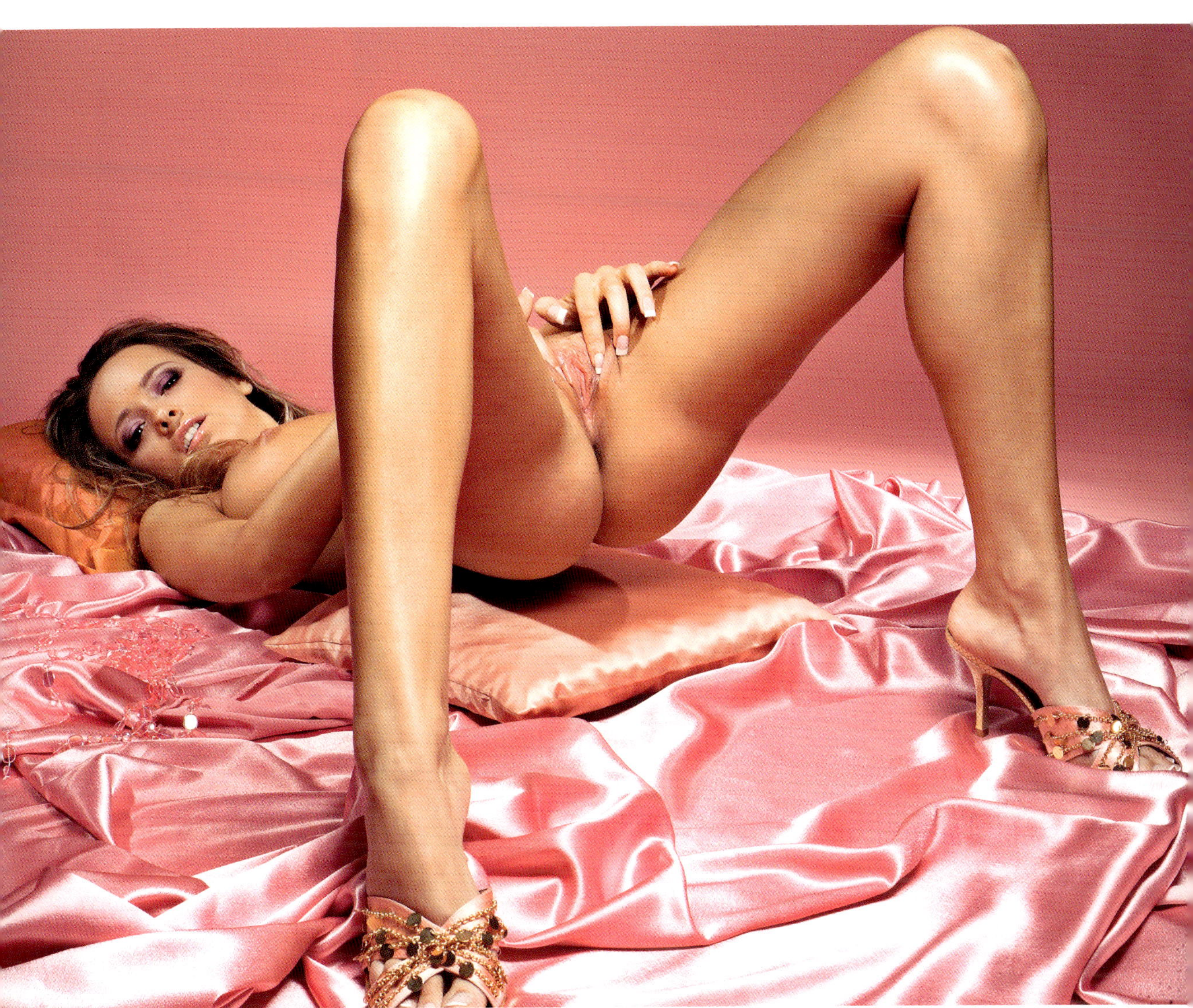

Klaudia

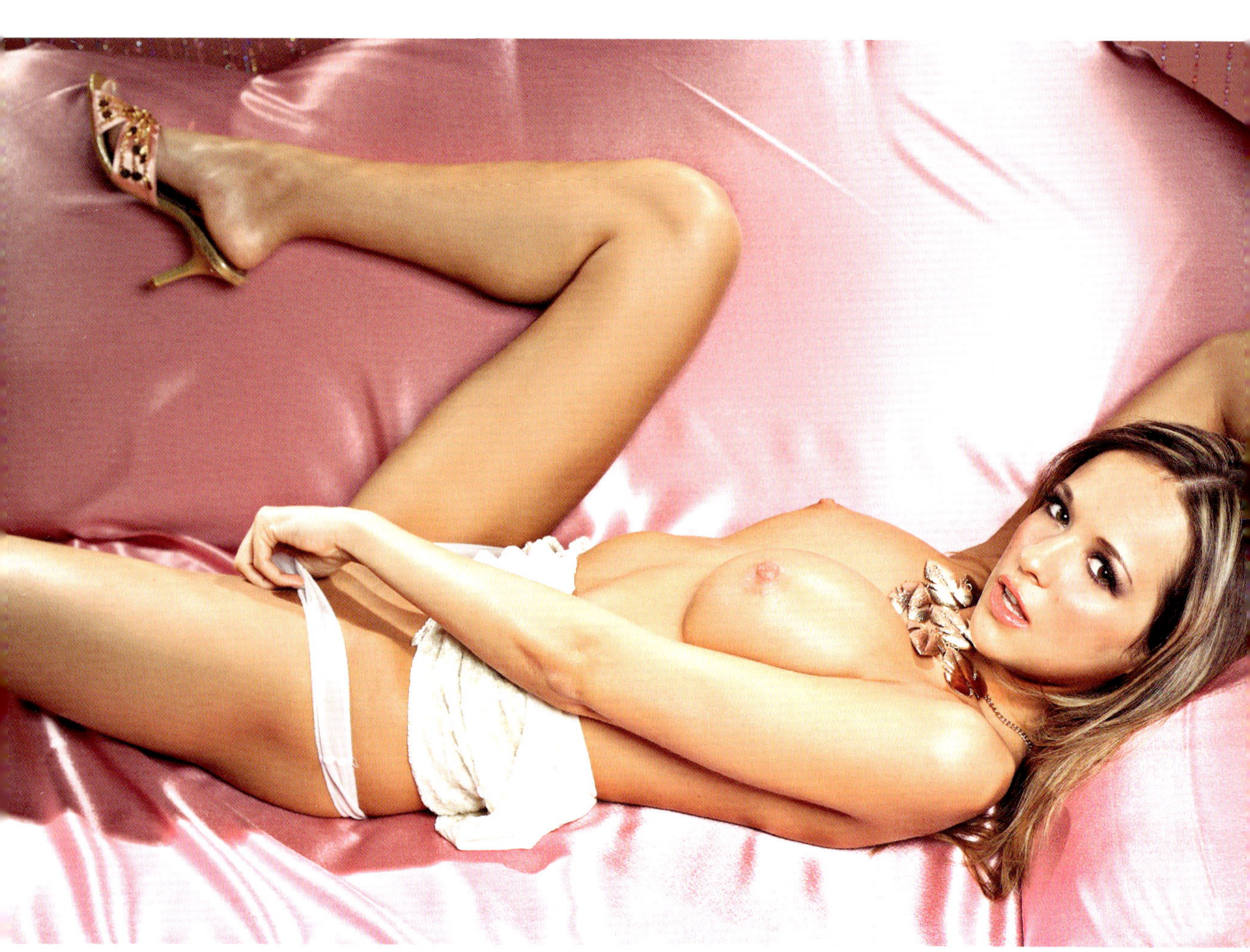

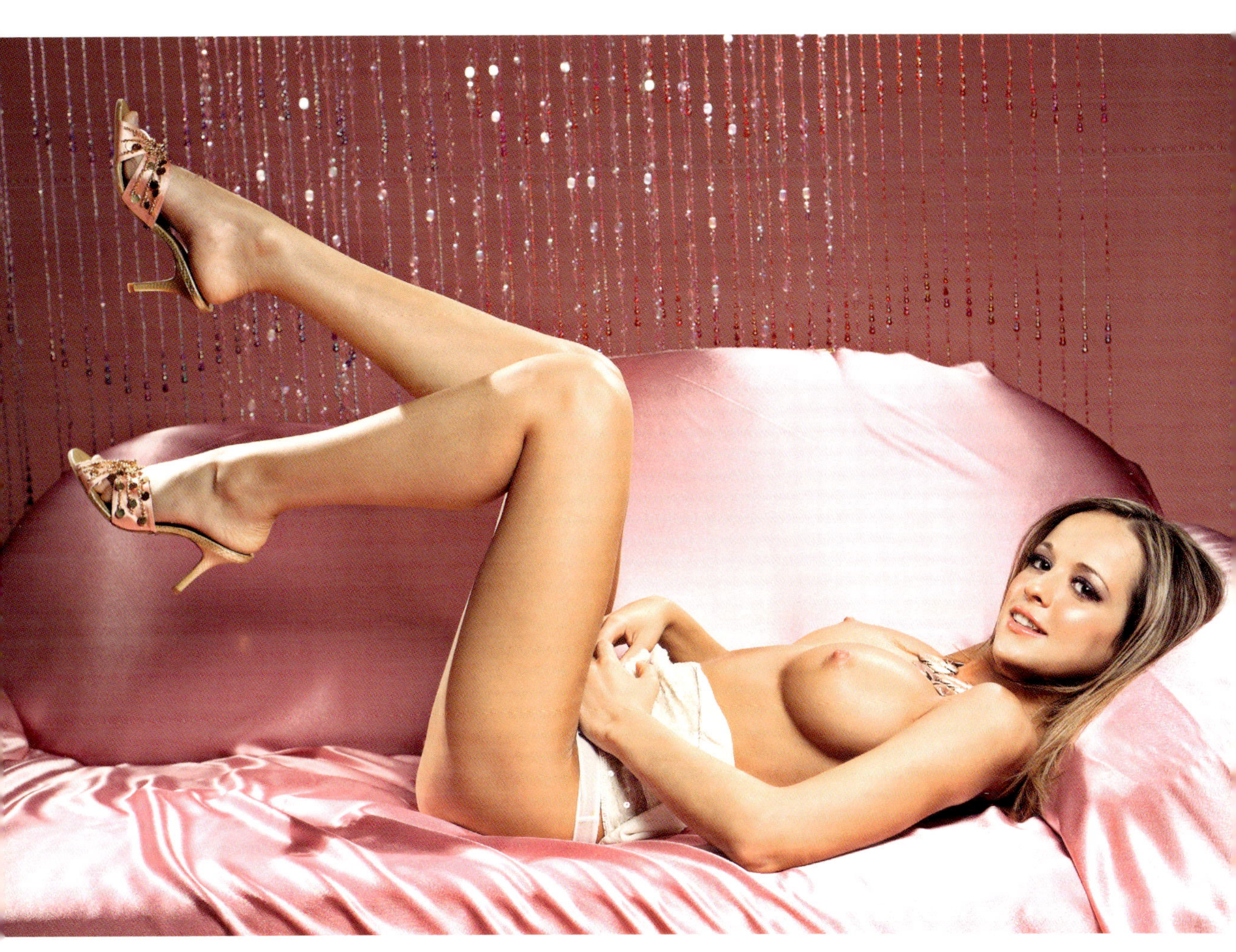

Klaudia

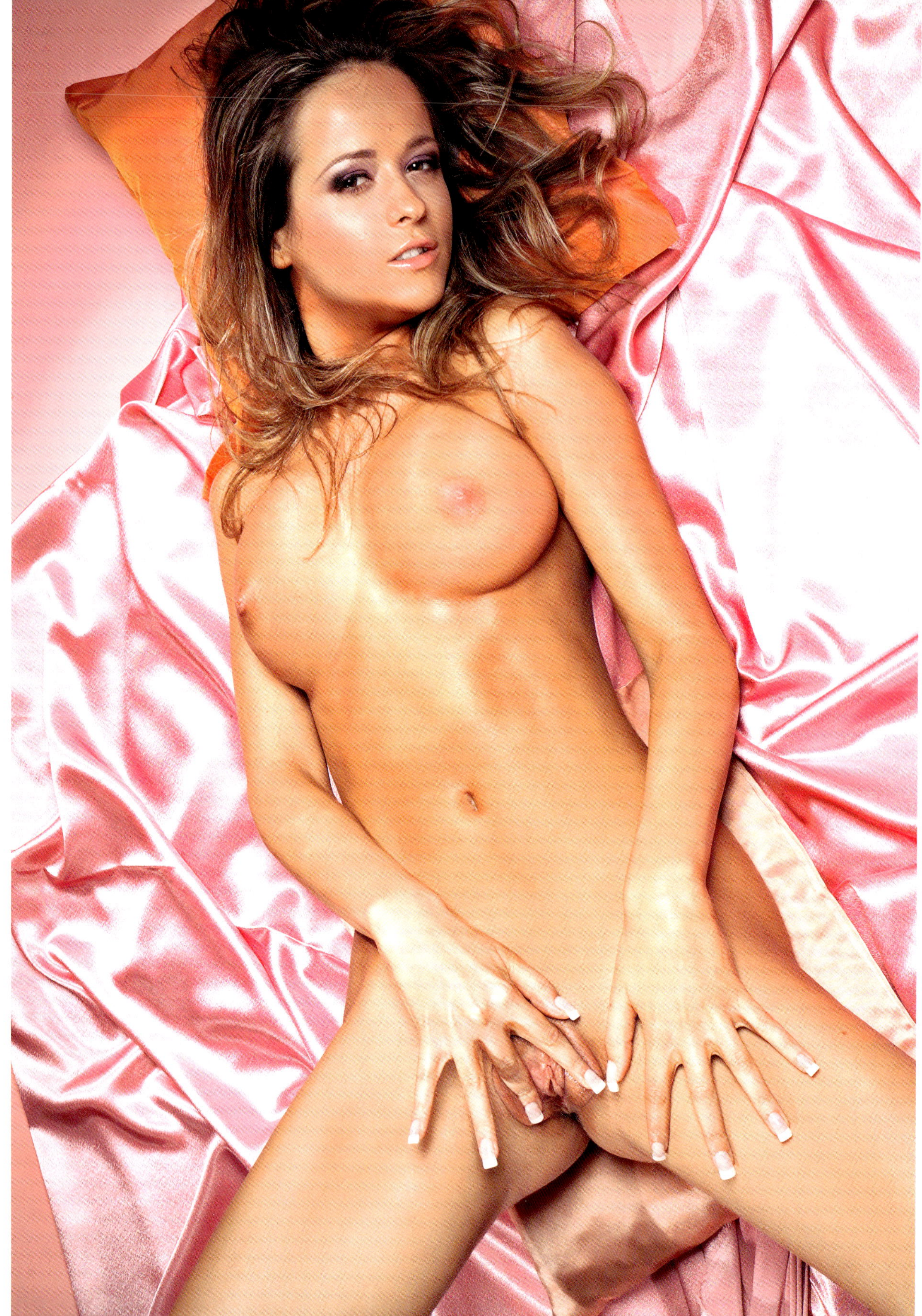